ave Street Gangs: 1991-1997

THE EUROGANG PARADOX

THE EUROGANG PARADOX

Street Gangs and Youth Groups in the U.S. and Europe

Edited by

Malcolm W. Klein
University of Southern California
Los Angeles, U.S.A.

Hans-Jürgen Kerner
University of Tübingen, Germany

Cheryl L. Maxson
University of Southern California
Los Angeles, U.S.A.

and

Elmar G.M. Weitekamp
University of Tübingen, Germany

KLUWER ACADEMIC PUBLISHERS
DORDRECHT / BOSTON / LONDON

A C.I.P. Catalogue record for this book is available from the Library of Congress.

ISBN 0-7923-6667-0 (HB)

Published by Kluwer Academic Publishers,
P.O. Box 17, 3300 AA Dordrecht, The Netherlands.

Sold and distributed in North, Central and South America
by Kluwer Academic Publishers,
101 Philip Drive, Norwell, MA 02061, U.S.A.

In all other countries, sold and distributed
by Kluwer Academic Publishers,
P.O. Box 322, 3300 AH Dordrecht, The Netherlands.

Printed on acid-free paper

Printed in the Netherlands.

TABLE OF CONTENTS

Preface

This volume has a very specific goal, to examine the common ground between the very extensive research and practical experience with American street gangs and the relatively new, sparse, but exciting research and experience with European street gangs. The natural tendency is to view the latter from the foundation of the former, and this raises some serious problems. This collection of papers, almost all of them developed for a special conference and published here for the first time, is designed to elucidate both the American and European gang situations and bring clarity to the problems of bridging them.

During two sabbatical leaves in Western Europe in 1985 and 1991, hosted by the University of Stockholm and the Swedish Council on Crime Prevention, editor Klein was able to survey the European street gang scene and note signs of change during that period. A literature search in the criminological archive, maintained by editors Kerner and Weitekamp at the University of Tübingen, revealed a paucity of research on gangs in Europe through 1991. Yet visits to scholars and officials in a number of cities rumored to be facing street gang problems revealed that such groups were indeed in existence. These initial visits yielded a list including London, Manchester, Stockholm, Zurich, Berlin, Frankfurt, Stuttgart, and Kazan among a number of Volga region cities. Yet almost no research depictions of street gangs in these or other cities were available (a notable exception being James Patrick's *A Glasgow Gang Observed*).

Continuing inquiries suggested that other cities were involved–and many others were not–and that a few researchers were undertaking gang studies in several locations. An initial body of knowledge about European gangs was evolving even while most policymakers were questioning or denying the existence of street gangs. This denial was often based on the disparities between European youth groups and what was thought to be the nature of American street gangs–"real gangs." The paradox here, from which this book takes its name, is that "real" gangs in America do not usually fit the stereotype that led to the denial of gangs in Europe.

In 1997, during a conference on restorative justice in Leuven, Belgium, a small group of scholars met to discuss this issue and to determine if there was sufficient interest to warrant further study. It was agreed that there was such interest and the group established itself as a steering committee to develop an approach. In addition to the four editors of this volume, the steering committee consisted of Peter van der Laan of Holland, Lode Walgrave and Conny Vercaigne of Belgium, Jerzy Sarnecki of Sweden, Ray Corrado of Canada, and Margaret Gatz of the U.S.

The work of this group over the following year led to the first Eurogang Workshop, held at a conference center in Schmitten, Germany. Approximately 40 participants from thirteen nations came together for three days, many with specially prepared papers and others with presentations that could be framed as formal papers. The first sessions were taken up with the American presentations of both gang substance and research methods. These were followed by presentations of European gang studies, and then in turn by presentations of additional European studies of other troublesome youth groups more generally that tested the boundaries of gang existence.

Finally, a full day was devoted to issues of gang knowledge and method as applied both to cross-national comparisons and to implications for public policy in Europe. In the minds of the steering committee members, it was also hoped that the discussion in Schmitten would lead to procedures for undertaking planned, comparative studies between European settings and perhaps between European and American settings.

To date, two principal products have resulted from this first Eurogang Workshop. One is this volume of collected papers by European and American researchers. The other is the convening of two follow-up workshops in 1999, one in Oslo, Norway, and the other in Leuven, Belgium. The work continues, and this is our best measure of success.

Acknowledgements

The convening of the Eurogang Workshop in Schmitten was made possible by grants from a variety of sources that, together, covered almost all travel and conference costs. We are grateful to the following for their support and participation:

- The Dutch Ministry of Justice
- The Dutch Ministry of the Interior
- The German Ministry of Justice
- The National Institute of Justice of the U.S. Department of Justice
- The Office of the Provost, University of Southern California
- The Social Science Research Institute, University of Southern California

In addition, several individuals merit special acknowledgment for their contributions. Peter van der Laan initiated discussions with the Dutch ministries and the National Institute of Justice. His efforts were pivotal in obtaining support from these agencies. Monica Whitlock and Margaret Gatz took on the difficult task of recording every word and nuance of the discussions. Their work was drawn upon throughout this volume, and especially in Part IV. Judith Webb has been our editorial advisor and handler of manuscripts, from the very beginning of the project to the completion of the book.

We acknowledge, with appreciation, permission to reproduce three previously published items, as follows:

- Oxford University Press, to reproduce the map used in Chapter Four. It appeared as figures 4-2 and 4-5 (pp. 92 and 95) in Malcolm W. Klein, *The American Street Gang*, New York: Oxford University Press, 1995.
- *Journal of Gang Research,* to reproduce portions of charts III and IV (pp. 37 and 39-40) in Cheryl L. Maxson and Malcolm W. Klein, Investigating Gang Structures, *Journal of Gang Research* 3(1), 1995. This material is incorporated into Chapter One of this volume.
- Kluwer Law International, to reproduce in full Hermann Tertilt, Patterns of Ethnic Violence in a Frankfurt Street Gang, *International Journal on Minority and Group Rights* 1997(4):341-352.

Finally, the editors are extremely grateful to all the authors and the Workshop participants for their professional and personal contributions. We are pleased to acknowledge them in the listing at the end of the book.

Malcolm W. Klein

Hans-Jürgen Kerner

Cheryl L. Maxson

Elmar G. M. Weitecamp

PART I

INTRODUCTION TO PART I

The authors of the papers in Part I were invited with a very specific purpose in mind: to represent current research, the current state of the art in American gang studies. We had noted a tendency among European scholars to consider the more classic American gang scholars–Thrasher, Cohen, Yablonsky, Walter Miller, Cloward and Ohlin, Short and Strodtbeck, for example–as the best windows on American gang studies. These were the pioneers, the standard setters, and the principal theoreticians of the field. Of those working the field prior to 1970, only Irving Spergel and Malcolm Klein have continued gang research to the present day. They and others have by now produced modern texts that more than adequately present the history and theory that has become so familiar to today's students of the street gang.

The reader will note that the chapters in Part I do not dwell on these matters. The authors were asked instead to present current trends against which the emerging gang scene might best be judged. In large part, this was sought to respond directly to the Eurogang Paradox, the tendency to deny the existence of gangs in Europe because they do not fit the stereotype derived from the earlier studies. Also contributing to this denial are careless media stereotypes of American gangs, false pictures of large, highly organized, stylistic, and violent youth in constant battles over turf and booty.

Along with the accelerated proliferation of America's gang-involved cities starting in the 1980s, some very important changes have characterized the American gang scene. Whereas formerly gang cities were principally the largest cities and some of their close-in suburbs, they are now to be found in all states, in urban, suburban, and even rural areas. This has changed the notion of gang structures.

The diffusion of "gang culture" to the point that it has been incorporated into a larger youth culture has meant the widespread adoption by youth of many of the symbols of gang life. With this, more and more youth who earlier would have eschewed gang behavior have been willing, even challenged to experiment with gang-like activity. Some have found the pattern rewarding, and new gang structures have evolved as a result.

Firearms, once rare enough to be a valued commodity in the gang "treasury," have become far more accessible and at the same time far more

M.W. Klein et al (eds.), The Eurogang Paradox, 3.

lethal. Thus gang rivalries have become more serious with shootings by any one group at another, more readily and normatively more demanding of a like response. More firearms are now carried on the person rather than stashed away in a safe place, meaning that more events, more crime scenes, more parties, and more confrontations involve the immediately available gun. Violence results, and violence increases. Over 90 percent of gang homicides now present firearms as the final weapon.

As gangs have changed and proliferated, so have gang researchers and their methods. More attention–finally–is being paid to gang structure and group process. More studies of female gang members have been produced, reducing some of the gender-related stereotyping of the previously sparse female gang literature. A far broader repertoire of research methods has appeared, expanding on the earlier patterns of gang observation and ethnography. Modern survey research methods are increasingly employed, more multi-site studies are reported, and far better archival research has been enabled by the increasing sophistication of police and court recording procedures. Not incidentally, more funding for gang research has brought in new researchers with interests that build upon but go well past those of the classic gang researchers.

Thus it was that the authors in Part I could be gathered together to inform their European colleagues where current gang knowledge in the U.S. stands, and what it might have to offer to other countries. We should note, however, that with one exception all the Americans represented in Part I were unfamiliar with the state of European gangs and knew next to nothing about the research under way in European nations. Thus the burden was truly upon the Europeans to draw out the implications of the American presentations for their own purposes; it was principally for them, the Europeans, to dispel the Eurogang Paradox.

The introductory chapter by Klein sets the stage for the workshop enterprise, with particular emphasis on group process and new data on gang structures. The following chapter by Decker reinforces the depiction of modern street gangs by using a three-city comparison that contrasts one stereotypic, highly organized gang with others that represent more typical patterns. Hagedorn's chapter depicts the developments in one city where the emergent gang picture is complicated by changing economic conditions in urban underclass settings, with potential parallels to other nations based upon patterns of globalization.

Thornberry and Porter show how crime patterns are affected by entry into gang membership in one emergent or new gang city, and then present an important contrast between traditional and the more common emergent cities, those more likely to offer parallels to Europe. Curry then demonstrates the enormous proliferation of such cities across America, using a newly developed national data base derived from police survey results. Esbensen and Lynskey's report of gang membership in a multi-site study using school survey data further exemplifies the current state of gang affairs, while Miller's review of the female gang literature stresses the importance to future research of including the gender issue.

The reader is invited to note, throughout Part I, the wide variety of methods and data that can be brought to bear on the gang problem. None of these studies rely on the same methods, and thus the field as so represented almost triangulates on street gangs to draw a far more comprehensive picture than can be offered by field observation alone, or survey methods alone, or archival methods alone. It is not a matter of which method is best, but of what each can contribute to a mosaic of gang knowledge.

Chapter 1

RESOLVING THE EUROGANG PARADOX

Malcolm W. Klein
University of Southern California

The goal of this volume is to share knowledge and ideas about street gangs, a matter that has long been an American staple and is now beginning to take on a European flavor. We are facing what I have come to call The Eurogang Paradox. The paradox has to do with denials that there are street gangs in Europe, because the gangs patterns don't fit the American pattern of highly structured, cohesive, violent gangs. But then neither do most American gangs fit the pattern.

I have spoken with a wide variety of European researchers, police, and public officials and, with a few exceptions, their report has been "We don't have gangs–we know what they're like in America, and we don't have that here." Berlin was an exception, as was Kazan, as well the gangs described in London and Manchester.

Interestingly, many American officials have also denied gangs in their cities, noting specifically that their groups don't resemble the gangs in Los Angeles. But then most Los Angeles gangs don't resemble those gangs either. In other words, we're facing a stereotype, the "West Side Story" or "Colors" image of urban gangs: good stories, but gross distortions of reality. This is why we have chapters by some American gang researchers in this volume describing the real, not the fantasy world of street gangs known to them. Included are their descriptions of the methods by which they have added to our gang knowledge. Maybe we'll learn that if American gangs really don't fit their stereotypes, then gang-like groups elsewhere should be more carefully scrutinized as well.

It is appropriate here to review a few issues that seem pivotal and were emphasized in the Eurogang Workshop. One of these is setting street gangs or

M.W. Klein et al (eds.), The Eurogang Paradox, 7–19.

youth gangs into the context of other forms of youth groups that many consider nongang. Let me illustrate this at the expense of a good friend and colleague from Stockholm, Professor Jerzy Sarnecki. Some years ago, Sarnecki published the results of his research on co-offenders arrested in a medium-sized Swedish city (Sarnecki, 1986; see also his chapter in this volume). He referred to these as gangs, and this work has been much cited by others as part of the gang literature (e.g., Reiss, 1986). When I read his report and later talked with him about it, I rather directly attacked his use of the term "gang" because it referred to temporary and usually small networks or companionships for which there was little evidence of group structure. Through several "dueling seminars" I got him to agree that the town of Borlange did not have gangs, but delinquent networks.

These discussions took place in the mid- to late 1980s. By 1992, Stockholm reports from research, police, and media alike, provided some consensus that immigrant and refugee groups of Turks, Kurds and others had formed rather stable gangs in housing areas like Rinkeby. The problem was serious enough to call forth a gang intervention program, gang data collection by the police, and a newspaper series depicting the characteristics of various delinquent groups and delinquent youth gangs.

Sarnecki's response now is to suggest that there are no gangs in Stockholm (even though he took me to observe the Rinkeby area as part of my gang review, and despite my evening with a Stockholm cop during which time we observed one such group closely). The groups he now studies and on which he and Pettersson report in their chapter in this volume have no gang reality, according to Sarnecki. But he is only able to say this because his methods don't test for gang structure. In any case, the illustration reminds us that defining gangs is a tricky business. We need to perfect the language for this.

A second issue emphasized in the Workshop had to do with ethnicities. Most American gangs are black or Hispanic, and unmixed. Other ethnic gangs–Polish, Irish, Italian, and so on–were common in the 1930s and 1940s in response to patterns of immigration and assimilation. They are seldom found now. The European gang reports also emphasize immigrant groups, and sometimes refugee groups. The most common pattern seems to be of groups of second generation youths–Turks and Kurds, Moroccans and Algerians, Yugoslavs of the various persuasions, Greeks, Chileans, Indians and Pakistanis and Afro-Caribbeans. Not infrequently, they may be ethnically mixed. They are often the off-shoot of guest-worker programs, and in most cases are the proof that it is not ethnicity *per se* that is at issue, but social marginalization and alienation. Shaw and McKay would nod their heads at this pattern, but be surprised at the failure of the concentric circle model. In many European cities, these groups are not concentrated in the inner city, as is the case in America, but in the low-income housing developments deliberately constructed on the outskirts.

This leads naturally to a third issue discussed at the workshop, the place of community in both the derivation and the control or prevention of street gangs. Community means different things to different people, and there are many kinds of communities. In earlier years, Shaw and McKay saw the inner-city community as both the source of and the solution to serious delinquency and gang problems. Gangs don't spontaneously generate like compost fires, but are spawned by the very nature of the structure and composition of our communities. Indeed, the proper study of street gangs provides a window on the nature of their own communities. We have learned how to crack down on gangs (usually not very effectively), but we are amazingly ignorant still about how to deal with them via community intervention. Most research disembodies gangs from their communities; we must find ways to conceive of them together.

This in turn brings us to a fourth issue to engage our interests, programs and policies of intervention. They range from social services for individual youth to special antigang legislation to crack down on and incarcerate gang members at greater levels than nongang offenders. In between are street worker programs, organizational change, community empowerment and police suppression programs. We heard much about these in the Workshop. Perhaps the most striking comment, however, is the almost complete lack of scientifically acceptable evidence for the success of any one of them, and the enormous complexity of attempting to implement a comprehensive approach involving a wide range of these approaches.

These, then, are four major themes we expected to run through the discussions: the youth group context, the role of marginalized populations, the role of community, and the range and questionable effectiveness of implemented policy. By design, we also heard about another set of issues, especially from the American presenters. There are several, very important generalizable characteristics of most American street gangs, characteristics that tend to get lost in the gang myths and stereotypes and lead directly to the Eurogang paradox. For now I'll merely mention them, but the reader of this volume should stay attuned to them because each is absolutely pivotal to bringing reality to our gang perspectives.

First, especially in the author's view, gangs are more than extreme examples of youth groups. Because of the interactions between gang members, between gangs, and between gangs and their communities, street gangs are, by and large, **qualitatively different from other youth groups**. To know street gangs, it is not sufficient merely to extrapolate from other youth groups. To prevent, intervene into, or control street gangs, it is not sufficient merely to apply more of the services and programs that have become traditional with other youth groups. To understand and deal with street gangs requires special knowledge–street gang knowledge. The gang is a group gone haywire, feeding on itself. When the ball team leaves the field, when the chess club ends its season, when the soccer rioters disperse to their homes, they revert to other, more permanent identities. But for many gang members, and for those fully committed ones that concern us the most, the gang becomes a "master identity." What is done to it, for it, and with it becomes a source of self-reinforcement. This is a major reason our programs fail: their effect is transformed by the gang members. The messages we send are not the messages received. The gang can contort, pervert, and transform our actions into meanings that increase their identity and cohesiveness. This is a pernicious process.

Second, most street gangs (though certainly not all) tend toward only moderate levels of organization, toward ill-defined and changing leadership, and a rhetoric of values and beliefs that is stronger in its statement than in its behavioral consequences. The "code" of the gang is weak. "West Side Story" is fiction, not fact.

Third, most street gangs–with an exception I will note later–tend toward a very versatile pattern of delinquent and criminal offending. They do everything and more often than not they–that is, the members–engage in minor offending: graffiti and vandalism, petty theft, minor fighting and threats, and various vices. While we hear much about violent gangs, or retreatist gangs, or smash-and-grab gangs, in fact these groups have received our labels based on only a portion of their behavior. We call this "cafeteria-style" offending. My friends know me as a red-meat eater, but I also eat white meats, vegetables, fruits and pastas. I am known as a Scotch drinker, but I also drink gin, ouzo, cognac, rum and beer; a little of this and a little of that is the rule both in food and in offending.

These several characteristics come together in yet a fourth theme, the amplification of criminal behavior by group processes within the gang. Over several decades, gang researchers using ethnographic or observational methods, and many police gang experts using their own mix of exposures, have been convinced that one major effect of group processes in gangs has been to increase the delinquent and criminal involvement of their members, beyond what those members might have done as individuals. Now, in the very recent reports of longitudinal projects in Rochester, New York (Thornberry et al., 1993), and Seattle (Battin, Hill, Abbott, et al., 1997), we have strong confirmation of this amplification or facilitation effect. The policy implications are fairly obvious for both gang members and their communities, for both are harmed by the consequences of gang membership. This is one of those factors that convince us that gangs are qualitatively different from other youth groups–they bear the seeds of their own bitter fruits.

A word about violence is also in order. As gangs amplify crime, they necessarily amplify violence, especially among territorial gangs that are in spasmodic or recurrent rivalries with other gangs. In the U.S., this is greatly enhanced by the number of and easy access to firearms. The lethal violence in particular is terribly disturbing. But while the media and the politicians allow gang violence to dominate their perspective, gang researchers must keep the cafeteria in mind. Gang crime comes in many forms, and violence is not the most common of these.

Finally, I want to offer some extended comments on street gang structures. Workshop participants had a chance to review the reprint on *Gangs in the United States and Europe* (Klein, 1996), but this material will be less familiar to American readers. The twin tendencies to stereotype gangs as all similar or to ignore the issue of gang structures have been harmful to research, to policy, and to public understandings of gangs. But as soon as we acknowledge the varieties of gang structures, we will have solved at least part of the paradox. Further, reviewing the varieties of gang structures helps to overcome some of the difficulties that stem from the absence of consensus on definitions of street gangs. Briefly, I suggest that most prior attempts at **defining** gangs have been nominal–using words and names to define informal youth groups that are so varied as to defy a single, inclusive characterization. An alternative approach is to adapt an **operational** definition, based on experiences with many gangs in many different settings. A typology of observed gang structures can supply such an operational definition.

It's not that we lack for gang typologies; these have been many but they have seldom been based on adequate data collection. In the U.S., we have well-known gang typologies from Cloward and Ohlin, Fagan, Huff, Taylor, Sanchez-Jankowski, Yablonsky, and even Klein in a 1971 review of the literature (see the review in Covey, Menard, and Franzese, 1997). And we have typologies derived from law enforcement. Both sources, the academic and the enforcement arenas, have emphasized one of two bases for gang types: race and ethnicity or behavior pattern. Almost none have been structural, that is, based on **group** properties of gangs.

In the U.S., earlier typologizing by ethnicity–Polish, Italian, Irish, black and so on–has been replaced by the threefold system of black, Hispanic, and Asian. The problem with a racial or ethnic typology is that it tells us far less than we assume. Certainly, there are some enduring cultural differences to be noted, but these are easily overwhelmed by the effects on all of them of racism and marginalization, by the common group processes to which I have alluded, and by the orientations to delinquent and criminal behaviors. The similarities far outweigh the differences.

Behavioral typologies would seem far more appealing: conflict, criminal, and retreatist gangs (Cloward and Ohlin); social, party, conflict and delinquent (Fagan); scavenger, territorial and corporate (Taylor); social, delinquent, and violent (Yablonsky); others abound. These were derived inductively from observational and survey research, but they don't hold up to empirical scrutiny because they fly in the face of crime versatility, of cafeteria-style offending. This is especially true if one applies self-report techniques which overcome the tendency of police to arrest, record, and report disproportionately those crimes of most concern to them–violence and drug sales. Gang members and gangs as units generally engage in many forms of crime and do not specialize in violence, or vandalism, or drug sales, or partying.

Since neither the ethnic nor the behavioral approach seems particularly accurate, Cheryl Maxson and I undertook a rather complex methodology–too complex to describe in detail here (see Maxson and Klein, 1995)–to derive **structural** patterns, if they really exist. Our data source was hundreds of police gang experts across the U.S. To avoid the *a priori* reliance on ethnic or behavioral (criminal) categories commonly used by police, we employed an inductive procedure in which these experts responded to individual "structural dimensions" of gangs. Specifically, they were asked to describe gangs known to them in terms of six dimensions–their size, duration, age range, subgroup organization, territoriality, and criminal versatility. Cohesiveness and leadership were omitted on the basis of earlier interviews that suggested police have stereotypic and unselected perspectives on these. Similarly, ethnicity and behavioral or criminal specificity were omitted.

Once we had a set of street gangs well known to the experts, each described by reference to these structural dimensions, an analysis of which dimensional positions were correlated with each other was performed. This yielded six potential patterns that were then cross-validated in interviews with 201 additional police experts. One of the six patterns did not hold up, so we have reported five fairly discrete gang structures arrived at inductively, and also have reported additional characteristics of them such as ethnicity and arrest patterns.

The results can be seen in Table 1, and in the brief descriptions that were used in the latter stages of our interviews and questionnaires with the police experts, as follows:[1]

Table 1. Characteristics of Five Street Gang Structures (In a sample of 201 cities)

	Traditional	Neotraditional	Compressed	Collective	Specialty
Average size	182	72	35	56	24
Sub-groups	Yes	Yes	No	No	No
Territorial	Yes	Yes	[No pattern]	[No pattern]	Yes
Crime versatility	Yes	Yes	Yes	Yes	No
Age range	Wide 20-30 yrs.	[No pattern]	Narrow <10 yrs.	Medium 10-20 yrs.	Narrow <10 yrs.
Duration	Long >20 yrs.	Short <10 yrs.	Short <10 yrs.	Medium 10-20 yrs.	Short <10 yrs.
Ethnicity					
Hispanic	57%	33%	27%	23%	20%
Black	20%	28%	31%	45%	32%
Asian	5%	10%	13%	21%	18%
White	12%	5%	13%	4%	10%
Mixed	6%	24%	15%	7%	20%
Number of cities	75	100	149	40	76*
Number of cities with 2:1 predominance	15	24	86	6	14
Number of gangs	316 (11%)	686 (24%)	1111 (39%)	264 (9%)	483 (17%)
Average arrest per month	10.9	9.2	6.1	7.4	5.7
Average arrest per person per month	.16	.20	.22	.17	.29

* Most common specialty focus was drugs (24), graffiti (20), assault (17). Other included burglary, auto theft, and robbery.

The Traditional gang: Traditional gangs have generally been in existence for twenty or more years–they keep regenerating themselves. They contain fairly clear subgroups, usually separated by age. O.G.s or Veteranos, Seniors, Juniors, Midget and various other names are applied to these different age-based cliques. Sometimes the cliques are separated as neighborhoods rather than by age. More than other gangs Traditional gangs tend to have a wide age range, sometimes as wide as from nine or ten years of age into the thirties. These are usually very large gangs, numbering one hundred or even several hundred members. Almost always, they are territorial in the sense that they identify strongly with their turf, 'hood, or barrio, and claim it as theirs alone.

In sum, this is a large enduring, territorial gang with a wide age range and several internal cliques based on age or area.

long-lasting
large
usually: distinct subgroups
wide age range
strongly territorial

The Neo-Traditional gang: The Neo-Traditional gang resembles the Traditional form, but has not been in existence as long–probably no more than ten years, and often less. It may be medium size–say fifty to one hundred members–or also into the hundreds. It probably has developed subgroups or cliques based on age or area, but sometimes may not. The age range is usually smaller than in Traditional gangs. The Neo-Traditional gang is also very territorial, claiming turf and defending it like the Traditional gang.

In sum, the Neo-Traditional gang is a newer territorial gang that looks on its way to becoming Traditional in time. Thus at this point it is subgrouping, but may not have achieved the size and wide age range of the Traditional gang. The subgrouping, territoriality, and size suggest that it is evolving into the Traditional form.

duration of ten years or less
medium to large in size
usually: distinct subgroups
strongly territorial

The Compressed gang: The Compressed gang is small–usually in the size range of up to fifty members–and has not formed subgroups. The age range is probably narrow–ten or fewer years between the younger and older members. The small size, absence of subgroups, and narrow age range may reflect the newness of the group, in existence less than ten years and maybe for only a few years. Some of these Compressed gangs have become territorial, but many have not.

In sum, Compressed gangs have a relatively short history, short enough that by size, duration, subgrouping and territoriality, it is unclear whether they will grow and solidify into the more traditional forms, or simply remain as less complex groups.

	short history
	small
usually:	no subgroups
	narrow age range

The Collective gang: The Collective gang looks like the Compressed form, but bigger and with a wider age range–maybe ten or more years between younger and older members. Size can be under a hundred, but is probably larger. Surprisingly, given these numbers, it has not developed subgroups, and may or may not be a territorial gang. It probably has a ten to fifteen year existence.

In sum, the Collective gang resembles a kind of shapeless mass of adolescent and young adult members that has not developed the distinguishing characteristics of other gangs.

	duration ten to fifteen years
	medium to large in size
usually:	no subgroups
	medium to wide age range

The Specialty gang: Unlike these other gangs that engage in a wide variety of criminal offenses, crime in this type of group is narrowly focused on a few offenses: the group comes to be characterized by the specialty. The specialty gang tends to be small–usually fifty or fewer members–without any subgroups in most cases (there are exceptions). It probably has a history of less than ten years, but has developed a well-defined territory. Its territory may be either residential or based on the opportunities for the particular form of crime in which it specializes. The age range of most Specialty gangs is narrow, but in others is broad.

In sum, the Specialty gang is crime-focused in a narrow way. Its principal purpose is more criminal than social, and its smaller size and form of territoriality may be a reflection of this focused crime pattern.

duration under ten years
small
usually: no subgroups
usually narrow age range
narrow criminal focus
territorial

The earlier paper (Klein, 1996) included my attempt to apply this five-structure paradigm to the reports I had gathered about gangs in Europe. Was it helpful? I think so, since it permitted me to clarify these reports in my own mind, and to locate different patterns within the same city in some cases, such as Stockholm. Here are other comments that could be made as well.

• Some of the so-called gangs in Europe probably are not gangs, but informal youth groups or networks. Having the five types makes this more obvious.

• Some of the gangs in Europe lack what has been thought of as a common feature in America–territoriality–probably because of the different locations of ethnic or national groups in many European cities. Gangs located centrally in the Kreuzberg section of Berlin are highly territorial; those in the Rinkeby outskirts of Stockholm are not.

• Some "marginal" gangs make it clear that the typology discovered for the U.S. needs continuing work. For instance, well-described Vietnamese gangs in the U.S. are far less territorial than others, and perhaps more focused on property crimes. Skinheads–more prominent in Europe than in the U.S.–stretch the meaning of street gangs; they are less street-oriented, and more focused on a particular crime pattern, for example. Yet I find I am comfortable placing them in the Specialty gang category of the paradigm, along with drug gangs, burglary gangs, and others.

Finally, let me add that we're in the midst of a four-year update of these gang structures. Of fifty-four gangs studied again, 20 percent have disbanded, either naturally or under police pressure. The Traditional and Compressed gangs remain the most stable, while 14 of 16 Neo-Traditional and Collective gangs have transitioned to one of the other forms. The smaller Specialty gangs disbanded at the highest rate. These stabilities and instabilities are roughly what we expected to see, although the amount of change surprises us. At any given time, the five structures still comprise the full census of gangs, but movement across types is important to keep in mind.

My hope in presenting these structural materials, along with the other facets of street gangs in this introductory paper, is that we can move rapidly toward research that will test their utility in Europe–and later elsewhere. The danger, of course, is that we create the phenomenon where it does not exist. Part of the paradox lies in the stereotype of the American gang; if we clarify the patterns of such gangs, we may reify a complex paradigm as a substitute for the stereotype.

And yet we can't afford to avoid seeking the patterns, because to deny gang existence is to allow them to emerge without understanding, without the capacity to form relevant and data-driven policy. As John Hagedorn (1998), among others, has illustrated, echoing the early remarks of Thrasher, many gangs evolve out of non-threatening, normal youth groups–play groups, music groups, special interest groups, and so on. When we can learn what it is that leads the minority of multitudinous youth groups to take on the mantle of the street gang, then maybe we can turn the corner from simplistic control to thoughtful prevention.

REFERENCES

Battin, S. B., K. G. Hill, R.D. Abbott, R.F. Catalano, and J.D. Hawkins (1997). The contribution of gang membership to delinquency beyond delinquent friends. Criminology 36(1): 93-115.

Covey, H. C., S. Menard, and R.J. Franzese (1997). Juvenile Gangs, Second Edition. Springfield, Illinois: Charles C. Thomas.

Hagedorn, J.M. (1998). People and Folks, Second Edition. Chicago: Lakeview Press.

Klein, M.W. (1996). Gangs in the United States and Europe. European Journal on Crime Policy and Research 4(2): 63-80.

Maxson, C. L. and M.W. Klein (1995). Investigating gang structures. Journal of Gang Research 3(1): 33-40.

Reiss, A.J. (1986). Co-offender influences on criminal careers. In A. Blumstein, J. Cohen, J.A. Roth, and C.A. Visher (eds.), Criminal Careers and "Career Criminals," Vol. II. Washington, D.C.: National Academy Press.

Sarnecki, J. (1986). Delinquent Networks. Stockholm: The National Council for Crime Prevention.

Thornberry, T.P, M. D. Krohn, A. J. Lizotte, and D. Chard-Wierschem (1993). The role of juvenile gangs in facilitating delinquent behavior. Journal of Research in Crime and Delinquency 30(1): 55-87.

ENDNOTES

1. Some of the materials are adapted from Maxson and Klein, 1995, and are reproduced here with the permission of the *Journal of Gang Research.*

Chapter 2

THE IMPACT OF ORGANIZATIONAL FEATURES ON GANG ACTIVITIES AND RELATIONSHIPS

Scott H. Decker
University of Missouri at St. Louis

What are the key structural features of gangs? How do these organizational characteristics affect gang activities? Law enforcement (Fox and Amador, 1993), media sources, the popular press and some government agencies (Conly, 1993) support the view that gangs are well organized and that gang activities reflect this reality. From this perspective, gangs are perceived as highly organized, well-coordinated, and efficient organizations that function much like a corporation. From this view, gangs have clearly articulated goals, motivate well-disciplined members toward the achievement of these goals, and operate with financial efficiency and rationality. Over time, disorganized aggregations of predatory individuals evolve into formal-rational gangs that purposively engage in crimes motivated and organized by the gang. However, an alternative view argues that most gangs are not well organized, and that the behavior of gang members reflects their status as adolescents. This issue has important implications for both prevention and intervention, and it bears on a central question about the nature of criminal behavior. However, little empirical evidence addresses these questions. In this paper, I review the results of interviews with gangs in three different cities, differentiating between the structural characteristics and organizational features of gangs. The emphasis is primarily on organizational features.

M.W. Klein et al (eds.), The Eurogang Paradox, 21–39.

GROUPS, GANGS AND CRIME

The structure of gangs and gang activity is an important issue in our understanding of gangs specifically and crime more generally. Drug sales provide insights into the relationship between structure and criminal behavior, because a large number of gang members sell drugs and a large amount of money is involved in the sale of drugs. Decker and Van Winkle (1995) suggest that there are two competing views of this relationship and that these views help shape the discussion of gang structure and organization. The instrumental-rational view is reflected in the work of Skolnick, Correl, Navarro, and Rabb (1988), Padilla (1992), Sanchez-Jankowski (1991), and Taylor (1990), who describe gangs as well-organized entrepreneurs who employ traditional economic strategies of marketing, structure, and profits that are re-invested in the gang. The gangs depicted in these works have a vertical structure, enforce discipline among their members, and are quite successful in defining and achieving group values. A contrasting view is found in the work of several well-known gang researchers, including Hagedorn (1988), Maxson, Klein and Cunningham (1991), Fagan (1989), and Klein (1995). Their research describes gang drug sales in starkly different terms, emphasizing the informal-individual characteristics of many youth gangs, and their difficulties organizing activities, producing consensus, and controlling profits. From this view, gangs are diffuse, self-interested and self-motivated aggregations of individuals, who mostly sell drugs for themselves. Decker and Van Winkle (1995) report results from their field study in St. Louis compatible with the latter conclusion. Indeed, their results support a view of drug sales as a rather haphazard, individually focussed activity.

The debate over the organizational level of street gang drug sales offers an important theoretical perspective on the issue of the organization of criminal activities. At the heart of this controversy is the extent to which offenders articulate and embrace common goals, motivate others to join them in a common enterprise, and maintain a structured monetary and emotional commitment to crime as a group enterprise. While there has been limited research on this topic in the matter of gangs, there has been considerable research regarding the stature of organizational structure among street criminals. This work generally shows that most of the individuals involved in crime are not well organized and have limited effectiveness in achieving common goals. For example, studies of active robbers (Einstadter, 1969;

Conklin, 1972; Wright and Decker, 1997) and burglars (Wright and Decker, 1994; Cromwell, Olsen, and Avery, 1991; Tunnel, 1995) concluded that these offenders rarely plan their offenses, do not work well in groups, and fail to use the proceeds of their criminality in ways to further their criminal activities. Indeed, these offenders act in a rather haphazard manner–Wright and Decker call it encapsulated, most often driven by drugs, drink, or desire to impress their friends. Beyond burglars and robbers lurks a broader group of street criminals, particularly those who engage in petty theft and drug sales. Best and Luckenbill (1994) suggest that independence among offenders is the norm, and that social organization is largely absent from the criminal involvement of these individuals. This view receives support from Irwin, who argues that "disorganized criminals" are:

> ... the largest category of active criminals, includes the less skilled, less sophisticated thieves who spend most of their time while not in prison hanging around, waiting for something to come along, and engaging in unplanned, unprofitable petty crimes, often on impulse (1972:122).

Adler (1985) suggests that while individual drug sellers are enmeshed in a broader organization of suppliers, that organization is more a consequence of social life being a series of relationships than the well-orchestrated efforts of a coordinated group. Indeed, many criminal activities require coordination at a minimal level, but are the consequence of short-term associations of convenience rather than organized crime.

This paper uses the results of interviews with active gang members from three cities, St. Louis, Missouri, San Diego, California, and Chicago, Illinois. In San Diego and Chicago, four gangs–one African-American and one Hispanic in each city were interviewed. The Chicago gangs were the Latin Kings and the Gangster Disciples, two of the city's most organized gangs. They fit the Maxson and Klein (1995) description of a "Traditional" gang, as they have been around for quite some time, are large with distinct subgroups, have wide age ranges and are strongly territorial. In San Diego, we interviewed members of an African-American gang (Lincoln Park Piru) and a Hispanic gang (Calle Triente). The Lincoln Park gang resembles the "Neotraditional" gang in the Maxson and Klein five-category typology. This gang has been in existence less than a decade, is medium to large in size and exhibits considerable territoriality. However, it does not have distinct subgroups as would be expected by the typology. Their Hispanic counterparts in San Diego look more like a "Collective" gang, with ten to fifteen years of existence, medium to large in size, no subgroups, and a considerable age range. The orientation to Hispanic cultural matters plays a large role in shaping the character of this gang. The St. Louis interviews are built on members from 29 different gangs (most of which were African-Americans), thirteen that claimed affiliations with Bloods and sixteen with Crips. By and large, these gangs resemble the African American gang studied in San Diego, emerging recently, with medium to large size memberships and strong territoriality. However, they do not have distinct subgroups.

The goal is to determine the extent to which gangs have begun to exhibit the characteristics of formal organizations. The interest here is not so much in structural characteristics of the gang, such as its longevity, size, territoriality, or age range. Rather, I have organized the results of our interview findings around three major categories: (1) organizational features of gangs, (2) gang activities, and (3) relationships with other gangs. This paper reviews evidence about the extent to which the organizational features of gang are formal or informal.

A key indicator of the extent to which gangs are evolving into more formal groups is how well organized they are to carry out gang activities. In this context it was determined whether gangs had levels of membership, leaders, regular meetings, written rules, and discipline of their members. Taken together, such features may provide operational indicators of a more organized gang.

The second set of indicators measured the criminal activities in which gang members engage. Many of these measures focused on drugs, such as selling drugs, organizing drug sales, supplying large quantities of drugs, or using drug money for gang purposes. The final measure of gang activities determines whether there were consequences for gang members who left the gang.

One consequence of the increasing organization and sophistication of gangs can be found in the relationships they maintain with other gangs and legitimate enterprises such as neighborhood stores. This can be measured by asking if gangs met together, sold drugs together, committed crime together, or partied together. In addition, we sought to determine the extent to which street gangs maintained relationships with prison gangs and legitimate political and neighborhood groups.

GANG ORGANIZATION

Levels of Membership

An important indicator of the level of gang organization is differentiation of membership levels within the gang. In general, the less differentiation there is between roles or levels of membership within the gang, the less developed the organization is, and the less effective it can be in generating common goals and producing compliance among members in the pursuit of those goals. Well-defined roles among Chicago gangs were found, but not among the gangs in San Diego or St. Louis. This reflects the "emerging" nature of the gang situation in San Diego and St. Louis, as well as the longer history of Chicago gangs. However, even some Chicago gang members expressed uncertainty about whether there were different levels of membership. In sum, the results support the contention that there are important differences in the degree of organizational differentiation between gangs in Chicago and those in St. Louis and San Diego. In the emerging gang cities, few members could offer distinctions between levels of membership or duties associated with those levels. In Chicago, however, role differentiation was greatest for the Gangster Disciples, although some of it appeared to take on a "mythic" character.

Leaders

A second characteristic of well-organized groups is the presence of leadership roles. Gang members were asked to elaborate specifically on the presence of leaders within their gangs, and whether leaders had any special roles, responsibilities, or skills. Again, the city was the most important dimension in determining whether leaders were present in the gang. Gangs in Chicago, especially the Gangster Disciples, reported that their gang had leaders, and the leaders performed different functions than regular members. Latin Kings described a less-defined leadership category. Virtually none of the St. Louis or San Diego gang members could tell us anything about leaders, except that where it existed, leadership was a characteristic of activities not individuals.

Regular Meetings

An important characteristic of organized groups is meetings. Meetings accomplish a variety of functions, including enhancing group cohesion, communicating responsibilities, and disseminating information. Almost all of our respondents told us that their gang had meetings, although the character of these meetings varied considerably. In Chicago meetings tended to occur more regularly and have a more formal character. This was not the case in St. Louis and San Diego.

Written Rules

Another characteristic of organized groups is their commitment to formal rules to enforce discipline and maintain order among members. Rules announce important organizational values, provide a means of forging consensus, and allow organizations to announce their boundaries by punishing unacceptable conduct. The great majority of the gang members interviewed indicated that their gangs did have rules. The character of those rules and their enforcement varied considerably within and between gangs. The view of rules in these gangs is consistent with the indicators of gang organization reviewed above. Only the Gangster Disciples stand apart from the other gangs in that they have a written constitution, acknowledged by all members. In this sense, consistency was found across the indicators of gang organization considered here, regardless of city.

GANG ACTIVITIES

I focus next on gang activities. Although a higher percentage of Chicago gang members reported involvement in criminal activities, the differences between Chicago gangs and those in St. Louis or San Diego were diminished compared to the results presented above. This indicates that while Chicago gangs are more organized, counterparts in emerging gang cities hardly lag behind them in the commission of criminal activities. One conclusion to be drawn from this set of findings is that levels of organization are not necessarily linked to increased involvement in crime, a finding true of the adult offenders studied by Best and Luckenbill (1994) and Adler (1985).

An important measure of gang organization may be found in the activities in which they engage. Here I examine five specific spheres of activity: (1) specialization within the gang, (2) organization of drug sales, (3) use of money made in gang endeavors, (4) ownership of legitimate businesses, and (5) gang involvement in political activities. It is not merely the involvement in these activities; rather, we sought to determine the extent to which activities are organized by the gang, involve a large proportion of gang members, and serve gang goals.

Specialization

A hallmark characteristic of organized groups, especially formal organizations such as corporations or public service groups, is specializing in a particular set of activities. Specialization requires expertise and technical skills in a defined area, recruiting and developing members with such skills, and establishing a reputation for that activity. Little evidence was found that any of the four gangs examined had developed such specialization. This finding is consistent with a long tradition of gang research that describes gang offending as "cafeteria style" (Klein, 1995) committing a variety of offenses with virtually no specialization. This style of offending by gang members is similar to that of adult offending described by Gottfredson and Hirschi (1989) in their "general" theory of crime. Other recent ethnographies of offenders (Cromwell, 1991; Wright and Decker, 1994) show that offenders rarely specialize and instead commit offenses in an opportunistic fashion.

Organization of Drug Sales and Use of Drug Money

Drug sales are a major activity among street gang members, and the gang members interviewed were no exception. A majority of the members of each gang told us that the gang played an active role in organizing drug sales, either by providing large amounts of drugs, managing money, or specifying roles in drug sales. If gangs are evolving into organized groups heavily involved in crime, they are most likely to do so in areas that involve considerable amounts of money, such as street drug sales. By choosing the two most organized gangs in the city with the most organized gangs (Chicago), we provided a direct test of this hypothesis.

The role of gangs in organizing drug sales in San Diego and St. Louis differed in several ways from Chicago gangs. While GDs and Kings could identify separate roles in drug sales, and some of the Chicago gang members pointed to a role for the gang in overseeing drug profits, no such roles were reported by San Diego or St. Louis gang members. Street gang drug sales in these cities conform to the balkanized and informal model found in a number of emerging gang cities described by Decker and Van Winkle (1995).

Clearly gang members are heavily involved in drug sales, and gangs play a role–largely through contacts that exist within the gang and cliques or subgroups of friends in the gang–in drug sales. But the level of organization is at best primitive, and at worst nonexistent. This view is consistent with the findings of Reuter et al. (1990) and Fagan (1992) who report drug sales of a rather haphazard nature at the street level.

Drug Profits Used for Gang Activities

One clear indicator of a formal organizational character among gangs would be the use of drug profits to further the interests of the gang. A key to understanding any organization involved in financial ventures is to follow the flow of cash. Thus, documenting how money is managed (its flow through the organization) and how it is spent should shed light on the level of gang organization. By and large, our respondents told us that the money they made from selling drugs remained with them for their own purposes, and most involved individual consumption of a rather immediate nature, such as clothes, parties, cars, and jewelry. Of course, this makes sense as it reflects the age-graded interests of most members.

Reflecting their more disorganized character, members of the San Diego and St. Louis gangs indicated that drug profits were used for individual purposes, especially those related to individual consumption. Most studies indicate that the primary (if not sole) use of drug profits among gang members is for individual consumption.

Gangs Own Legitimate Businesses

One measure of an increasingly organized gang would be efforts to find legitimate economic activities, such as businesses, that the gang could invest in and use to expand its criminal interests. This is a pattern that organized crime groups have used in the past to allow them to find legitimate roles for members and expand their influence in the community. In addition, by owning legitimate businesses gangs have the opportunity to exploit their own business-related enterprises for criminal purposes. Indeed, one of the great virtues of owning a legitimate business for crime groups has been the ability to use that business to pressure other legitimate businesses in ways that lead to illegal profits.

This is the first category where one of the gangs exhibited behavior consistent with higher levels of organization. The majority of Gangster Disciples identified legitimate businesses that their gang owned and operated. In most cases, these businesses did more than provide small-scale neighborhood services. Instead, these enterprises generated considerable sums of cash, allowing members of the GDs to launder drug money at these locations. This stands in contrast to the Hispanic gang in San Diego that identified car detailing businesses, usually run out of a parent's garage, as the means by which their gang had begun to penetrate legitimate businesses.

Political Activities

The final activity examined is the involvement of gang members in politics. Such involvement is evidence of increased organization on the part of gangs, as it may facilitate their ability to influence the political process. Given the volume of patronage jobs available to elected officials, especially in cities like Chicago, efforts to penetrate the political process have considerable benefits.

Nearly every Gangster Disciple identified political activities organized by the gang. These activities included passing out leaflets backing certain candidates, voter registration drives, soliciting contributions, and raising political awareness. A number of GDs mentioned the groups "21st Century Vote" and "Growth and Development" as vehicles through which the gang had become politically active. These groups have been active in Chicago, organizing neighborhood support for candidates sympathetic to their concerns for the last several years, albeit unsuccessfully. The political involvement of San Diego gang members is similar to that of the Latin Kings. One told us that voting was the political activity that some members participated in, and two said that the gang was active in politics but could not specify how. In general, St. Louis gang members were at a loss to understand how they could have an impact on the political process.

RELATIONSHIPS WITH OTHER GANGS

Relationships between gangs are important in attempting to determine whether gangs are becoming more like formal organizations. If street gangs are evolving from relatively disorganized groups to formal organizations, a series of mutually reinforcing relationships built on instrumental concerns should be observed. One measure of gang organization is a network of relationships between the gang and other groups. Such groups may include businesses in the neighborhood, gangs in other cities, prison gangs, and other criminal enterprises that provide opportunities for gangs and gang members. These four issues were explored in an attempt to determine the extent to which gang relationships were expanding beyond the narrow circle of gang members and neighborhoods.

Relationships with Neighborhood Stores

I first explore the relationships gangs have with businesses in their communities. In addition to a general question about relationships between the gang and neighborhood stores, it was asked whether gang members obtained credit from stores, protected stores, received payment to protect stores, extorted money from stores, or sold stolen goods to store owners. A consistent picture emerged as I talked to gang members about their relationships with local storeowners: only the Gangster Disciples had made significant inroads into the ownership or control of neighborhood stores. The great majority of members of other gangs seemed to barely understand these questions. It was as if they had never contemplated such matters. Most told us businesses in their neighborhood disliked them because gangs discouraged business and were viewed as a threat to commit crimes against those businesses.

There was considerable evidence among GDs that the gang was an important presence in the operation of neighborhood stores. This may stem from the large number, age, and concentration of GDs in many Chicago neighborhoods, as well as the more extensive participation of the gang in the ownership of legitimate businesses. Simply put, GDs shopped in, protected, and owned many such businesses. As such, they had a strong interest in these enterprises. A vastly different picture was found for the Latin Kings and the St. Louis and San Diego gangs. Only one King told us that gang members engaged in extortion, but the nature of this extortion more closely resembled individual property crime than an effort organized by the gang. Most members of the two San Diego gangs told us that they (and their gang) maintained good relationships with stores in their neighborhood. The hallmark of these relationships was the fact that the respondents regarded themselves as regular customers valued by the store. In St. Louis, gang members were most likely to respond that storeowners didn't like them around because they were bad for business, discouraging other customers and being under suspicion for shoplifting.

Relationships with Gangs in Other Cities

Police departments in the United States have talked a good deal about the "spreading tentacles" of gang membership. Such a statement clearly implies that gangs are being franchised, primarily out of Los Angeles or Chicago, to new gang territory. From this perspective, gangs from one city find a new territory, send veteran members to that territory to start new gangs, and reproduce themselves in a new city. A corollary to this argument is that networks among gangs exist across the country, exchanging cash, goods (primarily drugs and guns), and intelligence across a complex web of cities with inter-related gangs. Maxson, Woods, and Klein (1996) found little support for the "franchise" hypothesis, following interviews with knowledgeable law enforcement representatives in more than 200 cities. Rather, they concluded that most gang migration occurs primarily as a consequence of normal migratory pressures–family relocation, job opportunities, and the like–rather than concerted efforts to spread criminal activities by gangs.

These findings correspond closely to the Maxson and Klein conclusions about gang migration. Nearly every subject interviewed could identify other cities that were important to their gang or where relationships with other gang members were maintained. However, the origins of these relationships lacked the instrumental character associated with the view that gangs had actively franchised themselves across the country. The basis for much of the relationship with gangs in different cities was of an expressive nature, stemming from family or peer relationships. However, it is clear that the ability to buy or sell drugs and guns added an instrumental character to many of those relationships.

More Gangster Disciples maintained relationships with gangs in other cities, and those relationships were based on instrumental benefits. Latin Kings who commented on this issue told us that there were "Kings all over," but articulated the link between their gang in Chicago and those in other cities in far more tenuous terms. More often than not, the basis of such relationships was through family or friends. Despite their proximity to Los Angeles, members of each San Diego gang depicted their relationships with gangs in other cities in more general terms. They described weak linkages that provided few instrumental benefits to either party. A number of San Diego gang members described their relationship with Los Angeles gangs as based on dealing drugs together, although this was an exception. It was more likely that hanging out or ties to family formed the basis of such relationships. In St. Louis a similar picture emerged, with familial relationships a key to contacts with gangs in other cities.

Relationships with Prison Gangs

The past decade has seen a record pace for the use of incarceration in the United States. Because of their involvement in violence and drug sales, many gang members have been sent to prison during this time. Because prisons create the need for individual security and protection, they are ideal places for gangs to proliferate. The need for protection offers a rationale for the benefits of maintaining gang affiliations, but there are other reasons. Because a large number of gang members are imprisoned, they can use existing relationships to provide them with protection and commodities. Gang members who go to prison have a stake in maintaining ties to fellow gang members on the street, as they can lean on them for favors of a monetary, influential, or criminal nature. However, such relationships are functional for all inmates, not just gang members. Thus it is not surprising to find that gang members maintain relationships with gangs on the street. It is the *nature* of those relationships that tells us whether gangs are becoming more organized, moving down a path toward becoming formal organizations.

Gangs have existed in Illinois prisons for at least three decades, and Chicago gangs have been the most prominent of all such groups. The influence of prison gangs on street gang activity in Chicago is considerable. Prison gangs often call the shots for the street gang, identifying targets of violence, locations for drug sales, and other significant decisions about gang activity, criminal and non-criminal. In some ways this makes sense, as gang leaders are likely to be older, and older gang members face greater odds of being incarcerated owing to their lengthy involvement in criminal activities. Nearly every Chicago gang member told us that imprisoned gang members played a role in directing street gang actions. A very different picture emerged from our interviews with San Diego and St. Louis gang members. Although the majority told us that they stayed in touch with gang members in prison (as did prison gang members stay in touch with those on the street), the nature of such contacts had a more informal character, often based on familial relations. Ethnicity was a primary affiliational factor in prison gang associations. Imprisoned gang members tended to disregard divisive intra-ethnic gang affiliations from the street and associate primarily on the basis of ethnic identity while in prison. In sum, street gangs in all three cities maintained relationships with imprisoned gang members. For Chicago gangs, these relationships had a more instrumental character, providing formal linkages designed to provide direct input from the prison for the day-to-day operation of the street gang. In San Diego and St. Louis, such communication occurred along more informal lines, and was generally focussed on issues of family or friends.

Other Groups to Graduate to after the Gang

The review sought to determine whether street gangs are evolving into more formal organizations. To determine this, gang members were asked if their gang had relations with organized crime groups, and more importantly, if there were adult criminal groups gang members could join and with whom they could commit crimes. These are key issues in the evolution of gangs into more organized, efficient forms of committing crime. The results of this line of questioning can be summarized quite succinctly. Not a single respondent in any of the three cities were able to identify a crime group to which they could graduate, nor could a single respondent identify an organized crime group with which their gang could eventually affiliate.

CONCLUSION

This review has examined a central question in our understanding of contemporary American street gangs–the extent to which such groups are evolving into organized crime groups. I focussed on gangs in two emerging gang cities (San Diego and St. Louis) and two gangs from an established gang city (Chicago). Three spheres of gang activity were examined: (1) organization, (2) activities, and (3) relationships.

The results provide a number of important directions to the central question that motivated this review. In San Diego, the two gangs identified by law enforcement and social service providers had ceased to be central players on the street within a year of that designation. The disorganized character of these gangs is consistent with what Sanders (1994) and Pennell (1994) each found in their studies of San Diego gangs. Results of numerous studies of gangs in emerging gang cities such as St. Louis (Decker and Van Winkle, 1996), Milwaukee (Hagedorn, 1988), Denver, Cleveland and Columbus, Ohio (Huff, 1996), Seattle (Fleisher, 1995), Kansas City (Fleisher, 1999), and San Francisco (Waldorf, 1996) confirmed these findings, as well. Interestingly, the results for St. Louis parallel those for San Diego quite closely, as their gangs have been characterized as disorganized and ineffective criminal organizations (Decker and Van Winkle, 1996).

The story for Chicago is quite different. The Gangster Disciples exhibited many characteristics of formal groups, resembling in many respects organized crime groups. In organization, activities, and relationships, this gang has moved well beyond the rather disorganized, informal groups that have appeared in most American cities in the past decade. GDs also appear to have forged effective and solid relationships with gangs in prison, and to a lesser extent, gangs in other cities. Despite this, there appears to be virtually no penetration into traditional organized crime groups. Latin Kings represent a model of the cultural gang, as elements of Hispanic culture play a central role in the gang. And, while more organized than their San Diego counterparts, these gangs appear not to have embarked on the course followed by their African-American counterparts.

In addition to the substantive findings, this study has demonstrated the importance of comparative studies of gangs. Just as single city studies have documented the salience of neighborhood characteristics for gang organization, activities, and relationships, there are important city level differences and histories that affect these features of gang life. Clearly, the neighborhood, cultural, and institutional context of the city of Chicago has had a different impact on gangs than has been the case for most cities. This conclusion can be linked to the long history of gangs in Chicago, as well as the latent consequences of many gang prevention and intervention programs that strengthened rather than weakened the influence of these gangs.

I close this report with some observations about the relationship between group organizational development and crime. Because most crime committed by youths occurs in a group context and is organized to at least some limited degree, it is important to understand the role of gang organizational characteristics. The explanation of this issue has important consequences for how we view gang activities as they evolve over time. Clearly, the cultural and institutional features of the gang interact with the opportunity structure in communities, both licit and illicit, to produce a degree of organization. In addition, the level of organization of groups involved in crime is affected by the characteristics of individuals in the gang and the technology they use in pursuit of goals (Fickenauer and Waring, 1996). Each of the gangs examined had sufficient and appropriate culture to move them toward becoming organized crime groups. However, the institutional features of San Diego and St. Louis gangs were far less developed than were those of their Chicago counterparts, owing largely to the age of the gangs and their members. Haphazard, individually focussed economic pursuits require far less technology–and organization–than do more sustainable economic efforts. These organizational features make San Diego and St. Louis gangs and their activities resemble the disorganized groups described by Thrasher (1927) in the early stages of organization. However, Chicago gangs, particularly the Gangster Disciples, are more organized and are beginning to display some of the salient features of organized crime, particularly economic organization, penetration of legitimate businesses, and the maintenance of sustained intergenerational capability. These findings reinforce the centrality of understanding the forces that shape organizational characteristics of gangs, and their implications for crime.

This review concludes with two important recommendations for future research. First, it is critical to specify the organizational features of gangs and other groups involved in offending, and the role that such organizational features play in that offending. Our research has led us to identify a number of factors, which are subsumed under three headings, Organization, Activities, and Relationships. These are summarized in Table 1. These factors are suggestive of the sorts of issues that must be determined to identify the impact of gang structure on activities and relationships.

Table 1. Key Features of Gangs and Behavior

Organization	**Activities**	**Relationships**
Levels of Membership	Drug Sales	Engage in Crime Together
Leaders	Supplying Drugs	Contact with Prison Gangs
Meetings	Reinvesting Drug Profits	Legitimate Groups
Written Rules	Punishment for Leaving Gangs	Neighborhood Groups
Discipline	Gang	
Post Gang Groups		

These topics provide suggestions for future research, particularly in locales where gangs are less well understood. As a gang exhibits more of these variables, and more of each of them, it takes on the attributes of a formal organization. This is important because formal organizations are capable of completing a greater number of complex acts than are their underdeveloped counterparts. In particular, we suggest that the variables in the first column (Organization) are the most important set to understand. It is useful from this perspective to think of groups as tools. The ability of a tool to complete a discrete task is enhanced to the extent that it contains the capability to do so. As organizations, gangs may be inefficient–though perhaps not always ineffective–in completing crimes that call for specialization, sustainability, a division of labor, and the ability to motivate the troops. When these organizational features are found in combination with activities and relationships, gangs have become more powerful forces to deal with.

It is also important to specify the factors that may account for these features. Why is it that gangs in Chicago are more organized than their counterparts in other cities? In Table 2, I suggest a list of key variables that may account for the variation in gang organization and structure across cities. These are structural and institutional characteristics of cities that may provide fertile territory for the initial development of gangs as well as an increased level of organization. It is important to understand the attributes of gangs as well as the broader context within which they operate, as the latter affects the former.

Table 2. Features that Affect Gang Organization and Structure

City Size–Larger cities are more likely to have highly organized structures than are smaller cities

Nature of the Gang Problem–Chronic gang cities are more likely to have highly organized gangs than do emerging gang cities.

Proximity to Chronic Gang Cities–Cities in close proximity to chronic gang cities (and their more organized gangs) are likely to have more organized gangs. Transportation access, particularly interstate highways, freeways, or motorways enhance proximity.

Ethnicity–Gang organizational structure is likely to vary by ethnicity, particularly as cultural factors play a role in organizing the gang and activities in the neighborhoods where gang members reside.

Underclass–The isolation of an urban underclass will have an impact on gang organization. Generally, underclass neighborhoods will not produce the most organized gangs; they will be found where legitimate and illegitimate opportunity structures are better developed.

Institutional Opposition–The degree of institutional opposition will strengthen gang organization. Gang cohesion in particular is enhanced by external threats to the gang.

Age of Gangs–The longer gangs have existed in a city, the more organized they may become. This is especially true where gangs have begun to penetrate the legitimate institutional structure.

Presence of Organized Criminal Groups–The presence of organized criminal groups in a city will lead to more organized gangs. This as much reflects the availability of organized crime opportunities as it does the penetration of organized crime groups by gangs.
Age of Gang Members–As gangs include more, older members, their ability to lead and control member behavior will increase, as will the sophistication of gang crimes.

This list is by no means exhaustive. However, the list does suggest important avenues for investigating the characteristics that lead to more organized gangs. The findings from this review suggest that the level of gang organization affects the nature of involvement in crime and relationships with other groups. In addition, this review suggests that the institutional and cultural context within which gangs evolve plays a critical role in determining the nature of gangs that emerge and the nature of their development.

REFERENCES

Adler, P. (1985). Wheeling and Dealing. New York: Columbia University Press.
Best, J. and D. Luckenbill (1994). Organizing Deviance. Englewood Cliffs, NJ: Prentice Hall.
Conklin, J. (1972). Robbery. Philadelphia: J.B. Lippincott.
Conly, C. (1993). Street Gangs: Current Knowledge and Strategies. National Institute of Justice, Issues and Practices.
Cromwell, P., J. Olson, and D. Avery (1991). Breaking and Entering: An Ethnographic Analysis of Burglary. Beverly Hills, CA: Sage.
Decker, S.H. and B. Van Winkle (1995). Slinging dope: Drug sales and gangs. Justice Quarterly 11: 1001-1022.
Decker, S. H. and B. Van Winkle (1996). Life in the Gang: Family, Friends, and Violence. New York: Cambridge University Press.
Einstadter, W. (1969). The social organization of robbery. Social Problems 64-83.
Fagan, J. (1989). The social organization of drug use and drug dealing among urban gangs. Criminology 27: 633-669.
Fagan, J. (1992). Drug sales and work in the inner city. In A. Harrell and J. McCarthy (eds.), Drugs, Crime and Social Isolation. Urban Institute Press.
Fleisher, M. (1999). Dead End Kids: Gang Girls and the Boys They Know. Madison, WI: University of Wisconsin Press.
Fox, R. W. and M.E. Amador (1993). Gangs on the Move. Placerville, CA: Copperhouse.
Gottfredson, M. and T. Hirschi (1990). A General Theory of Crime. Stanford, CA:Stanford University Press.
Hagedorn, J. (1988). People and Folks. Chicago: Lakeview Press.
Huff, C. R. (1996). The Criminal Behavior of Gang Members. Final Report to the National Institute of Justice.

Irwin, J. (1972). The inmates perspective. In J.D. Douglas (ed.), Research on Deviance. New York: Random House.
Klein, M. (1995). The American Street Gang. New York: Oxford University Press.
Klein, M., C. Maxson, and L. Cunningham (1991). Crack, street gangs, and violence. Criminology 29(4): 623-650.
Maxson, C. and M. Klein (1986). Street Gangs Selling Cocaine "Rock." University of Southern California. Social Science Research Center.
Maxson, C., K. Woods, and M. Klein (1996). Street gang migration: How big a threat? Research in Action, National Institute of Justice Journal (February): 26-31.
Maxson, C, and M. Klein (1995). Investigating gang structures. Journal of Gang Research 3:33-40.
Padilla, F. (1992). The Gang as an American Enterprise. New Brunswick, N.J.: Rutgers.
Pennell, S. (1994). Gangs in San Diego. Final Report submitted to the Department of Health and Human Services, Administration of Children and Families. San Diego Association of Governments.
Reuter, P., R. MacCoun and P. Murphy (1990). Money from Crime: A Study of the Economics of Drug Dealing. Santa Monica: Rand.
Sanchez-Jankowski, M. (1991). Islands in the Street. Berkeley, CA: University of California Press.
Sanders, W. (1994). Drive-bys and Gang Bangs. New York: Aldine.
Skolnick, J., T. Correl, E. Navarro, and R. Rabb (1988). The Social Structure of Street Drug Dealing. Sacramento: Office of the Attorney General of the State of California.
Taylor, C. (1990). Dangerous Society. Lansing, MI: Michigan State University Press.
Tunnel, K. (1995). Choosing Crime: The Criminal Calculus of Property Offenders. Chicago: Nelson-Hall.
Waldorf, D., C. Reinerman and S. Murphy (1996). Cocaine Changes. Philadelphia: Temple.
Wright, R. and S.H. Decker (1994). Burglars on the Job. Boston, MA: Northeastern University Press.
Wright, R. and S.H. Decker (1997). Armed Robbers in Action. Boston, MA: Northeastern University Press.

Chapter 3

GLOBALIZATION, GANGS, AND COLLABORATIVE RESEARCH

John M. Hagedorn
University of Illnois-Chicago

Sometimes new facts are right there staring us in the face, but we fail to see them. U.S. gangs are like that. They have been undergoing some sweeping changes in the last decade, but we've sometimes failed to notice some rather significant facts.

It is clear to me that gangs in the United States today are straddling two eras. There are still thousands of male and female youth gangs that look much like the gangs that formed in American cities over the last hundred years. But the urban neighborhoods where gangs have always formed are witnessing the formation of new types of post-industrial gangs which play important economic roles within an expanding neighborhood informal economy (see the theoretical review in Hagedorn, 1998b).

Klein's "Eurogang Paradox" (see Chapter 1, this volume) argues that one reason we may not find U.S.-style gangs in Europe is that such gangs don't exist in the U.S. either–or more precisely, few U.S. gangs closely resemble their media stereotype. But this should not be taken to mean that media claims of increased U.S. gang violence and drug involvement are completely inaccurate. Whether Europe is likely to witness the emergence of U.S.-style gangs, of either the industrial or post-industrial variety, was a central question of the Eurogang Workshop and is the object of needed research.

This essay briefly outlines some differences between industrial era and post-industrial era U.S. gangs and explores some implications of these changes for

M.W. Klein et al (eds.), The Eurogang Paradox, 41–58.

European gangs and youth groups. It then argues for collaborative methodologies as one way to clarify the nature of European gangs and help make international comparisons.

INDUSTRIAL ERA GANGS

Industrial era U.S. gangs of the 19th and much of the 20th centuries were primarily the product of the problems of assimilation of immigrant and migrant groups into the dominant American culture. Gangs of that time, Frederic Thrasher (1927/1963) pointed out, typically formed as a result of lack of adult control over youthful playgroups in immigrant and migrant communities. Industrial era gangs were also a kind of anticipatory rebellion against a dreary future life in the factory–and for girls an often dreary future as housewives or in menial jobs. In other words, in some poor and working class U.S. neighborhoods, groups of kids formed playgroups with one another and some became socialized to the streets rather than to conventional institutions. They called themselves a gang or some such term and had the capacity to reproduce themselves. This process is probably universal in developed countries with considerable immigration (see Moore, 1998). Presenters at the Eurogang Workshop described youth groups fitting this description in several countries, with some of them calling themselves gangs, or "bande," or "Chefoors," or some similar term. But many others clearly did not consider themselves "gangs" of any type. Gangs, as Moore argues, are not defined fundamentally by what law enforcement, or the media, label as gangs (see Moore, 1998), but to a greater extent by how groups of street youth see themselves.

The minority gangs which formed in Milwaukee in the late 1970s and early 1980s looked very much like those described sixty years earlier by Thrasher (1927/1963) and they called themselves gangs. But while earlier Milwaukee gangs of Germans, Polish, and Italians had dissipated when good jobs allowed their ethnic group to move out of the central city, things were different for the African American and Latino communities. In the twilight of the industrial era, the good jobs just weren't there to help the new minority working class climb up the ladder of mobility. As Bernard (1970) notes in her critique of Thrasher's and Park's Chicago School of Criminology, the concept of "ethnic succession" didn't work very well for African Americans.

Our data confirmed Bernard's critique, at least for males. Most of the girls in our study left the gang as teenagers, to take care of their children and get on with their lives. Some things don't seem to change. But while Milwaukee's 1980s male gangs started out like earlier German, Irish, or Polish gangs, something different happened to the minority men as they were ready to "mature out" of delinquency. Young adult gang men, many who were already fathers, had a difficult time adopting the expected male role of breadwinner. Since stable legal work was disappearing, many young men, including adult gang members, turned toward the illegal opportunity structure to survive. Crime has always been a means of ethnic mobility, as shown by Bell (1960), Cloward and Ohlin (1960), Ianni (1975) and others.

But conditions today are different than in the industrial era. The 1980s were globally a decade of industrial capitalism undergoing a massive restructuring into information capitalism. The 1980s marked the beginnings of a world-wide economic system based no longer on the mass production of goods by industrial workers, but rather on the global processing of information by highly-educated information workers (see Castells, 1996; Sassen, 1998). Peter Drucker (1993:186) points out that by 1990 all developed countries spent one fifth of their entire Gross National Project (GNP) on processing information. In the 1950s a majority of all U.S. workers were engaged in making and moving goods but today these occupations make up less than one fifth of the work force. But what does that have to do with gangs?

POST INDUSTRIAL GANGS

Information-age capitalism has transformed the opportunity structures in poor neighborhoods where gangs have always been found. Many of the generic-labor jobs–factory work which requires little skill or education–have moved away from inner cities. It was these jobs that had always helped young men "mature out" of their gangs. Generic jobs today are the most unstable kind of jobs, with the flows of information capitalism ready to uproot low skill work from any one spot and move it to the other side of the world in search of higher profits. Most well paid jobs now require high levels of education or advanced technical skills, human capital which is in short supply in poor neighborhoods where gangs are found.

In the 1980s, as the U.S. economy restructured, legitimate opportunities in poor neighborhoods fatefully constricted. In these conditions, young men began to sell drugs on a never-before-seen scale (Fagan, 1996; Gunst, 1995). A sharp rise in violence accompanied the carving out of new crack markets (Blumstein, 1995). Many gangs transformed their character, offering illicit employment opportunities for young adults and providing heavily armed support. "Unwired" poor communities began to resemble areas of the Third World, with a burgeoning informal economy taking the place of lost legal jobs (Portes and Sassen-Koob, 1987; Sassen, 1994). This informal neighborhood economy includes off-the-books enterprises, like street-side car repair, hair styling, house-painting, child care, and street vending, as well as a host of illegal activities (Portes, Castells, and Benton, 1989). And the most profitable informal enterprise is the business of drugs (Hagedorn, 1998c). Poor neighborhoods, as Castells (1998) points out in his sweeping review of the information age, are becoming the "shop-floor" of the international drug economy.

Detailed studies of gang involvement in drug selling have been made in cities across the US. For example, Taylor's in Detroit (1989), Padilla's (1992) and Venkatesh's (1996) in Chicago, Waldorf's (1993) in San Francisco, Sullivan's (1989) in New York, Decker and Van Winkle (1996) in St. Louis as well as in my own fifteen years of research in Milwaukee. These and other studies have documented the trend toward adult involvement with gangs as well as different kinds of gang drug organization. Klein (1995) makes a sharp separation between drug gangs and street gangs, and points out that not all gangs sell drugs and gangs do not do most drug selling. Admittedly, most U.S. gangs can be fit into the five different types Klein (1996) describes. However, we need to understand why at this time in history gangs in so many U.S. cities have added economic functions.

The curtailing of the welfare system is also bound to have major implications for women and female gangs. However, we have only sketchy research on female involvement in the still mainly male gang drug operations and scattered reports on all-female drug rings. There are few, if any reports of adult female gangs or female prison gangs, while there are thousands of adult male gangs, and gangs in almost every male prison. This is evidence for the relative stability of gender roles, rather than their responsiveness to even massive economic change, but we are badly in need of feminist research (see Chesney-Lind and Hagedorn, 1999).

FIVE RELEVANT ISSUES IN MILWAUKEE'S GANG RESEARCH

Five issues have arisen in the course of our Milwaukee research that may have international relevance. First, gangs in Milwaukee began just as gangs have always begun: among alienated youth, typically among immigrants or powerless minority groups. The industrial era youth gang is basically a wild adolescent peer group that becomes attached more to peers and the wild life than to conventional institutions. As they conflict with authorities and other peer groups they take on a deviant identity and organize themselves. This classic pattern, first described by Thrasher (1927/1963), fits the gangs I studied in Milwaukee, which progressed from kids hanging out and fighting one another, to adopting the identity of "gang," "set," or street "organization." This pattern also appears to reflect the experience of most contemporary U.S. youth gangs (see Klein, 1995).

There is much that I find familiar in the descriptions of delinquent youth groups in Stockholm, Brussels, Athens, Paris, Slovenia, and some cities in Germany. These groups may or not call themselves "gangs," but the processes of gang formation are similar to what we have long found in the U.S. Wacquant (1997) compares delinquent youth in the U.S. "black belt" with the French "red belt." He sees similarities in the nature of oppression and stigmatization in Chicago's Cabrini-Green projects and the Quatre Mille housing project in Paris. He argues, sensibly, that race is much more salient in the American ghetto than in France. He also argues that alienation of youth in the banlieu (or working class suburb) is a class and space-related characteristic, and not related just to immigrants. However, both Touraine (1995a:184), who dissects the causes of gang development in France; and Yaeger (1997:159), who surveys the literature on immigration, stress a relationship between ethnic identity, gangs, and crime. Pfeiffer (1998: 436-438), using some standard criminological concepts, finds the causes of French youth violence as income polarization and the social "exile" of youth.

The similarities with industrial-era U.S. gangs can be seen even more clearly in Werdmolder's (1997) ethnography of a Moroccan gang in Amsterdam. Werdmolder observed the "Marnel" group for two years and then returned to study them as young adults, in the kind of longitudinal work that is much needed on both sides of the Atlantic. The Marnel group started as rowdy teens with a troubled family life complicated by discrimination, problems with school, and drug use. When Werdmolder returned four years later, the young adults of the group had largely "aged out" of the gang and out of criminal activity (73). The Marnel group is supporting evidence for Moore's (1998:73) conclusion that "preconditions are ripe for the development of American-style gangs" in Europe.

But, second, here is where European/American differences strongly emerge. In Milwaukee, unlike in Amsterdam, the wild gang kids didn't mature out of the gang and criminal activities (Hagedorn, 1998a). In Milwaukee, most male gang members sold drugs as adults, as well as participated in a variety of off-the-book enterprises. The sales of drugs, as part of a larger informal economy, exerted a major force in poor neighborhoods. Our research in three small neighborhoods of Milwaukee, comprising a total of 116 blocks, found more than 600 people employed in the drug game with drug sales grossing over $17 million per year. We concluded that the drug economy probably employed about one in ten minority males in Milwaukee aged 18-29. If our estimates are even close to accurate, the drug business now employs more young, minority males than any other sector of the Milwaukee economy.

Not all adult gang members in Milwaukee sold drugs. Many landed jobs though most were part time and often short-term. Long prison terms interfered with their capacity to settle down. Many adult gang members looked to off-the-books businesses for survival and success. A few invested drug profits in licit restaurants, stores, or other retail firms. But more utilized their skills as carpenters, auto mechanics, or salesmen to set themselves up into their own businesses, competing with more formal businesses by charging much less for the same services (Sassen, 1994).

Do these developments appear in Europe? On the one hand, there is not the long-standing tradition of youth gangs in Europe that could transform into drug gangs. By any reports, the gang phenomenon in Europe is much smaller than in any region of the U.S. (Klein, 1995). On the other hand, there are scattered reports of European drug gangs, notably in Kazan in Russia, Italy, and England, and reports of Turkish drug gangs in Germany. In North America, gang "business organizations" similar to U.S. drug gangs were found in Vancouver, Canada (Gordon and Foley, 1998). The Kazan gangs seemed to be the product of the new capitalism and the utter disorganization of the no longer socialist economy (see Savelsberg, 1995), while the Italian drug gangs were thought to have ties to the Mafia. Immigrants were deeply involved in the drug business in England, Germany, and Vancouver. London appears to be polarizing in a way quite similar to New York (Gordon and Harloe, 1991; Small, 1997). What stands out from the papers presented at the Workshop, however, was the strong separation of an organized drug business from most delinquent youth groups, whether they are seen as "gangs" or not.

Globalization has been seen by some as bringing to Europe "Americanized" poverty (Wacquant, 1997; Castells, 1997; 1998) with European trends toward greater inequalities following inexorably in U.S. footsteps. In 1995, according to the editors of the Economist, 46 percent of Europe's unemployed were out of work for at least a year (Micklethwait and Wooldridge, 1996: 206). Some observers argue that the "Rhine model" of social welfare capitalism cannot work in a global economy (Thurow, 1997: 31-322), and that globalization is inevitable (e.g., Kantor, 1995). On the other hand, others like Touraine (1995b) warn that free markets are a major threat to European life and call for resistance to what Gray (1995:181) calls the "hegemony of global markets and technology." Gray argues, as a conservative, that globalization demands England reconsider adopting a more equitable social policy. Sassen (1998: 138) concurs:

> To a considerable extent these trends toward greater inequality and insecurity are most advanced in the United States because the government has never been as concerned with regulating economic and social conditions as is typical in Western European countries. An important research question is how far the European countries will go toward deregulation of the economy and thereby stimulate some of these new trends.

At this point, the post-industrial gang, as seen in the United States, does not seem to have a consistent counterpart in Western Europe. It should be noted in Werdmolder's (1997) study that the same social worker who worked with the Marnel group when they were teen rowdies was still there trying to help them as adults, a level of continuous social service almost unheard of the in the U.S. Werdmolder also explains that most of the unskilled and under-educated immigrant youth he studied will end up on "social security," beneficiaries of the Dutch welfare state. Only one or two of the 34 members of the Marnel group eventually became serious adult criminals, much like the small number of "residuals" Thrasher (1927) described in the 1920s as graduating from the teen gang into adult criminality. Whether youth groups or immigrant gangs will transform into drug gangs or "business organizations," as they have in Milwaukee and many other U.S. cities, will probably be related to the degree of economic mobility within poor and immigrant European communities and the continuing health of their welfare states.

A third relevant issue in our research is that Milwaukee gang men are focused on economics, not politics. Our research shows that the substantial pull of the underground economy has not diverted adult gang members from a persistent, if often futile, search for legitimate jobs (e.g., Hagedorn, 1994). Being a member of a gang is not the same thing as being a career criminal, nor are many gang members revolutionaries. There are a only handful of gang members who have joined the criminal drug capitalists, and fewer who have joined left wing or nationalist political organizations. The vast majority of adult male gang members barely make a living wage, though the few studies of average income from drug sales find that it triples what could be earned at part time minimum wage jobs (MacCoun and Reuter, 1992). Still the risks are great. Male gang members bob in and out of the formal economy, looking for a good job and wanting to settle down to a conventional life, rather than continuing to risk arrest and violence. The need to survive takes on a full time character, with hustling an all-day chore of "hard work" (Valentine, 1978; Simon and Burns, 1997). There has been little rebellion or political activity among gangs to date in Milwaukee.

Gangs in the United States have always been more alienated and survival-focused rather than political (Miller, 1976), even in the turbulent sixties (Short, 1976). But, compared to most American gangs, youth groups in Germany were heavily politicized by right wing ideologies, often directed at foreigners and "Gast Arbeiters" (Bergmann, 1998; Kersten, 1994). In the U.S., despite occasional forays of gangs into politics (e.g., Royko, 1971; Thrasher, 1927/1963: 313; Rodriguez, 1993; Shakur, 1993; Dawley, 1992) and some more recent reports of organizing against police (e.g., Hamid and Curtis, 1996; DiChiaria, 1997), there has historically been more hostility to authority than political participation. There appears to be a much stronger political orientation of German youth groups than in contemporary American gangs, sensible when we consider Europe's long tradition of collective political violence (Tilly, 1969). The politicization of youth in Germany is likely to be a "protective factor" in preventing street gang formation, though the substitution of right wing hate groups for gangs is a dubious benefit.

Fourth, our research in Milwaukee questions those sociologists who see drug selling in poor neighborhoods as an example of a deviant subculture. Rather, we find that drug dealing is strongly related to an over-commitment to the root American–and now global–capitalist value of making money (Hagedorn, 1998a; 1998d; 1998e). The gang members we studied were immersed in the TV and movie culture of affluence. They don't lack successful role models, as some say, but are severely strained by having so many rich and successful role models invade their homes and minds through the TV networks daily. Some male gang members revel in the violent life of the drug seller as basically an act of rebellion from a lost capacity to be the revered breadwinner in a patriarchal family. On the streets, masculinity, to many cultural observers, is measured by the size of a man's gun (see Hagedorn, 1998f). I've concluded the real problem of gangs is not some deviant ghetto subculture, but the nature of mainstream American culture, the definition of masculinity, and lack of economic opportunity.

The impact of U.S. style capitalist culture can be felt everywhere in Europe. Savelsberg (1995:219) reviews crime trends in Eastern Europe and argues that criminal behavior is "an adaptive strategy for dealing with strain" in a classic Mertonian cultural analysis. Violence, James (1995) speculates, is closely tied to a Ronald Reagan and Margaret Thatcher inspired "winner-loser" culture. It may surprise some that America's leading export is not manufactured goods but *movies* (Thurow, 1997). Klein (1995) commented on the considerable impact of U.S. youth culture on the European gang scene (see also Short 1996). This point was brought home at the Workshop when we were shown newspaper pictures of Dutch "Crips," complete with tattoos, colors, and gang attire. The widespread influence of American youth culture will surely lead some impressionable wild youth to copy the "baddest" American media stereotypes they can find.

A final issue of international relevance from our research is that rates of violence are falling in Milwaukee and many U.S. cities. Still, by far the greatest decreases in homicide rates have been in the global cities like New York and Los Angeles, centers of concentrations of both old and new wealth (see Soja, 1991, for a comparison). It is a shocking realization that 1997 homicide rates in Milwaukee, Indianapolis, Nashville and other medium sized cities were higher than in New York, Los Angeles, Boston, or San Francisco. There has been little consensus on reasons for between-city variations in violence in the United States. While some attribute declines to stepped up police restoration of order (Bratton, 1995; Kelling and Coles, 1996) others suggest the stabilization of drug markets and the increasing age of many drug dealers, among other factors (Blumstein and Rosenfeld, 1998; Hagedorn, 1998c). It does appear that in both Europe and America, those cities that relied on an industrial base and are now being by-passed by the new information technologies, may be in for severe shocks and unprecedented social problems (Sassen, 1998).

What is important for the international audience is that rates of violence do not have to be uniformly high, even when they are related to gangs and the drug trade. While overall levels of violence in Europe are much lower than in the U.S., there is no intrinsic reason for homicide rates to undergo the kind of wild fluctuations as they have in America, even if gangs in Europe become more prevalent. Still, one most take note of the increased youth violence in most European countries, though rates of violence among foreign-born youth are declining in Germany (Pfeiffer, 1998: 400). A sturdy welfare state, economic opportunity for immigrants and the poor, rejection of American-style "winner-loser" culture, and an anti-drug policy that is less obsessed with incarceration may soften the effects of globalization on youth groups. One can hope these policies may forestall most European gangs from transmogrifying into post-industrial economic criminal organizations.

COMPARATIVE AND COLLABORATIVE GANG RESEARCH

Comparative research is a good way to make sense out of diverse European developments. Researchers need to pay attention to ethnic and cultural differences, but also to labor market and social welfare differences and variations between cities. In the new post-industrial era, broader literatures than standard criminology may be useful. As this essay suggests, urban political economy may be an important field in understanding the evolution of post-industrial gangs. There is much merit in the notion of a "T" model, discussed at the Eurogang meeting, of combining both broad and deep research of a city's gang problem (see Chapter 23, this volume).

But in order to understand gangs fully, some studies have to be undertaken which seek to understand the world from the perspective of gang members. The collaborative research methods I learned from Joan Moore (1978, 1991) are well suited to this task and can be replicated in Europe and elsewhere. Moore's research team in East Los Angeles was made up of former gang members who were trained to follow a structured interview questionnaire and interview their homeboys and homegirls.

In Milwaukee, I had both a low cost and a high cost strategy. In my first study over a decade ago (1988), I had little money and so worked closely with one gang member I trusted, who had worked for me when I ran a gang diversion program. He and I interviewed 47 young men and women who were the founding members of Milwaukee's major gangs, including 11 of the 16 gang-leaders. When the National Institute on Drug Abuse (NIDA) gave us considerable research money to conduct follow-up studies, we were able to hire a complete research team made up of male and female gang members and conducted interviews with 90 men and 84 women over five years. My staff had helped write the proposal, participated in developing the interview questionnaire, did more than three quarters of the interviews, helped code and enter the data, and went over drafts of the articles. Staff accompanied me to many professional meetings and assisted with presentations. In my most recent study (Hagedorn, 1998c) I was forced to return to a low cost strategy of utilizing long time associates from the gangs as "community researchers."

Gang research has always had to deal with the suspicion of gang members, that, in Yablonsky's (1966) words, every researcher could be a cop. This issue is even more important today, when drug selling gang members have so much to hide and gang members and researchers alike know by heart media stereotypes of what gang members really "look like." The problem isn't getting a gang member to talk but getting behind the facade of gang member denials of, or "hype" about, drug selling and violence. Peer interviewing at times produces a very different view of reality than the typical law enforcement-centered research.

But collaborative research has its problems. For example, sometimes respondents try to normalize their behavior, rather than report a sordid reality.

Since relationships between academics and gang members are close, both staff and respondents may have something to gain from cooperation. The researcher may speak to a judge on the gang member's behalf, or help him/her find a job. This can help build rapport, but it also can provide reasons for a gang members to make him or herself appear "reformed." Retrospective data are also subject to distortions from a faulty memory or redefinition of old events. The old stand-by of multiple measures is the proper treatment. We also interviewed several people within each gang so we could compare accounts and construct a more balanced version of events (see Hagedorn, 1996).

But collaborative research has more strengths than weaknesses, and addresses many of the shortcomings of other research designs. One of the most serious problems in all kinds of gang research is selection effects: interviews often are with self-nominated gang members who refer the researcher to their friends, who often look a lot like them. American gangs are made up of different kinds of neighborhood kids, from different kinds of families. For example, in Milwaukee, a third of all parents of gang members we interviewed owned their own home. While a quarter of both male and female gang members come from homes where the family had a long history of drug or alcohol use, criminality, or gang involvement, half came from families with much less serious problems. Another quarter came from conventional two parent families with no observable problems. If you only interview kids from street families and their similar wild friends, you may get a very different picture of the gang than if you interview everyone on a roster or sample representatively.

In Milwaukee, our collaborative team was able to develop validated rosters of the entire gang membership and we were able in some instances to interview everyone on the roster. When we didn't interview everyone, we used Biernacki and Waldorf's (1981) advice to ask people to nominate someone different than they are for an interview, searching for representativeness. We constructed various typologies of gang members–e.g., "homeboys," "legits," "dope fiends," and "new jacks" for males–that further aided in sampling (Hagedorn, 1994). It also gave us a more rounded picture of the moral difficulties gang members had as players in a drug game most considered immoral.

Collaborative research is practiced best over a long period of time, when academics and gang members can learn to trust one another. In Milwaukee, our research has tracked the 234 male and 176 female founding members of 14 male and 8 female gangs since their origins in the late 1970s. We have seen the gangs change and watched the young boys and girls turn into men and women. Since we have been involved with the lives of so many gang members from early on, we also have built up a certain amount of legitimacy on the streets. We have promised our respondents to do our best to advocate policies that soften the impact of the drug war and develop a safe house for female gang members at risk of sexual and physical abuse in gangs. Our practical efforts on these subjects give us credibility among our respondents, and we hope demonstrate responsibility in research.

When any social formation, like gangs, is undergoing sweeping change, it is important to develop methodologies that can throw off the "yoke of those empirical categories that long habit often make tyrannical" (Durkheim, 1982: 73). This radical suggestion does not imply a rejection of surveys or analyses of official data, but rather an emphasis on good field research to explore the nature of some long-held concepts, to see if they fit new realities (see Hagedorn, 1990, for a much-maligned treatment of this issue). The collaborative method is a promising research strategy as part of a broader comparative international undertaking. In the best case scenario, at least some European researchers would make commitments to study gangs and youth groups within individual cities, over time, in a collaborative manner.

CONCLUSION

The process of globalization is jarring every society on earth. Prosperity for the middle and upper classes in the developed world has meant the crystallization of a "dual city" in the metropolis worldwide (Castells and Mollenkopf, 1991). The informal or underground economy appears to be a structural development of the post-industrial information age, and not just a new version of "How the Other Half Lives" (Riis, 1894/1957). The new dual city contains multiple conflicting strata and no longer represents the industrial era bourgeois/proletarian dichotomy (see Castells and Mollenkopf, 1991, for a discussion of different strata and Kantor, 1995, for a comparison between "cosmopolitan" and "local" elite). The end of the industrial era has meant the transition of many U.S. gangs into new kinds of economically focused, post-industrial gangs. But what does this mean for Europe?

I learned two major lessons at the Eurogang Workshop. First, as in the U.S., there is wide variation in youth formations, not only between countries, but also within countries, and probably within cities. Gangs and youth groups in each country are still the result of local conditions, as well as broader economic trends. The gangs in Kazan, for example, did not resemble in any way the youth networks of Stockholm, the wild youth of Brussels, the hate groups of Germany, nor the "Chefoor" of Slovenia. And we heard very little of female gangs, though there is little reason to think there won't be any in Europe.

On the other hand, the relative absence of densely packed ethnic neighborhoods in many European cities is a factor not favorable to the formation of U.S. industrial-style gangs, which have always been neighborhood based. For example, in the heterogeneous Paris banlieux where youth groups hang out, Wacquant (1997: 347) notes there is nothing similar to U.S. "turf," nor any "ordered segmentation" in Suttles (1968) sense (see a similar comment on London by Gordon and Harloe, 1992). Still, immigration and ethnicity–despite Wacquant's arguments–seem to be related to European gang and youth group formation in many cities, just as has always been the case in the United States (Yaeger, 1997).

Second, despite some examples of drug gangs in England, Italy, Germany and Russia, there don't appear to be widespread post-industrial gangs similar to what has developed in Milwaukee and some other U.S. and Canadian cities. What I believe, and I think this view is shared by many, is that if Europe follows the laissez-faire American road and dismantles their welfare states as they globalize their economies, then increased inequalities are bound to give birth to American-style problems. If European countries want to emulate the United States, then they can have U.S.-style gangs as well.

REFERENCES

Bell, D. (1960). The End of Ideology: On the Exhaustion of Political Ideas in the Fifties. New York: The Free Press.

Bergmann, W. (1998). Collective violence as social control. In M.W. Watts (ed.), Cross-Cultural Perspectives on Youth and Violence. Stamford, CN: JAI Press.

Bernard, J. (1970). The Sociology of Community. Glenview, Illinois: Scott, Foresman and Company.

Biernacki, P., and D. Waldorf (1981). Snowball sampling: Problems and techniques of chain referral sampling. Sociological Methodology 10:141-163.

Blumstein, A. (1995). Youth violence, guns, and the illicit-drug industry. The Journal of Criminal Law & Criminology 86:10-36.
Blumstein, A. and R. Rosenfeld (1998). Assessing the recent ups and downs in U.S. homicide rates. NIJ Journal 237(Oct): 9-11.
Bratton, W.J. (1995). Great expectations: How higher expectations for police departments can lead to a decrease in crime. In Measuring What Matters: Prepared Papers. Washington D.C.: National Institute of Justice.
Castells, M. (1996). The Information Age: Economy, Society and Culture, Volume I: The Rise of the Network Society, 1. Malden, Mass: Blackwell.
1997 The Information Age: Economy, Society and Culture, Volume II: The Power of Identity, 2. Malden, Mass: Blackwell.
1998 The Information Age: Economy, Society and Culture, Volume III: End of Millennium. Malden, Mass: Blackwell.
Castells, M. and J. H. Mollenkopf (1991). Conclusion: Is New York a dual city? In J.H. Mollenkopf and M. Castells (eds.), Dual City: Restructuring New York, pp. 399-417. New York: Russell Sage.
Chesney-Lind, M. and J. M. Hagedorn (eds). (1999). Female Gangs in America: Essays on Girls, Gangs, and Gender. Chicago: Lakeview Press.
Cloward, R. and L. Ohlin (1960). Delinquency and Opportunity. Glencoe, Ill: Free Press.
Dawley, D. (1992). A Nation of Lords: The Autobiography of the Vice Lords. Prospect Heights, IL: Waveland Press.
Decker, S., and B. Van Winkle (1996). Life in the Gang: Family, Friends, and Violence. New York: Cambridge.
DiChiaria, A. (1997). Gangs as Families. Presented at the American Society of Criminology meeting, San Diego.
Drucker, P.F. (1993). Post-Capitalist Society. New York: Harper Business.
Durkheim, E. (1982). The Rules of Sociological Method and Selected Texts on Sociology and its Method. New York: The Free Press.
Fagan, J. (1996). Gangs, drugs, and neighborhood change. In R.C. Huff (ed.), Gangs in America: Second Edition, pp. 39-74. Thousand Oaks, CA: Sage.
Goffman, E. (1959). The Presentation of Self in Everyday Life. New York: Anchor Books.
Gordon, R. M., and S. C. Foley (1998). Criminal Business Organizations, Street Gangs and Related Groups in Vancouver: The Report of the Greater Vancouver Gang Study. Department of Justice: Canada.
Gordon, I., and M. Harloe (1992). A dual to New York? London in the 1980s. In J. H. Mollenkopf, and M. Castells (eds.), Dual City: Restructuring New York, pp. 377-395. New York: Russell Sage.
Gray, J. (1995). Enlightenment's Wake: Politics and Culture at the Close of the Modern Age. London: Routledge.
Gunst, L. (1995). Born Fi' Dead: A Journey Through the Jamaican Posse Underworld. New York: Henry Holt & Company.

Hagedorn, J. M. (1998a). People and Folks: Gangs, Crime, and the Underclass in a Rustbelt City, second ed. Chicago: Lakeview Press.

1998b Post-industrial gang violence. In M. Tonry, and M. H. Moore (eds.), Youth Violence, pp. 365-419. Chicago: University of Chicago.

1998c The Drug Business in Milwaukee. Milwaukee, Wisconsin Policy Research Institute.

1998d As American as apple pie: A case study of gang violence. In M.Watts (ed.), Cross-Cultural Perspectives on Youth, Radicalism, and Violence, pp. 79-98. Hartford, CN: JAI Press.

1998e Homeboys, new jacks, and anomie. Journal of African American Men 3:7-28.

1998f Frat boys, bossmen, studs, and gentlemen: A typology of gang masculinities. In L. Bowker (ed.), Masculinities and Violence, pp. 152-167. Thousand Oaks, CA: Sage.

1996 The emperor's new clothes: Theory and method in gang research. Free Inquiry for Creative Sociology 24(2):111-122.

1994 Homeboys, dope fiends, legits, and new jacks: Adult gang members, drugs, and work. Criminology 32:197-219.

1990 Back in the field again: Gang research in the nineties. In C.R. Huff (ed.), Gangs in America, first edition, pp. 240-259. Beverly Hills, CA: Sage.

1988 People and Folks: Gangs, Crime, and the Underclass in a Rustbelt City, first edition. Chicago, IL: Lakeview Press.

Hamid, A., and R. Curtis (1996). State-sponsored violence in New York City and indigeneous attempts to contain it: The mediating role of the Third Crown (Sgt. at Arms) of the Latin Kings. Paper presented at the American Sociological Association annual meeting, New York.

Huff, R. (1989). Youth gangs and public policy. Crime and Delinquency 35:524-537.

Ianni, F. (1975). Black Mafia. New York: Simon & Schuster.

James, O. (1995). Juvenile Violence in a Winner-Loser Culture. London: Free Association Books.

Kantor, R. M. (1995). World Class: Thriving Locally in the Global Economy. New York: Touchstone.

Kelling, G. L., and C.M. Coles (1996). Fixing Broken Windows: Restoring Order, and Reducing Crime in Our Communities. New York: Touchstone Books.

Kersten, J. (1994). Feindbildkonstruktionen und gewalthandlungen bei gruppierungen junger manner. In W. Bergman and R. Erb (eds.), Neonazimus und Rechte Subkultur. Berlin: Metropol.

Klein, M.W. (1995). The American Street Gang: Its Nature, Prevalence, and Control. New York: Oxford University Press.

1996 Gangs in the United States and Europe. European Journal on Criminal Policy and Research 4:63-80.

MacCoun, R., and P. Reuter (1992). Are the wages of sin $30 an hour? Economic aspects of street-level drug dealing. Crime & Delinquency 38:477-491.

Micklethwait, J., and A. Wooldridge (1996). The Witch Doctors: Making Sense of the Management Gurus. New York: Random House.

Miller, W. (1976). Youth gangs in the urban crisis era. In J. Short (ed.), Delinquency, Crime, and Society, pp. 91-122. Chicago: University of Chicago.

Moore, J. W. (1998). Understanding youth street gangs: Economic restructuring and the urban underclass. In M. Watts (ed.), Cross-cultural Perspectives on Youth, Radicalism, and Violence, pp. 65-78. Stamford, CN: JAI Press.

1991 Going Down to the Barrio: Homeboys and Homegirls in Change. Philadelphia: Temple University Press.

1978 Homeboys: Gangs, Drugs, and Prison in the Barrios of Los Angeles. Philadelphia: Temple University Press.

Padilla, F. (1992). The Gang as an American Enterprise. New Brunswick: Rutgers University Press.

Pfeiffer, C. (1998). Juvenile crime and violence in Europe. In M. Tonry and M. Moore (eds.), Crime and Justice: An Annual Review of the Research, pp. 383-456. Chicago: University of Chicago.

Portes, A., and S. Sassen-Koob (1987). Making it underground: Material on the informal sector in Western market economies. American Journal of Sociologiy 93:30-61.

Portes, A., M. Castells, and L. A. Benton (1989). Conclusion: The policy implications of informality. In A. Portes, M. Castells, and L.A. Benton (eds.), The Informal Economy: Studies in Advanced and Less Advanced Countries, pp. 298-311. Baltimore: The Johns Hopkins Press.

Riis, J.A. (1894/1957). How the Other Half Lives. New York: Hill and Wang.

Rodriguez, Luis J. (1993). Always Running: La Vida Loca: Gang Days in LA. New York: Simon & Schuster.

Royko, M. (1971). Boss. New York: Signet.

Sassen, S. (1998). Globalization and Its Discontents. New York: The New Press.

1994 Cities in a World Economy. Thousand Oaks: Pine Forge Press.

Savelsberg, J. J. (1995). Crime, inequality, and justice in Eastern Europe: Anomie, domination, and revolutionary change. In J. Hagan and R.D. Peterson (eds.), Crime and Inequality, pp. 206-224. Stanford, CA: Stanford University Press.

Shakur, Sanyika (1993). Monster: The Autobiography of an LA Gang Member. New York: Penguin Books.

Short, James F. (1996). Forward: Diversity and change in U.S. gangs. In C. R. Huff (ed.), Gangs in America: Second Edition, pp. vii-xviii. Thousand Oaks, CA: Sage.

1976 Gangs, politics, and the social order. In J.F. Short (ed.), Delinquency, Crime, and Society. Chicago: University of Chicago.

Simon, David, and Edward Burns (1997). The Corner: A Year in the Life of an Inner-City Neighborhood. New York: Broadway Books.

Small, Stephen (1997). Racism, Black people, and the city in Britain. In C. Green (ed.), Globalization and the Black Diaspora: The New Urban Challenge, pp. 357-377. Albany: State University of New York.

Soja, Edward W. (1991). Poles apart: Urban restructuring in New York and Los Angeles. In J.H. Mollenkopf and M. Castells (eds.), Dual City: Restructuring New York, pp. 361-375. New York: Russell Sage Foundation.

Sullivan, Mercer L. (1989). Getting Paid: Youth Crime and Work in the Inner City. Ithaca: Cornell University Press.

Suttles, G.D. (1968). The Social Order of the Slum. Chicago: University of Chicago.

Taylor, C. (1989). Dangerous Society. East Lansing, Michigan: Michigan State University Press.

Thrasher, F. (1927/1963). The Gang, 1927 edition. Chicago: University of Chicago.

Thurow, L.C. (1997). The Future of Capitalism: How Today's Economic Forces Shape Tomorrow's World. New York: Penguin Books.

Tilly, C. (1969). Collective violence in European perspective. In H.D. Graham and T.R. Gurr (eds.), The History of Violence in America, pp. 4-45. New York: Frederick A. Praeger.

Touraine, A. (1995a). Critique of Modernity. Oxford: Blackwell.

1995b Beyond social movements. In S.M. Lyman (ed.), Social Movements: Critiques, Concepts, Case-Studies, pp. 371-393. New York: New York University Press.

Valentine, B.L. (1978). Hustling and Other Hard Work. Glencoe, Illinois: Free Press.

Venkatesh, S.A. (1996). The Gang in the community. In C. R. Huff (ed.), Gangs in America: Second Edition, pp. 241-256. Thousand Oaks, CA: Sage.

Wacquant, L.J.D. (1997). Urban Outcasts. In C. Green (ed.), Globalization and the Black Diaspora: The New Urban Challenge, pp. 331-355. Albany: State University of New York.

Waldorf, D. (1993). Don't be your own best customer: Drug use of San Francisco gang drug dealers. Crime, Law and Social Change 19:1-15.

Werdmolder, H. (1997). A Generation Adrift: An Ethnography of a Criminal Moroccan Gang in the Netherlands. London: Kluwer Law International.

Yablonsky, L. (1966). The Violent Gang. New York: The MacMillian Company.

Yaeger, M.G. (1997). Immigrants and criminality: A cross-national review. Criminal Justice Abstracts 29:143-171.

Chapter 4

ADVANTAGES OF LONGITUDINAL RESEARCH DESIGNS IN STUDYING GANG BEHAVIOR

Terence P. Thornberry and Pamela K. Porter
University at Albany, New York

INTRODUCTION

Many prior studies of gangs are based on ethnographic methods in which an observer spends a substantial period of time on the street with one or more gangs, observing the relationships of the gang members and their behaviors. Other studies are comparative; researchers sample gang members and compare their behaviors and attitudes to those of non-members. While our understanding of gangs and gang members has been greatly enhanced by these studies, they often fail to address developmental issues. Observational and comparative studies open rather narrow windows into the life course of gang members, studying their behavior only during their period of active gang membership. These studies often contain little information on the lives of gang members before and after their active gang membership.[1] Failure to highlight developmental and life-course issues with respect to gang membership limits our understanding of both the antecedents and consequences of gang membership. Developmental issues such as these are best examined in the context of prospective, longitudinal studies. In these studies the individual gang member is the unit of analysis; in contrast, in many previous gang studies the gang itself is the unit of analysis. This chapter examines both the

M.W. Klein et al (eds.), The Eurogang Paradox, 59–77.

advantages and limitations of studying gang behavior within the context of longitudinal studies in which individuals, not groups, are followed over time. Several advantages to this approach are illustrated using data from the Rochester Youth Development Study.[2]

ADVANTAGES AND DISADVANTAGES OF LONGITUDINAL DESIGNS

Focusing on the careers of individual gang members has some distinct disadvantages. It limits our ability to study group processes and the way in which group processes influence the behaviors of gang members. It tends to decontextualize the deviant behavior of gang members and makes it difficult, if not impossible, to distinguish between delinquent acts committed by gang members as individuals and delinquent acts committed by gang members for the gang or at least in the context of gang activities. These and other important analytic issues cannot be easily addressed in this type of design.

Despite limitations of this nature, a developmental approach to the study of gangs also has distinct advantages, addressing substantive issues that cannot easily be examined when the gang is the unit of analysis. It allows for a clearer identification of the prior attributes of the individual that increase the risk of becoming a gang member and eases, but does not eliminate, the difficult challenge of identifying the causes of gang membership. It allows for the study of gangs to be informed by a consideration of dynamic and reciprocal influences, recognizing that while family and school factors may influence the probability of joining a gang, gang membership may also have an impact on family and school relationships. A developmental approach allows for the examination of the influence of gang membership on life-course trajectories and is consistent with the transient character of gang membership. Most gang members, at least in emergent gang cities, remain in the gang for less than one year and proportionately few remain members for multiple years. Given this distribution it is important to understand why adolescents join and leave gangs and how their period of active membership affects other aspects of their lives.

In our view, a developmental approach complements the very detailed understanding that prior research has presented about periods of active gang membership, and both types of studies are needed to understand fully the phenomenon of street gangs. In many ways an ideal design would be to embed the study of gangs and gang processes within an ongoing longitudinal study so that the findings of one approach can inform the findings of the other. Such designs would be difficult and expensive to implement and, while we await them, the best we can do is present the results from these different, but complementary approaches to the study of street gangs.

In the remainder of this chapter we provide two illustrations of the types of issues that can be examined in individual-based longitudinal designs. The first concerns the amplification effect that gang membership has on delinquent behavior; the second concerns the long-term consequences of gang membership on life-course development.

GANGS AND THE AMPLIFICATION OF DELINQUENCY

Prior studies have demonstrated that gang members have significantly higher rates of delinquency than non-gang members and that they account for a disproportionate share of the crime problem relative to their representation in the population. Since gangs clearly connote groups that have a deviant or criminal orientation, it is not surprising that there is a strong relationship between gang membership and high rates of delinquency. What prior studies do not identify, however, are the social processes which bring about the association between gang membership and higher rates of delinquency.

In earlier work (Thornberry et al., 1993; Thornberry, 1998), we identified three competing models that could account for the strong relationship between gang membership and delinquency. They are social selection, social facilitation, and a mixed model combining both selection and facilitation effects.

A selection or "kind of person" model posits that gangs recruit their members from adolescents who have a high propensity for delinquency and who will engage in delinquency and drug use regardless of their membership in gangs. If a selection model were accurate we would expect to observe, first, that gang members have higher rates of delinquency than non-gang members, and second, that this would hold across time–before, during, and after their membership in the gang.

Second is a social facilitation or a "kind of group" model, positing that gang members are intrinsically no different from non-members in terms of delinquency. Upon joining a gang, the normative structure and group processes of the gang are likely to bring about high rates of delinquency and drug use. If the social facilitation model is accurate, gang members will differ from non-gang members in terms of delinquency and drug use only when they are active members of a gang. Before and after membership they should not differ substantially from non-gang members.

Third is a mixed or enhancement model that combines the other two. It suggests that both selection and facilitation effects operate to generate high levels of delinquency. A mixed model predicts that even when they are not active members, gang members would have higher rates of delinquency than non-gang members and that delinquency rates would be particularly high when they are active gang members.

In an earlier analysis of the Rochester data, Thornberry et al. (1993) tested these competing models. Based on a comparison of the male gang members and non-members they report strong support for the facilitation model and virtually no support for the selection model:

> Perhaps the strongest support for the social facilitation model is found in the analysis of the type of behavior most often associated with gangs–crimes against the person... Gang members have higher rates of person offenses only when they are active gang members. Of particular interest is the drop-off in the rate of person crimes once boys leave the gang. The means for crimes against the person for boys when they are active members of the gang are, by and large, at least twice as high as when they are not. Clearly, being in the gang is generative of violent behavior among these boys (Thornberry et al., 1993:80-81).

In those analyses each individual acts as his own control since we are examining changing patterns of behavior for the same individual as that person enters and leaves gangs. Doing so helps control the impact of a number of possible covariates.

An alternate strategy is to explicitly control the impact of major risk factors for both gang membership and delinquency in multivariate equations. Doing so allows us to assess whether gang membership still has an impact on delinquency and drug involvement after the risk factors are held constant. Major risk factors for gang membership and for delinquency include social class position, family, school, peer and individual characteristics, and prior delinquency.

We estimate separate regression equations at each of four annual observation points, using data from the Rochester Youth Development Study.[3] In each equation, the risk factors are measured in the year immediately prior to the measurement of the dependent variable and three dummy variables are incorporated to assess the impact of gang membership. The first is Current Gang Member, indicating whether a respondent is a gang member during the year in which the dependent variable is measured. The second is Past Gang Member, indicating whether he was a gang member in some prior wave but not in the current one. The third is Future Gang Member, indicating that he will become a gang member in a future wave but has not yet joined a gang. The omitted category is Never Gang Member.

Finding a significant impact only for the variable signifying current gang membership would indicate a facilitation effect. That is, deviance would be elevated only during periods of active gang membership (net of other risk factors) but one's status as either a past or future gang member would have no significant impact on current levels of deviance. In contrast, a selection effect would be consistent with the additional finding that the impact of the variables representing future and past gang membership is significant. If future gang member is significant, it would suggest that adolescent males who will become gang members already exhibit elevated rates of deviance and that gang members are recruited or selected from among a more highly delinquent portion of the population.[4]

In Table 1 we present results predicting the frequency of general delinquency (logged) for Years 1 through 4. In all four equations the coefficient for current gang member is positive and significant. These coefficients are approximately the same magnitude as the coefficients for association with delinquent peers and prior delinquency, typically two of the strongest predictors of deviant behavior. These results indicate that active gang membership facilitates involvement in delinquency even when major risk factors are held constant.

Table 1. Predicting the Incidence of Self-Reported General Delinquency, Rochester Youth Development Study, Males Only (Standardized OLS regression coefficients)

	Self-Reported General Delinquency (logged)			
Risk factors	Year 1[a]	Year 2[b]	Year 3[c]	Year 4[d]
Current gang member	.26**	.29**	.27**	.22**
Future gang member	.10**	.12**	.06	-
Past gang member	-	.03	.09*	.02
Family poverty level	.02	.00	-.04	-.02
Parental supervision	-.07*	-.01	-.01	-.10*
Commitment to school	-.12**	-.15**	-.21**	-.04
Association with delinquent peers	.31**	.12**	.14**	.22**
Negative life events	.17**	.14**	.19**	.16**
Prior general delinquency	.23**	.15**	.15**	.13**
Adjusted R	.56	.34	.37	.26
N	520	528	481	428

[a] Year 1 general delinquency combines data from Waves 2 & 3; risk factors are from Wave 2.
[b] Year 2 general delinquency combines data from Waves 4 & 5; risk factors are from Wave 3.
[c] Year 3 general delinquency combines data from Waves 6 & 7; risk factors are from Wave 5.
[d] Year 4 general delinquency combines data from Waves 8 & 9; risk factors are from Wave 7.
*p<.05; **p<.01

The coefficient for the variable future gang member is significant at Years 1 and 2 but not at Year 3; the coefficient for the variable past gang member is significant only at Year 3. Moreover, the coefficients for these variables are of fairly modest size and well less than half the size of the coefficients for current gang members.

These results are quite similar to those observed by Thornberry et al. (1993) where a simpler tabular form of analysis was used. Overall, there appears to be a substantial facilitative effect of gang membership on delinquency (represented here by the variable current gang member) and a lesser selection effect (represented here by the variables future and past gang member). Importantly, these effects are observed when important risk factors for both gang membership and delinquency–family poverty level, parental supervision, commitment to school, association with delinquent peers, negative life events, and prior delinquency–are controlled.

Similar results are observed for violent delinquency (data not presented). When drug use and drug sales are examined, the evidence for a gang facilitation effect is even stronger. When equations parallel to those reported in Table 1 are estimated, current gang membership exerts a strong positive impact on drug use and on drug sales in all four years. In contrast, none of the coefficients for future gang member and only one of the coefficients for past gang member (at Year 4 for drug use) attain statistical significance.

In this section we adopted an analytic strategy for assessing facilitation and selection effects that is possible only with longitudinal data that follow the same individual across time and which allow for a comparison of gang members and non-members. The multivariate models allow us to control explicitly for important antecedent variables generally identified as risk factors for both gang membership and for deviance.

Net of the impact of family poverty, parental supervision, commitment to school, association with delinquent peers, negative life events, and prior deviance, current involvement in street gangs increases delinquency, violence, drug use, and drug sales at all four years. The coefficients associated with future gang members and past gang members are of smaller magnitude and are less consistently significant, however.

LIFE-COURSE CONSEQUENCES OF GANG MEMBERSHIP

The contemporaneous and short-term effects of gang membership are generally well understood, but considerably less is known about the long-term consequences of gang membership on life-course development. Does being a member of a street gang contribute to disorder in the life course, for example, by decreasing the chances of making successful transitions to adult statuses, such as stable employment, completion of education, and on-time onset of marriage and parenthood?

A growing number of studies have found that involvement in delinquent behavior decreases the likelihood that a person will make successful transitions to adult statuses but relatively little is known about whether involvement in deviant social networks, as opposed to deviant behavior, also contributes to these outcomes. Street gangs can be viewed as prototypical deviant social networks in which actors are embedded in a culture and behavior system that facilitates deviance. Being a member of a gang should have an effect on life-course transitions over and above the effect of just having delinquent friends or of just engaging in delinquent behavior. Moreover, members of a gang who are more committed to that social network should be particularly likely to experience problematic transitions. Hence, gang members who remain in the gang for an extended period of time are hypothesized to be more likely to experience problematic transitions than are short-term members and non-members. To illustrate the examination of this type of hypothesis, we look at the relationship between gang membership and early adult unemployment. Unemployment is a particularly salient life-course transition for males since the ability to establish a stable occupational career is central to virtually all aspects of adult development.

The unemployment variable is calculated as the percentage of months from ages 19 to 21 that the subject did not have a job. For our purposes, respondents were considered "employed" if they were working, in the military, or still attending school. We test this hypothesis separately for male and female respondents. For the males we compare respondents who were never gang members to short-term gang members and to more stable, long-term members. We hypothesize that non-members are the least likely to experience unemployment and that stable gang members are the most likely to do so. Because of the smaller number of cases for the females, we use a simple ever-prevalence measure, comparing non-members to those who were ever members of a street gang.

Table 2 shows the bivariate relationship between gang membership and early adult unemployment. For the male respondents, on average, those who were never members of a gang were unemployed 17 percent of the time from age 19 to 21. For short-term gang members, this percentage was higher (21%); for stable gang members it was still higher (26%). Thus, not only is there a general effect of gang membership, there is an increased impact with long-term exposure to the gang environment.

Table 2 also shows the bivariate relationships for the female respondents. Again, we see that the amount of time unemployed is higher for the gang members (35%) than the non-members (29%), although the difference is not statistically significant.

Table 2. Bivariate Relationship between Gang Membership and Early Adult Unemployment (in percentages)

	Males		Females	
	Average percentage of months unemployed, ages 19-21	n	Average percentage of months unemployed, ages 19-21	n
Gang Membership				
Never	17	395	29	156
Short-term	21	68	--	
Stable	26	72	--	
Ever	--		35	54
F	3.387		1.273	
P<	.035		.261	

While there appears to be a fairly strong relationship between adolescent gang membership and early adult unemployment, that relationship could be spurious, that is, produced by common antecedent variables. To examine this possibility we regress early adult unemployment on the measures of gang membership, holding other effects constant. Because the distribution of the unemployment variable is highly skewed, we use Tobit to estimate the equations. We also present OLS estimates. Because OLS is robust, we anticipate similar results to the Tobit estimates but with a more intuitive interpretation.

The specific control variables are percent poverty in the census tract of residence, family poverty level income, parental unemployment, number of family transitions, CAT math score, self-esteem, attachment to parent, parent attachment to subject, attachment to teachers, parenthood, graduated from high school by age 19, and race/ethnicity. For the male subjects, the trichotomous measure of gang membership is used, with non-members as the omitted category. The bivariate results reported above are replicated in the multivariate analysis (see Table 3). For males, stable gang membership has a moderate impact on early adult unemployment, net of the control variables. This is evident for both the Tobit and OLS estimates. However, the effect of short-term gang membership is not significant. For the female respondents, as expected, gang membership is not statistically significant.

Table 3. Multivariate Model for Gang Membership and Early Adult Unemployment

	Males		Females	
	OLS[a]	**Tobit**	**OLS[a]**	**Tobit**
Family background				
Area poverty	.09*	.18*	.07	.14
Family poverty level	.16*	6.66	.01	-2.75
Principal wage earner unemployed	.16*	13.38*	.01	4.91
Number of family transitions	-.01	.35	.04	1.41
Human capital				
Math score-CAT	-.01	.01	-.17*	-.28*
Self esteem	.03	.27	-.14*	-13.26*
Social bonding/social capital				
Attachment to parent	.04	2.74	-.07	.12
Parent attachment to child	-.09*	-4.49*	-.14*	-10.11*
Attachment to teachers	-.07	-1.61	-.14*	-10.81*
Gang membership				
Short-term	.01	.13	--	--
Stable	.12*	7.95*	--	--
Ever	--	--	-.07	-2.91
Life course transitions				
Parenthood by Wave 12	-.07	-4.58*	.32*	24.23*
Graduated high school by age 19	-.25*	-10.60*	-.23*	-11.53*
Race/ethnicity				
African American	-.18*	5.80*	-.05	-5.21
White	.04	-4.01	-.00	-4.14
R2	.24	--	.31	--
Sigma	--	30.14	--	30.67
Scale Factor	--	.56	--	.71
Log likelihood function	--	-1227.37	--	-542.86
N	414	412	159	160

[a] Standardized OLS regression coefficients are reported.
* $p < .05$ (one-tailed)

Late adolescence is a critical time in the life course when youth are expected to prepare for and make successful transitions into adult roles and statuses. Events, behaviors, and associations all play important roles in determining whether those transitions are made at the appropriate time, in the normative order, and, ultimately, whether they lead to successful adult outcomes.

As an important and powerful social network, the gang constrains the behavior of its members, limits access to prosocial networks that may act as social capital in facilitating adult transitions, and increases the criminal embeddedness of its members. All of these characteristics cut the individual off from conventional pursuits and increase the chances of disorder in the life course. Based on this, we expected that gang membership would reduce the stability of employment. For males, the results show some support for the general conclusion that being a member of a gang increases the likelihood that youth will experience off-time and unsuccessful transitions to adult statuses. For females, however, this relationship is not supported by the current analysis.

To this point we have discussed some of the advantages and disadvantages of studying gang members within the context of individual-based longitudinal studies. We illustrated this research strategy by examining two issues with data from the Rochester Youth Development Study. To situate these results within the larger literature on gangs, it helps to consider the issue of gang studies conducted in larger and smaller, as well as older and newer, gang cities.

GANGS IN LARGER AND SMALLER CITIES

Rochester, NY, the site of our study, is probably typical of many mid-sized, gang-involved American cities. Indeed, many of our results on gangs are quite similar to those found in Denver (Esbensen and Huizinga, 1993) and Seattle (Battin-Pearson et al., 1998), but Rochester is probably different from many larger cities which have yielded the best known gang data.

There has been a tremendous proliferation of street gangs in American cities in the past 10 to 15 years (Maxson, 1998). While at one time street gangs were only found in the largest cities, such as New York, Chicago, and Los Angeles, gangs have recently emerged in medium- and small-sized cities throughout the country. Although gangs are found in cities of all sizes (Curry et al., 1996; Klein, 1995) there appears to be a relationship between city size and several important characteristics of street gangs. Three can be mentioned.

Prevalence

The largest American cities have nearly reached saturation level with respect to gangs. Curry et al. (1996) found that 89 percent of the cities with a population of over 200,000 had active gangs. In contrast, as one moves down the continuum of city size, the proportion of cities reporting active gangs diminishes. Howell (1997) reports that 50 percent of American cities and towns with populations under 25,000 reported a gang problem in 1993. Thus, while gang activity is sizable in cities of all sizes, it is most prevalent in the largest cities.

Onset

In our nation's largest cities, such as New York, Philadelphia, Chicago, and Los Angeles, gangs have existed for decades, if not for the past century. While activity has waxed and waned, gangs have been a steady part of the history and tradition of these cities for quite some time. Because of that, gangs and gang activity are well understood by the residents of neighborhoods in which gangs flourish.

In contrast, gang activity is a relatively new phenomenon in smaller and mid-sized cities. The set of maps presented by Klein (1995) showing the growth of gang activity across America gives vivid illustration to this fact. Two of his maps (Klein, 1995: 92 and 95) are reproduced here as Figures 1a and 1b. In 1960 (Figure 1a) it is easy to identify the clustering of gangs in and around major metropolitan areas. By 1992 (Figure 1b), the gang situation was vastly different; the American landscape was littered with active street gangs, in cities both large and small.

Given this temporal distribution, gang researchers typically refer to smaller and mid-sized cities as "emergent" gang cities (see Spergel and Curry, 1990). Gangs are not part of the tradition or history of these cities and they are much less well understood by residents, including residents of active gang neighborhoods.

Figure 1a: Cities with Gangs through 1960 (number of cities = 58)

Figure 1b: Cities with Gangs Through 1992 (number of cities = 769)

Figure1. Geographical Distribution of Street Gangs in America, 1960 and 1992. Source: Klein, 1995:92 and 95

Types of gangs

Klein (1996) has identified five types of street gangs (see Chapter 1, this volume). Among them are "traditional" and "compressed" gangs. Traditional gangs have been around longer, existing in the same neighborhoods across multiple generations. They are larger, have distinct subgroups, a wide age-range, and are strongly territorial. In contrast, compressed gangs have a much shorter history, are smaller in size, do not have distinct subgroups, and have a narrow age-range. They may or may not be territorial.

Traditional gangs are more often found in older gang cities, which are also the largest cities in American society. Smaller and mid-sized cities, as newly emergent gang cities, are far more likely to have compressed gangs or "neo-traditional" gangs that appear to be mid-way between traditional and compressed gangs in Klein's typology.

In sum, while gangs exist across the continuum of American cities, they are not equally distributed across that continuum. If we contrast smaller and mid-sized cities with America's largest cities, the following portrait begins to emerge. First, somewhere between one-half and two-thirds of the smaller and mid-sized cities are likely to have gangs, while virtually all of the larger cities are likely to have gangs. Second, mid-sized cities are more likely to be "emergent" gang cities, with gang activity a relatively recent phenomenon. In contrast, the largest cities are more likely to have experienced gangs for long periods of time. Third, mid-sized cities are more apt to have compressed gangs while the largest cities are more apt to have traditional gangs. In the remainder of this section we explore the research and policy implications that follow from these observations. These implications may apply not only to the American situation, but to new gang situations in other nations as well.

Research Implications

Ideally, one would study gang behavior in cities distributed along the full continuum of city size and the various methods of studying gangs would also be distributed along this continuum. Unfortunately, gang studies are not evenly distributed. A vast amount of the gang literature derives from studies in a few very large cities; there are fewer gang studies in mid-sized cities, and yet fewer in small cities. Thus, our understanding of gangs, in general, is biased toward findings that derive from studies in very large cities (see also, Klein, 1996:70).

In addition, as in any field of inquiry, there are a handful of "classic" gang studies that disproportionately influence our theoretical and empirical understanding of gang behavior. They include the work of Thrasher (1927), Short and Strodtbeck (1965), Klein (1971), Miller (1966), Moore (1978), Spergel (1964), and a few others. All of these classic studies were conducted in Chicago, Boston, or Los Angeles! Thus, the image of gangs that predominates in the U.S. and elsewhere is heavily biased toward the image of gangs from these cities as presented in these classic studies.

The situation is further confounded if one takes into account research design. Perhaps the most common way of studying gangs and gang behavior is through observational or ethnographic methods. More recently, studies have begun to examine the behavior of gang members within the context of longitudinal panel studies of general population samples, such as in the Rochester study reported above.

Having alternative methods for studying the same phenomenon is one of the bed-rocks of scientific inquiry. Unfortunately, in the study of gangs there is relatively little overlap in the cities in which these varying methods have been used. Panel studies have only been conducted in mid-sized, newly emergent gang cities. In contrast, observational studies, while existing in a broader array of cities, have clustered in the larger, more traditional gang cities. Thus, it is hard to determine if the findings produced by these different methods are a function of the research designs or the research settings. For example, the panel studies indicate that gang membership during adolescence is quite fluid, with most gang members remaining in a gang for less than a year. That image is very discordant with the image of gang membership based on observational studies. We do not yet know if this discrepancy is a function of the different methods, different research settings, or both.

Does it make a difference where gang research is conducted? It appears that it does and that this difference affects our image of gangs and gang members and therefore theoretical and policy issues that flow from the empirical data.

Curry (forthcoming) presents data comparing gangs in larger cities with gangs in smaller cities. As compared to smaller cities, gangs in larger cities are more likely to be composed of minority group members and males and to commit more serious and violent crimes. Klein (1996) has noted that larger cities are more apt to have traditional gangs while smaller and mid-sized cities are more apt to have compressed gangs. Finally, gang membership in emergent gang cities tends to be more fleeting, while gang membership in larger cities appears to persist across longer periods of the life course.

Overall, some very basic research findings seem to vary depending on the site of the gang research. These discrepancies appear to contribute heavily to the Eurogang paradox. We are not implying that either depiction of gangs in America is wrong. Studies appear to describe gangs accurately as they exist in larger, traditional cities and in smaller, emergent cities. But a full description of gangs and gang behavior would require that both depictions be taken into account, and ideally that various types of gang studies would be conducted across a full continuum of city size.

Policy Implications

These different descriptions of gangs and gang behavior have important implications for policy issues as well. The image of street gangs generally held by the media, politicians, and policymakers, is heavily influenced by the classic studies conducted in the largest and most traditional gang cities. Thus, there is an image of gang members as racial and ethnic minority males and of gangs extensively involved in serious violent crime. But, as we just showed, this image is somewhat biased and does not appear to apply equally well to gangs and gang behavior in smaller and emergent gang cities. As a result, general gang prevention and suppression policies are based on data drawn from gangs at the most extreme end of the continuum and applied, perhaps inappropriately, to gangs found all along the continuum. Years ago Leslie Wilkins (1969) reminded us that it is not wise to base policy decisions on extreme cases. Policies appropriate for large traditional gangs in Chicago and Los Angeles may not be appropriate for the run-of-the-mill gangs found in newly emergent gang cities.

The irony, of course, is there are always relatively few "extreme cases" and many more run-of-the-mill cases. Thus, our image of the phenomenon is typically shaped by the extreme cases that lead to the formation of policies; those policies are then applied across the board. If the general population differs in significant ways from the extreme ends of the continuum–and there is every theoretical and empirical reason to expect that they do–then we may have a serious problem of ill fit between the nature of the phenomenon and the nature of our interventions. More systematic attention needs to be given to this issue so that we can arrive at more balanced and more effective policy decisions.

REFERENCES

Battin-Pearson, S.R., T.P. Thornberry, J.D. Hawkins, and M.D. Krohn. (1998). Gang membership, delinquent peers, and delinquent behavior. Juvenile Justice Bulletin, Office of Juvenile Justice and Delinquency Prevention. Washington, DC.

Curry, G.D. (Forthcoming). Race, ethnicity, and gender issues in gangs: Reconciling police data. In Problem Oriented Policing, Vol. 2. Washington, DC: Police Executive Research Forum.

Curry, G.D., Ball, R.A., and Decker, S.H. (1996). Estimating the national scope of gang crime from law enforcement data. Research in Brief (August), National Institute of Justice, U.S. Department of Justice.

Esbensen, F. and D. Huizinga. (1993). Gangs, drugs, and delinquency in a survey of urban youth. Criminology 31:565-589.

Hagedorn, J. (1988). People and Folks: Gangs, Crime and the Underclass in a Rustbelt City. Chicago: Lake View Press.

Howell, J.C. (1997). Youth gangs. OJJDP Fact Sheet (#72). U.S. Department of Justice, Office of Juvenile Justice and Delinquency Prevention. Washington, DC.

Klein, M.W. (1971). Street Gangs and Street Workers. Englewood Cliffs, NJ: Prentice-Hall.

Klein, M.W. (1995). The American Street Gang: Its Nature, Prevalence, and Control. New York, NY: Oxford University Press.

Klein, M.W. (1996). Gangs in the United States and Europe. European Journal on Criminal Policy and Research 4:63-80.

Maxson, C.L. (1998). Gang members on the move. Juvenile Justice Bulletin, Office of Juvenile Justice and Delinquency Prevention. Washington, DC.

Miller, W.B. (1966). Violent crimes by city gangs. Annals of the American Academy of Political and Social Science 364:96-112.

Moore, J.W. (1978). Homeboys. Philadelphia: Temple Press.

Moore, J.W. (1991). Going Down to the Barrio: Homeboys and Homegirls in Change. Philadelphia, PA: Temple University Press.

Short, J.F. and F.L. Strodtbeck. (1965). Group Process and Gang Delinquency. Chicago: University of Chicago Press.

Spergel, I.A. (1964). Slumtown, Racketville, Haulburg. Chicago: University of Chicago Press.

Spergel, I.A. and G.D. Curry (1990). Strategies and perceived agency effectiveness in dealing with the youth gang problem. In C.R. Huff (ed.), Gangs in America. Newbury Park, CA: Sage Publications.

Thornberry, T.P. (1998). Membership in youth gangs and involvement in serious and violent offending. In R. Loeber and D.P. Farrington (eds.), Serious & Violent Juvenile Offenders: Risk Factors and Successful Interventions, pp. 147-166. Thousand Oaks, CA: Sage.

Thornberry, T.P., M.D. Krohn, A.J. Lizotte, and D. Chard-Wierschem. (1993). The role of juvenile gangs in facilitating delinquent behavior. Journal of Research in Crime and Delinquency 30:55-87.

Thrasher, F.M. (1927). The Gang: A Study of 1,313 Gangs in Chicago. Chicago: University of Chicago Press.

Tracy, P.E. (1979). Subcultural Delinquency: A Comparison of the Incidence and Seriousness of Gang and Nongang Member Offensivity. Unpublished manuscript, University of Pennsylvania, Center for Studies in Criminology and Criminal Law.
Vigil, J.D. (1988). Barrio Gangs: Street Life and Identity in Southern California. Austin, TX: University of Texas Press.
Wilkins, L. (1969). Evaluation of Penal Measures. New York: Random House.

ENDNOTES

1 There are several exceptions to this general tendency; see, for example, studies by Moore (1978, 1991), Vigil (1988), Short and Strodtbeck (1965), Hagedorn (1988), and Tracy (1979).

2 A description of the Rochester Study and the gang measures can be found in Thornberry et al. (1993).

3 Because of the limited number of female gang members, especially after Year 2, this analysis is conducted only for males.

4 We recognize that temporal order is in some sense inverted for the variable of future gang member since a future status is being used to "predict" a current behavior. Nevertheless, the typology of past, current, and future gang members can be accurately created from the longitudinal data in the Rochester project. Also, since the coefficient for the dummy variable of future gang member is interpretable and helps distinguish between the facilitation and selection models, the analysis is valid.

Chapter 5

THE PROLIFERATION OF GANGS IN THE UNITED STATES[1]

G. David Curry
The University of Missouri, St. Louis

To speak of the proliferation of gangs in the U.S. in the last two decades requires some care. First, each of the three veteran scholars most closely associated with recognizing and documenting this proliferation has at one time implied the need for theoretical caution. The range of evidence for the existence of gangs historically and internationally prompted Irving Spergel's suggestion (1990:174) that "youth gangs may be an endemic feature of urban culture." While Malcolm Klein (1995b) has pointed out that the recent history of gang problems can only be described as an "extended upswing," he has also spoken of "gang cycles." In answer to the question of the possibility of "a new wave of gang violence" in the early 1970s, Walter Miller (1982:7) characterized the U.S. gang problem as a series of waves,

> There was no new wave, but rather a continuation of an old wave–a wave that strikes with great fury at one part of the shore, recedes, strikes again at another, ebbs away, strikes once more...

On the other hand, the case for labeling what has happened to gangs between the 1970s and the present as proliferation has been well made by each of these scholars: Miller (1996), Spergel (1995), and Klein (1995a). The mark for the low tide in U.S. gangs or at least interest in U.S. gangs was the publication of Bookin-Weiner's and Horowitz's (1983) "The End of the Youth Gang: Fad or Fact?" In the article, the authors examined whether the decline in

M.W. Klein et al (eds.), The Eurogang Paradox, 79–92.

research on gangs was a function of an actual decline in gang problems or a shift of research focus in crime from a social to an individual phenomenon. Whatever the reason for the perceived diminished importance of gangs as a research problem, the attention given the Bookin-Weiner and Horowitz article has made the task of arguing for a proliferation in gangs in the decade and a half since somewhat easier.

Second, as most of us know who've examined data on the "spread" or "appearance" (Klein's preferred term) of youth gang problems, we are studying community reactions to gangs and perceptions of gangs as much as we are studying gangs themselves. Hence, I wish to continue to stress the special roles that definition and social policy have played in any perceived proliferation. Below, I will briefly review the evidence for proliferation and offer some preliminary findings on the process of proliferation.

BACKGROUND

In 1994, the Office of Juvenile Justice and Delinquency Prevention (OJJDP) of the Department of Justice established the National Youth Gang Center in Tallahassee, Florida. The establishment of the Center marked the U.S. government's first continuing commitment to generating and compiling national level statistics on gang problems. Constructing national statistics on gang crime by consulting local law enforcement agencies follows the model of the Uniform Crime Reports (UCR). Administered by the FBI since 1930, the UCR tabulates data on incidents of crime from over 16,000 police departments across the nation. The UCR has never collected data on gang-related crime. Prior to the establishment of the National Youth Gang Center, what we knew about the scope and dynamics of the U.S. gang problem came from a handful of studies.

In 1975, Walter Miller conducted the first of several national studies. Under OJJDP's sponsorship, Miller employed purposive samples of jurisdictions and interviews from diverse agencies at each site to produce the first national estimates of the U.S. gang problem. A random sample of police departments in jurisdictions with 100,000 or more population was used by Jerome Needle and William Stapleton (1983) to support and extend many of Miller's findings. In 1988, Spergel and Curry (1993) screened 98 jurisdictions that Spergel identified from his personal knowledge and notes as potentially having gang problems. From these 98 jurisdictions, sites with promising programs were identified for more intensive study, and updated national statistics produced. With National Institute of Justice funding, Curry and colleagues conducted national surveys of law enforcement data on gangs in 1992 and 1994. The 1992 Curry survey included the 79 largest U.S. cities and the remainder of jurisdictions from Spergel's 1988 screening list that were not among the population of largest cities. In 1994, Curry, Ball, and Decker extended the 1992 survey sample by adding all cities with populations over 150,000 and a random sample of cities with populations between 25,000 and 150,000.

Curry and his co-authors (Curry, Ball, and Decker, 1996; Curry and Decker, 1998) have reviewed the results of these surveys as a method of documenting the proliferation of gang problems in the U.S. Critics have correctly noted that this was a history of study results rather than a systematic study of the proliferation of the U.S. gang problem. Each successive study's results were based on different sampling strategies and instruments. It was not possible to separate out what were actual changes in the scope of the U.S. gang problem and what were changes in research methodology. The only sample of cities that was consistently rechecked between 1988 and 1994 was the sample of cities that Spergel developed from his knowledge and notes as they stood in 1988. Before proceeding to approach proliferation with a different methodology, I think it's important to review two other efforts to trace the proliferation of the U.S. gang problem, each of which relies on the knowledge and notes of a veteran gang researcher other than Irving Spergel.

While I was attempting to assess the changing magnitude of the U.S. gang problem building on cities first identified by my mentor Irving Spergel, another effort to map the proliferation of gangs in the U.S. was already underway by Malcolm Klein. Klein (1995a:18) described his effort as an initially personal one. "Over the years," he had "been collecting a list of cities that seemed to reliably have gangs." By 1990, Klein's list had grown from "about 50" to over 100. In just over one additional year, his list had increased to 187 and was still growing. In 1991, Klein had begun calling cities in a more systematic fashion. By the end of 1991, he had identified 261 gang cities based on phone calls to 316 cities. Klein (1995a: 32-37) described the nature of gang problems in these 261 cities in some detail. In contrast with the practice used by Miller and Spergel of obtaining multiple agency interviews, and Curry's practice of obtaining only the official administrative line of law enforcement agencies,

Klein used his knowledge of gangs to select respondents from each site. He selected those who appeared to be knowledgeable of the actual rather than officially recognized status of gang crime problems in each jurisdiction. "Most" of his respondents were therefore "gang investigators and gang unit supervisors" (32).

Using data accumulated from several surveys, Klein and Cheryl Maxson (Maxson, Woods, and Klein, 1996) constructed a sample of 1,019 police departments for their study of gang migration. From this sample, they identified 790 cities with local gangs. Using respondents' estimates of the year of onset of local gangs, Klein constructed a series of maps of the United States for 1960, 1970, 1980, and 1992 (see Chapter 4, this volume). These maps depict the proliferation of gangs from 58 in 1960 to 769 cities that provided dates of gang emergence in 1992. Unlike reviews of studies with different methodologies over time, the Klein study portrayed the proliferation of gangs in the United States using a consistent methodology over multiple points in time.

The submission of Walter Miller's last project report in 1982 did not constitute an end to his research on the scope of the U.S. gang problem. Miller had constructed a computerized database of gang localities in 1970 and routinely supplemented it thereafter. Of the observers of the U.S. gang problem from the 1960s through the 1970s, Walter Miller used the broadest range of information sources. He has collected agency reports, products from commissions and conferences, published and non-published academic manuscripts, and media reports including those available online. In 1996, Miller submitted the result of his quarter century of gang research in the form of an OJJDP draft report. Miller's tabulation of every locality that had reported the presence of gang activity between 1970 and 1995 constituted an unparalleled effort. The number of cities and towns with gang problems increased from 201 in 1970 to 1,487 in 1995. The number of counties with gang problems identified by Miller grew from 73 in 1970 to 706 in 1995. As with Klein's research, Miller's effort provided a measurement of the proliferation in the U.S. gang problem using a single set of definitional and selection criteria over time.

The National Youth Gang Center

The National Youth Gang Center (NYGC) has conducted three national surveys since its founding. The first served a useful but different function from the latter two. In the first survey in 1995, the Center attempted to validate and update prior samples. Using lists of localities (obtained from Miller, Spergel, Curry, and Klein/Maxson), lists of gang-problem cities identified by the National Drug Intelligence Center, the Bureau of Alcohol, Tobacco and Firearms, and member agencies in the Regional Information Sharing Systems (RISS), a purposive sample of 4,120 law enforcement agencies was produced, representing 2,820 cities and 1,300 counties. With an 83 percent response rate, the resulting database of 3,440 jurisdictions makes it possible to update to 1995 specific information on most jurisdictions surveyed in earlier studies. New jurisdictions (especially smaller ones) allowed Miller (1996: 57) to extend his count of gang cities to 2,100 and gang counties to 900.

The second and third NYGC surveys administered in 1997 and 1998 had a different purpose and employed a different and statistically representative sampling strategy. These surveys included all cities with populations over 25,000, a representative random sample of cities with populations between 1,000 and 25,000, all counties identified as suburban by the Census, and a representative random sample of rural counties. In addition, the NYGC solicited updated information on all jurisdictions included in the Center's 1995 survey that were not encompassed by the 1996 sampling strategy. The result are two separate data sets: one that provides representative samples of U.S. city and county jurisdictions and the other that provides updated information on cities and counties studied in earlier surveys.

METHODS

Here I re-examine the proliferation of gang problems in the U.S. with the advantage of having access to a number of the data sets used in prior studies. For this exercise, I had access to the computerized data sets from the 1988 Spergel and Curry survey, the 1992 Maxson-Klein migration survey, the 1992 Curry, Ball, and Fox NIJ survey, the 1994 Curry, Ball, and Decker NIJ survey, and the 1995 and 1996 NYGC surveys. In addition, I had the written reports from Miller's studies and Needle and Stapleton. This availability has allowed me to examine multiple retrospective measures of when gang problems were reported to have emerged as well as whether a gang problem was reported on the date of a particular survey.

FINDINGS

Dates of Problem Emergence

An important preface to this discussion requires assessing the utility of retrospective estimates of when gang problems in a jurisdiction began. In order to examine this issue, I used the retrospective measures from three studies–the Maxson-Klein migration survey in 1992, the Curry, Ball, and Fox NIJ law enforcement survey from 1992, and the 1996 National Youth Gang Survey. For comparison, I have selected seventy of the largest U.S. cities included in all three studies. I have eliminated cities such as Washington, D.C., Philadelphia, New York City, Baltimore, Memphis, Richmond, Pittsburgh, and Newark each of which has experienced policy discontinuities in their responses to youth gangs over the past decade. Of these seventy cities, 49 reported a date for the origin of their gang problem to all three surveys. The other 21 reported a date for the origin of their gang problem to two of the surveys. Reporting was higher to the Maxson-Klein migration study (n = 69) and the Curry, Ball, and Fox NIJ law enforcement survey (n = 67). Only 53 of the cities reported a date for the origin of their gang problem to the NYGC survey. Anaheim was not a respondent in the Maxson-Klein study. Detroit, Honolulu, and Albuquerque did not respond to this particular question in the Curry, Ball, and Fox study.

It was pleasing to discover that there was little difference between the two studies sponsored by NIJ in 1992. The average difference between the Maxson-Klein data and the Curry, Ball, and Fox data was only 1.7 years. This is not statistically significant under a dependent pairs t-test. The difference between the two 1992 studies and the 1996 NYGC survey was statistically significant. Still, eliminating cases with dates prior to 1960 from the analysis, the average differences between the dates recorded by NYGC in 1996 and the two earlier studies was about four years.

Denial, Exaggeration, and Moral Panic

In studying the emergence of gang response policies in Ohio cities, C. Ronald Huff (1989) observed that the recognition of gang problems was not simply a matter of empirical evidence. A range of social issues and conditions play a role in whether or not law enforcement agencies officially acknowledge the presence of gangs. From his assessment of gang problems in Milwaukee, Hagedorn (1988) emphasized both conservative and liberal motivations that affect how local agencies respond to gangs. Concerns for a municipality's commercial and tourist images can quite quickly, with a catalyzing event, turn into politically visible patterns of suppression. Curry, Ball, and Fox (1994b) observed that jurisdictions facing rapidly changing violent gang problems frequently vacillate greatly in their identification of causal processes and rational responses. As Hagedorn has noted, politically liberal responses are just as likely as conservative ones to generate into moral panics. Among the largest cities, examples of uncertain official reactions to gang problems are well known. The District of Columbia has persisted in insisting on the uniqueness of the capitol's "crew" problem. New York City and Philadelphia, two cities with gang problems in the 1960s and 1970s have consistently thwarted gang researchers by "re-adjusting" to response strategies and statistics over the years. Both acknowledged having gang problems to the 1997 NYGC survey, but expressed their official doubts about available statistics. Pittsburgh and Columbus, Ohio have in the 1990s both been marked by policies no more stable than local political power balances. Southeastern cities such as Raleigh, Memphis, Baltimore, and Richmond have long-term patterns of denial followed by recent, sometimes post-dated recognition. Each of these cities reported no gang problem origin dates to the two 1992 surveys and dates prior to 1990 to the 1996 NYGC survey. Memphis reported most recently that its gang problem started in 1960. Even Newark reported gangs in 1997 and identified the problem as beginning in 1987. While it is difficult to control for these types of policy changes, it is possible to use responses to earlier studies as guidelines in accepting retrospective problem origin dates from any survey at face value.

City Size and Proliferation

By the time I began presenting the results that were later published as Curry, Ball, and Fox (1994a), it was fairly obvious that gang problems were ubiquitous in the largest U.S. cities. Despite the fluctuations in gang response policy in several large cities noted above, it is generally agreed that almost every U.S. city with a population over 200,000 had a gang problem or had been challenged by local media as ignoring a gang problem. With these routine shifts in policy, the largest cities will perpetually level off at about 90 percent, until there is some evidence of the kind of extended downswing that would be necessary for confirming any theory of cycles or waves.

In the 1994 NIJ law enforcement survey, Ball, Decker, and I used a random sample of 284 cities with populations between 25,000 and 150,000 population. I was able to match 260 of those cities with their responses to either the 1995 or 1996 NYGC surveys. My goal was to estimate the rate of emergence of gang problems for that range of cities between 1994 and 1995. The results are shown in Table 1. Not counting the fifteen communities that had reported that they no longer had a gang problem in 1995, the proportion of municipalities reporting a problem increased from 49.2 percent to 73.4 percent. Since there were 1,126 cities within this population range in the 1990 census from which the random sample was selected, the increase of 24.2 percent represents an increase of 272 municipal jurisdictions in approximately a year. While the 1995 proportion was still less than the 90 percent prevalence rate exhibited for the very largest cities, there were not enough cities without gangs in this population range for a comparable increase to occur between 1995 and 1996.

Table 1. Gang Problems in Municipal Jurisdictions of Population 25,000 to 150,000 for the Years of 1994 and 1995

Problem reported for 1995	Problem reported for 1994	
	Yes	No
Yes	128 (49.2%)	63 (24.2%)
No	15 (5.8%)	54 (20.8%)

In order to identify patterns in how the proliferation has occurred, I have looked at two variables using the 1997 NYGC data. The first is size of municipality. The 1996 NYGC study surveyed all cities with populations over

25,000 and took a random sample of cities and towns with populations between 1,000 and 25,000.

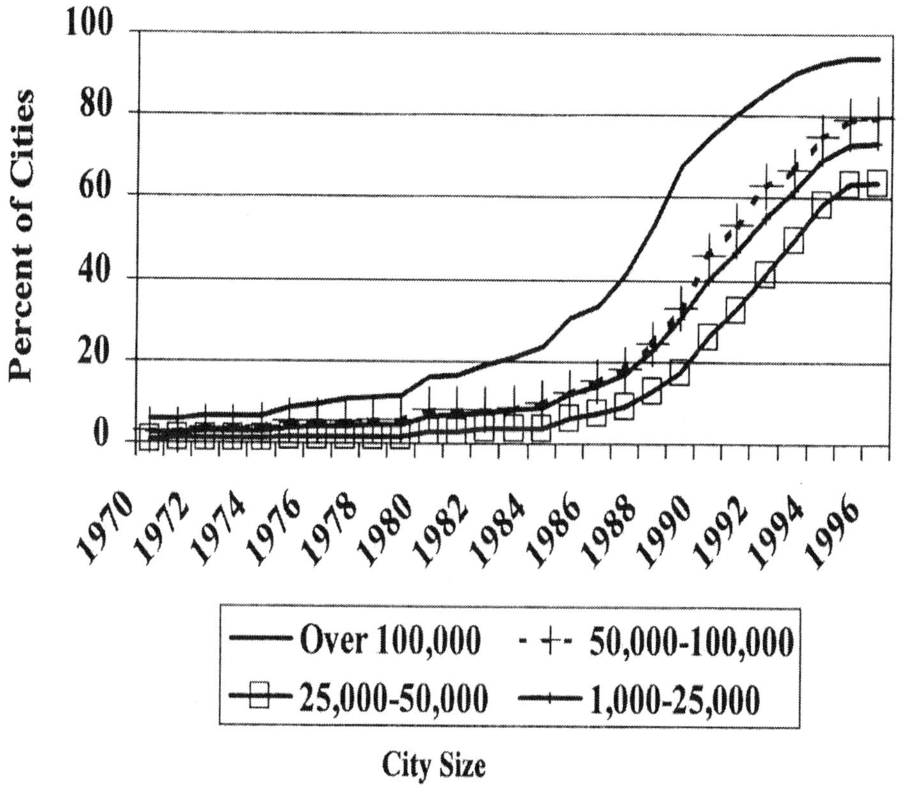

Figure 1. Patterns of Gang Proliferation by City Size

Dividing cities into several population categories, I created cumulative percentage graphs from 1970 to 1996. Since I found that cities with populations over 100,000 were comparatively homogeneous in the pattern of proliferation, I combined all cities of that size into a single category for this analysis. The different patterns of proliferation for four categories of city size are displayed in Figure 1. Even among the largest cities, gang problems were comparatively rare prior to 1970. Increases in the largest city category are gradual until 1980 when the slope becomes steeper, as also appears in 1985. Distinct annual increases continue into the early 1990s. Without question, the proportion of municipalities with populations over 100,000 reporting gang problems has consistently exceeded that for all other categories in any given year.

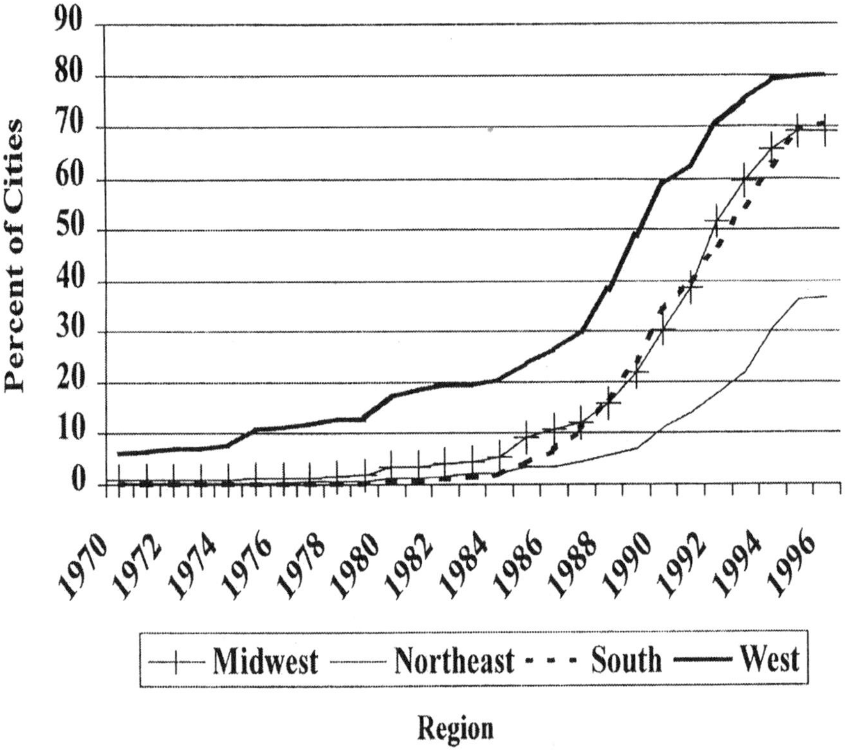

Figure 2. Patterns of Gang Proliferation by Region

Region and Proliferation

Miller (1982) argued that the relationship between city size and the likelihood of gang problems held in every part of the U.S. except for California.

Figure 2 repeats the analysis that I did for city size by region of country using only four large regional divisions. The earlier periods of proliferation in the West are clearly discernible. The comparatively low prevalence of gang problems in the Northeast is associated with a much more recent proliferation. The proliferation of gangs in the Midwest and South comes after the initial proliferation in West and falls somewhere between the patterns in West and the Northeast.

THE UTILITY OF LAW ENFORCEMENT DATA

OJJDP's Comprehensive Community Response to Gangs (more generally referred to as the "Spergel Model") places special emphasis on the importance of law enforcement participation and data. A call (Spergel, 1995:194) is made for specialized law enforcement information systems with common definitions of gang members and gang incidents (Spergel et al., 1994:6-7). Area-specific statistics on gang-related crimes derived from such information systems are identified as the primary measures for baseline and outcome measures of effectiveness for gang crime reduction programs. In the best known application of the Spergel Model in the Little Village community of Chicago (Spergel and Grossman, 1997), reductions in levels of gang violence as recorded by police served as the primary evidence of program success. For the prototype models being tested in selected cities across the U.S., OJJDP has stressed the importance of law enforcement data in program development and evaluation. In 1996, the Justice Department's Office of Community Oriented Policing Services (COPS) selected sites for its Anti-Gang Initiatives on the basis of pre-existing law enforcement data on gang-related crime.

Even where the focus is on a local problem, researchers of crime and particularly journalists seem to prefer to cite "national-level statistics." In his general criticism of law enforcement data, John Hagedorn (1988:21) noted that the national surveys of law enforcement agencies were "the only recent scientific nation-wide data collected concerning gang developments." Between the time of Miller's surveys and the publication of the Spergel and Curry (1993) estimate, it was not uncommon for writers to quote Dolan and Finney's (1984) estimate of 100,000 gang members. In the years immediately following my work with Spergel on his 1988 national survey of promising gang programs, I was continually surprised by how often agency representatives, journalists, and even other researchers contacted me requesting "specific numbers" that could be used to represent the magnitude of the U.S. gang problem. When I began to report the tentative findings of the 1992 NIJ survey, many of my colleagues argued that tabulating numbers simply because they were available leads to more distortion than awareness. Still, there was a shared sense among those requesting and using the "numbers" that statistical estimates were part of the assessment required for effectively responding to the problem. By the time that the estimates from the 1994 NIJ survey were being circulated, remarkably similar estimates for the magnitude of the U.S. gang problem were being offered by Malcolm Klein and George Knox.

Besides providing a sense of security to those who require numbers before they can begin conscientiously to respond to a social problem, national surveys now have a less "psychological" utility. Each of the prior surveys in which data were tabulated for a specific city at a specific point in time constitutes a data element that can be combined with more recent systematic data to develop an understanding of the process of proliferation of U.S. gangs. If there is to be any evaluation of the national and local commitments of resources to overcoming gang crime problems, it will depend on the analyses of the national surveys of law enforcement agencies, as a collective archive of historical information. In addition to being able to recognize when and if the proliferation of U.S. gangs begins to ebb it may even be possible to speculate about how and why or why not the patterns of change occurred. However, there is a clear caveat to all this: reliability of police survey data does not guarantee the **validity** of these data. Until agreement is achieved on defining gangs, gang-related crime, and the like, gang proliferation estimates remain just that–estimates.

REFERENCES

Bookin-Weiner, H., and R. Horowitz (1983). The end of the gang: Fad or fact? Criminology 21: 585-602.

Curry, G. D., R.A. Ball, and S.H. Decker (1996). Estimating the National Scope of Gang Crime from Law Enforcement Data. National Institute of Justice Research in Brief. Washington, DC: U.S. Department of Justice.

Curry, G. D., R.A. Ball, and R.J. Fox (1994a). Gang Crime and Law Enforcement Recordkeeping. National Institute of Justice Research in Brief. Washington, D.C.: U.S. Department of Justice.

Curry, G. D., R.A. Ball, and R.J. Fox, (1994b). Criminal justice reaction to gang violence. In M. Costanzo and S. Oskamp (eds.), Violence and the Law, pp. 203-225. Thousand Oaks, CA: Sage.

Curry, G. D., and S.H. Decker (1998). Confronting Gangs: Crime and Community. Los Angeles: Roxbury.

Dolan, E. F., Jr., and S. Finney (1984). Youth Gangs. New York: Julian Messner.

Hagedorn, J. M. (1988). People and Folks: Gangs, Crime and the Underclass in a Rustbelt City. Chicago: Lake View Press.

Huff, C. R. (1989). Youth gangs and public policy. Crime & Delinquency 35: 524-537.

Klein, M.W. (1995a). The American Street Gang. New York: Oxford University Press.

Klein, M.W. (1995b). Street gang cycles. In J.Q.Wilson and J. Petersilia (eds.), Crime, pp. 217-236. San Francisco: Institute for Contemporary Studies.

Maxson, C.L. (1999). Gang homicide. In M.D. Smith and M. Zahn, (eds.), Studying and Preventing Homicide, pp.197-220. Newbury Park, CA: Sage Publications.

Maxson, C., K. Woods, and M. Klein (1996). Street gang migration: How big a threat? NIJ Journal, 230:26-31.

Miller, W. B. (1982). Crime by Youth Gangs and Groups in the United States. Washington, D.C.: Office of Juvenile Justice and Delinquency Prevention, U.S. Department of Justice.

Miller, W. B. (1975). Violence by Youth Gangs and Youth Groups as a Crime Problem in Major American Cities. Washington, D.C.: U.S. Government Printing Office.

Miller, W. B. (1996). The Growth of the Youth Gang Problem in the United States 1970-1995. National Youth Gang Center. Draft report to OJJDP.

National Youth Gang Center (1997). 1995 National Youth Gang Survey. Washington, D.C.: Office of Juvenile Justice and Delinquency Prevention, U.S. Department of Justice.

Needle, J., and W.V. Stapleton (1983). Report of the National Juvenile Justice Assessment Centers, Police Handling of Youth Gangs. Washington, D.C.: Office of Juvenile Justice and Delinquency Prevention, U.S. Department of Justice.

Spergel, I. A. (1990). Youth gangs: Continuity and change. In M. Tonry and N. Morris (eds.), Crime and Justice: A Review of Research. Volume 12. Chicago: University of Chicago Press.

Spergel, I. A. (1995). The Youth Gang Problem: A Community Approach. New York: Oxford University Press.

Spergel, I. A., and G.D. Curry (1993). The National Youth Gang Survey: A research and development process. In A. Goldstein and C. R.Huff (eds.), Gang Intervention Handbook. Champaign-Urbana: Research Press.

Spergel, I. A., and S.A. Grossman (1997). The Little Village Project: A community approach to the gang problem. Social Work 42: 456-470.

Spergel, I., R. Chance, K. Ehrensft, T. Regulus, C. Kane, R. Laseter, A. Alexander, and S. Oh (1994). Gang Suppression and Intervention: Community Models. Research Summary. Washington, DC: U.S. Department of Juvenile Justice and Delinquency Prevention.

ENDNOTES

1 This research would not have been possible without the access to data afforded to the author by the National Youth Gang Center, the Office of Juvenile Justice and Delinquency Prevention, Cheryl L. Maxson, and Malcolm W. Klein. The opinions expressed in this publication are those of the author and do not necessarily represent those of the cooperating agencies and colleagues.

Chapter 6

YOUNG GANG MEMBERS IN A SCHOOL SURVEY

Finn Aäge Esbensen and Dana Peterson Lynskey
University of Nebraska at Omaha

The past one hundred years have produced volumes of research describing gangs, gang members, and gang activity. Currently there is heightened– concern that while the American violent crime rate is declining, the juvenile violent crime rate is increasing (Fox, 1996). Some commentators have suggested that juvenile gangs are in part responsible for this increase due to their involvement in drug trafficking and other illegal activities (Spergel, 1995). Combined with the stereotypical image of gang members (e.g., an African-American or Hispanic male), this belief of gang-based drug sales serves to reinforce the myth that the American crime problem is a male and "minority" problem. Is this an accurate reflection of the problem or is it possible that methodological approaches have unintentionally perpetuated this stereotype?

METHODOLOGICAL ISSUES

Juvenile gangs have often served as the focal point for delinquency research and theoretical development (e.g., Cloward and Ohlin, 1960; Cohen, 1955; Miller, 1958; Short and Strodbeck, 1965; Thornberry, Krohn, Lizotte, and Chard-Wierschem, 1993). Historically, the study of gangs has been descriptive in nature (e.g., Asbury, 1927; Campbell, 1991; Hagedorn, 1988, 1994; Moore, 1978; Puffer, 1912; Spergel, 1966; Thrasher, 1927; Vigil, 1988), relying chiefly

M.W. Klein et al (eds.), The Eurogang Paradox, 93–114.

upon observational methods and, in so doing, providing a wealth of information about specific gangs and their members. In spite of some excellent descriptive accounts provided by recent gang researchers (e.g., Campbell, 1991; Decker and Van Winkle, 1996; Hagedorn, 1988, 1994; Harris, 1988; Sullivan, 1989; Vigil, 1988), little information exists regarding the composition of gangs relative to the adolescent population as a whole. Bursik and Grasmick (1995:154) have summarized gang research by stating that the "emphasis has been on the depth of data, rather than the breadth."

More recently, social scientists have turned to two types of quantitative data. First, some gang researchers rely on law enforcement records to describe gang offenses and gang members (e.g., Curry, Ball, and Decker, 1996; Curry, Ball, and Fox, 1994; Maxson and Klein, 1990; Spergel, 1990). This body of research echoes the general picture of gang members being disproportionately male and from ethnic/racial minorities, an image often reinforced by the popular press. Given enforcement strategies that tend to target individuals with these characteristics, in conjunction with a general reluctance to discredit the notion that girls can possibly be gang members, this finding is not surprising.

A second quantitative approach employs survey methods to study gang behavior (e.g., Esbensen and Huizinga, 1993; Esbensen, Huizinga, and Weiher, 1993; Fagan, 1989; Thornberry et al., 1993; Winfree, Backstrom, and Mays, 1994). Interestingly, regardless of study design or research methodology, considerable consensus exists regarding the high rate of criminal offending–including crimes against person and property, substance use, and drug distribution and sales–among gang members.

As with gang research in general, much of what is known about ethnicity and gangs is derived from case studies of specific gangs or cities. Even the more general surveys of youth have not included diverse enough samples to address adequately the race/ethnicity composition of gangs. The Denver and Rochester longitudinal studies (e.g., Bjerregard and Smith, 1993; Esbensen and Huizinga, 1993; Thornberry et al., 1993) were concentrated in high-risk neighborhoods which, by definition, included disproportionate representations of racial and ethnic minorities. Such samples hardly allow for examination of gang membership by ethnicity.

Estimates of the prevalence of females in gangs varies greatly, as do descriptions of their involvement in gang activities (e.g., Bjerregard and Smith, 1993; Cohen, Williams, Bekelman, and Crosse, 1995; Curry et al., 1994; Esbensen and Huizinga, 1993; Goldstein and Glick, 1994; and Klein and

Crawford, 1995). Most estimates place the figure in the single digits and perpetuate the stereotype of girls being auxiliary members and relegated to gender specific activities (i.e., seducing males, concealing weapons, and instigating fights between rival male gangs). A growing number of studies, however, suggest that girls are significantly more gang-involved than commonly believed. The discrepancy may be attributed to two primary sources: 1) the research methodology utilized to produce the data and 2) the age of the sample members studied. Case studies, observational studies, and those relying upon law enforcement data tend to produce lower estimates of female involvement while general surveys tend to find a greater level of female gang involvement. This may well be an artifact of differential recording policies for males and females.

The second methodological issue, age of sample, may be the more significant factor. The Esbensen and Huizinga (1993) study reported a lower percent of girl gang members as the sample aged. There is additional evidence to suggest that girls mature out of gangs at an earlier age than males (e.g., Fishman, 1995; Harris, 1994; Moore and Hagedorn, 1996). According to Harris (1994), girls are most active in gangs between 13 and 16 years of age. She (1994:300) suggests that "by 17 or 18, interests and activities of individual members are directed toward the larger community rather than toward the gang, and girls begin to leave the active gang milieu." Thus, gang samples consisting of older adolescents or gang members in their 20s are apt to produce a substantially different picture than studies focusing on middle school and high school aged youths.

In spite of consensus on the extent of gang members' involvement in criminal activity, a lack of consensus exists with regard to other elements of gangs, including gang member demographic characteristics, structural and organizational aspects of the gang, and reasons for joining gangs. Our objectives in writing this chapter are two-fold: first, we examine the extent to which similarities exist in cross-city comparisons of gang member characteristics (demographic and perceived organizational aspects) and gang member involvement in delinquent activity. Second, we discuss the feasibility, including methodological concerns, of using school-based surveys to study youth gangs.

RESEARCH DESIGN

This investigation is part of the National Evaluation the Gang Resistance Education and Training (G.R.E.A.T.) program, a school-based gang prevention program. Site selection and sampling procedures were dictated by the objectives associated with the evaluation. Since the G.R.E.A.T. program is a seventh grade curriculum, eighth grade students were surveyed to allow for a one-year follow-up while at the same time guaranteeing that none of the sample was currently enrolled in the program. During the Spring of 1995, this multi-site, multi-state cross-sectional survey was conducted in eleven cities (Kansas City, Missouri; Las Cruces, New Mexico; Milwaukee, Wisconsin; Omaha, Nebraska; Orlando, Florida; Philadelphia, Pennsylvania; Phoenix, Arizona; Pocatello, Idaho; Providence, Rhode Island; Torrance, California; Will County, Illinois). For a description of the sampling and site selection, consult Esbensen and Winfree (1998).

This public school-based sample faces the standard limitations associated with school-based surveys (i.e., exclusion of private school students, exclusion of truants, sick, and/or tardy students, and the potential under-representation of "high-risk" youth). With this caveat in mind, the current sample is comprised of all eighth grade students in attendance on the days questionnaires were administered in eleven cities. The sample includes primarily 13 to 15 year old students attending public schools in a cross-section of communities within the continental United States. This is not a random sample and generalizations can not be made to the adolescent population as a whole. However, students from these eleven jurisdictions do represent the following types of communities: large urban areas with a majority of students belonging to a racial or ethnic minority (Philadelphia, Phoenix, Milwaukee, and Kansas City); medium-sized cities (population ranges between 100,000 and 500,000) with considerable racial and/or ethnic heterogeneity (Providence and Orlando); medium sized cities with a majority of white students but with a substantial minority enrollment (Omaha and Torrance); a small city (less than 100,000 inhabitants) with an ethnically diverse student population (Las Cruces); a small racially homogenous (i.e., white) city (Pocatello); and a rural community in which more than 80 percent of the student population is white (Will County). This diversity in locations and in sample characteristics allows for exploration of the distribution of gang affiliation and delinquent activity in an age group generally excluded from "gang research."

The student questionnaire consisted of demographic, attitudinal, and behavioral measures. In this chapter, the focus will be on the gang-specific questions, with an emphasis on describing gang members (e.g., gender, age, race/ethnicity, and family composition) and their perceptions of their gangs. A comparison of the self-reported delinquency and victimization of the gang members across the 11 sites will also be provided. Even though there is a lack of consensus about what constitutes gang membership and numerous definitional issues arise, we chose to utilize a self-nomination procedure. This self-definition method has become the standard not only in survey research, but is widely accepted in law enforcement practice. In the current research, two filter questions introduce the gang-specific section of the questionnaire: "Have you ever been a gang member?" and "Are you now in a gang?" Given the current sample, with almost all the respondents under the age of 15, even affirmative responses to the first question followed by a negative response to the second may still indicate a recent gang affiliation. In an attempt to limit our sample of gang members to "delinquent gangs," we employed a restrictive definition of gang status. Thus, only those youths who reported ever having been in a gang and who reported that their gangs engaged in at least one type of delinquent behavior (fighting other gangs, stealing cars, stealing in general, or robbing people) were classified as gang members. This definition resulted in the identification of 623 gang members representing 10.6 percent of the entire sample.

This large sample of gang members provides the opportunity to examine the extent to which gang members are similar across a variety of cities. Since gang membership remains a relatively rare phenomenon, most general surveys do not contain adequate numbers of gang members to make such comparisons. Thus, the purpose here is to provide a descriptive account of gang members drawn from a general survey of middle school students.

RESULTS

Prior to exploring the characteristics of gang members, we will describe the entire sample of eighth grade students (tables 1a and 1b). Approximately half of the sample is female (52%) and most of the respondents live in intact homes

(62%), that is, they indicated that both a mother and father (including step parents) were present in the home. The sample is ethnically diverse, with Whites accounting for 40 percent of respondents, African-Americans 27 percent, Hispanics 19 percent, Asians 6 percent, and Other 8 percent. As would be expected with an eighth grade sample, most of the respondents were between 13 and 15 years of age, with 60 percent being 14 years old. Based on data provided by the school districts included in this study, the sample characteristics are similar, indeed, virtually identical to the districts' student profiles. For example, in Las Cruces Middle Schools, 36 percent of students are Caucasian, 61 percent are Hispanic, and four percent are classified as Other. Our Las Cruces sample is 34 percent Caucasian, 57 percent Hispanic and nine percent Other. In Milwaukee, our sample contains 27 percent White and 56 percent African-American students compared to 25 percent and 61 percent respectively in the district.

As has been reported elsewhere (Esbensen and Winfree, 1998; Esbensen and Deschenes, 1998), this sample of eighth grade students provides a different picture of American gang members than is traditionally the case. The aggregated data from all 11 sites reveals that 1) there are more girls in gangs than is commonly assumed and 2) whites comprise a larger portion of gang members than official reports suggest. Consistent with much of the emerging gang research but contrary to prevailing stereotypes about the male dominated nature of gangs, fully 38 percent of the gang members in this eighth grade sample are females. While this figure still indicates that females are proportionately under-represented among gang members, it is to a far lesser extent than is commonly found when older samples are studied. Also, contrary to popular perception, 25 percent of the gang members are White. While minority youths account for the majority of gang members, the White youths are not as absent as "official" estimates suggest. As previously discussed, much of the prior gang literature has relied upon case studies of gangs or surveys limited to predominantly minority samples. The racial composition of gang members in this sample reveals that White youths are less likely to be involved in gangs than are African-American and Hispanic youths, but not to the extent that prior research has suggested. In fact, if we include some of the Other category which includes White youths who identified themselves as American, Italian, German, Portuguese, and the like, the difference in gang membership by ethnicity is even further reduced.

Table 1a. Demographic Characteristics of Gang Members by Site

	Age			Family structure		
Site	**<13**	**14**	**>15**	**Intact**	**Single parent**	**Other**
Kansas City	16%	56%	29%	48%	45%	7%
Las Cruces	10%	71%	19%	57%	38%	5%
Milwaukee	12%	53%	35%	35%	49%	16%
Omaha	16%	61%	22%	42%	41%	18%
Orlando	15%	63%	23%	37%	49%	14%
Philadelphia	9%	63%	28%	31%	56%	13%
Phoenix	11%	65%	25%	56%	27%	17%
Pocatello	22%	61%	17%	58%	36%	6%
Providence	23%	58%	19%	56%	28%	16%
Torrance	36%	55%	10%	57%	31%	12%
Will County	39%	61%	0%	63%	34%	3%
Total gang (n=623)	**17%**	**61%**	**23%**	**47%**	**40%**	**13%**
Total nongang (n=5,312)	**31%**	**60%**	**9%**	**64%**	**30%**	**7%**

Consistent with earlier assessments of the demographic characteristics of gangs, this sample reveals that younger youths are under-represented in gangs and gang members are more likely to live with a single parent. Even within this limited age sample, the youths 13 and under accounted for only 17 percent of gang members while they represented 31 percent of the non-gang sample. At the other extreme, 23 percent of gang members were 15 years old or older while only nine percent of non-gang members were this old. A minority of youths lived in single parent homes but gang members reported living in single parent homes more frequently (40%) than did non-gang youths (30%).

Table1b. Demographic Characteristics of Gang Members by Site (continued)

Site	Gender		Race			
	Male	**Female**	**White**	**African American**	**Hispanic**	**Other**
Kansas City	66%	34%	14%	68%	7%	11%
Las Cruces	59%	41%	21%	2%	71%	7%
Milwaukee	62%	38%	12%	57%	8%	23%
Omaha	63%	37%	38%	36%	9%	18%
Orlando	59%	41%	27%	31%	25%	18%
Philadelphia	75%	25%	13%	51%	13%	22%
Phoenix	59%	41%	3%	21%	66%	10%
Pocatello	58%	42%	65%	3%	9%	24%
Providence	63%	38%	9%	18%	24%	48%
Torrance	51%	49%	33%	5%	21%	40%
Will County	59%	41%	69%	3%	9%	19%
Total Gang (N=623)	**62%**	**38%**	**25%**	**31%**	**25%**	**20%**
Total Nongang (n=5,312)	**46%**	**54%**	**42%**	**26%**	**18%**	**14%**

Given the one-site nature of most gang research, what can we learn from multi-site comparisons? To what extent are these sample characteristics of gang members found in each of the eleven study sites? With respect to the number of gang members, we found quite a range, with as few as 5 percent of students in Will County claiming to be gang members and as many as 16 percent in Phoenix and Milwaukee.

Examination of gang member demographics reveals considerable variability across the eleven sites. With the exception of age (14 years of age was the modal age in all sites) gang demographics varied by community. Gender composition, for instance, varied considerably, with males accounting for only 51 percent of gang members in Torrance but 75 percent in Philadelphia. With respect to family status, 31 percent of Philadelphia gang members reported living in intact homes compared to a high of 63 percent in Will County. Correspondingly, the percent of gang members living in single parent homes ranged from 27 percent in Phoenix to 56 percent in Philadelphia. It is with race, however, that we notice the largest site-specific differences. While 25 percent of the entire gang sample was White, this varied from a low of three percent in Phoenix to a high of 69 percent in Will County. Similarly, the percent of gang members indicating they were African American ranged from two percent in Las Cruces to 68 percent in Kansas City. Hispanics comprised seven percent of gang members in Kansas City compared to 71 percent in Las Cruces. From this we can conclude that site selection shapes the image of gangs and gang members; they are a reflection of their communities rather than some stereotypical LA or Chicago gangster.

Organizational Characteristics of Gangs

The gang members were asked to respond to a series of questions assessing the level of gang organization. Among the questions assessing gang structure and organization were the following: there are initiation rites; the gang has established leaders; the gang has regular meetings; the gang has specific rules or codes; the gang has symbols or colors; and there are specific roles for girls. Responses to these questions indicate a fair degree of consistency across the 11 sites, although the range of affirmative responses to these gang descriptors was substantial. For instance, while approximately 40 percent of gang members in Omaha and Philadelphia indicated they held regular meetings, over 70 percent of gang members in Pocatello and Orlando stated that they met regularly (Table 2). The diversity of responses is less for the other gang characteristics, but one could develop a different impression of the level of gang organization depending on which site was studied. Philadelphia appears to differ significantly from the other sites, with those gang members reporting the lowest degree of gang organization. Only 39 percent of those youths indicated that their gangs held regular meetings, and approximately half of the gang members stated that their gangs had initiation rites, had established leaders, and had symbols or colors. This contrasts to Orlando where more than 90 percent of the gang members indicated that their gangs had established leaders, had specific rules for gang members, and had symbols or colors. Gang members in the remaining sites fell between these two extremes, but tended to provide responses more similar to the Orlando situation than the one in Philadelphia.

Table 2. Gang Characteristics by Site

Site	Initiation rights	Established leaders	Regular meetings	Specific rules	Colors	Roles for girls
Kansas City	70%	82%	55%	78%	95%	46%
Las Cruces	89%	84%	58%	70%	95%	66%
Milwaukee	85%	87%	66%	91%	97%	44%
Omaha	80%	70%	42%	67%	99%	53%
Orlando	79%	94%	79%	94%	92%	70%
Philadelphia	50%	53%	39%	61%	55%	37%
Phoenix	68%	71%	50%	71%	99%	68%
Pocatello	80%	91%	72%	91%	89%	59%
Providence	70%	85%	58%	72%	91%	48%
Torrance	90%	79%	67%	79%	88%	48%
Will County	88%	90%	61%	75%	97%	53%
Total	**77%**	**79%**	**57%**	**77%**	**92%**	**54%**

Gang Activities

The gang members were also asked to comment on the range of illegal activities in which the gang was involved. Clearly, these gangs are criminally active groups; the majority of members reported their gangs engaged in the following things: get in fights with other gangs; steal things; rob other people; steal cars; sell marijuana; and damage or destroy property (Table 3). With the exception of Philadelphia, these figures indicate considerable consistency in the range of criminal activity of gangs across all sites. Eighty-five percent or more of gang members in all sites indicated that they fight other gangs and, with the exception of Philadelphia, 70 percent or more of gang youth in the other ten sites stated that their gangs stole things, sold marijuana, and destroyed property.

Table 3. Illegal Activities of Gangs by Site

Site	Fight other gangs	Steal things	Rob people	Steal cars	Sell marijuana	Destroy property
Kansas City	95%	70%	73%	71%	87%	79%
Las Cruces	97%	79%	61%	50%	86%	83%
Milwaukee	85%	71%	67%	74%	89%	72%
Omaha	98%	71%	55%	76%	81%	79%
Orlando	94%	75%	57%	67%	75%	78%
Philadelphia	88%	57%	57%	60%	60%	61%
Phoenix	99%	74%	61%	81%	87%	90%
Pocatello	94%	83%	60%	74%	83%	94%
Providence	94%	70%	46%	67%	73%	70%
Torrance	95%	85%	66%	63%	92%	85%
Will County	91%	100%	66%	75%	75%	88%
Total	**94%**	**74%**	**61%**	**70%**	**82%**	**79%**

Reasons for Joining the Gang

In attempts to understand the allure of gangs, the gang members were asked why they joined their gang. They were provided a list of reasons for joining gangs and asked to circle each separate reason for why they joined. Of interest is the diversity of reasons provided and the lack of agreement among gang members. Clearly, adolescents are attracted to gangs for a variety of reasons, and these reasons appear to be particular to specific sites. Contrary to common perception, very few (7%) indicated that they were forced to join. The most common reason for joining the gang was for protection (54%), although this varied substantially across sites (from 37% in Philadelphia to 74% in Will County). A common belief is that youths join gangs because their friends or siblings are gang members. This was not as common a reason for joining as anticipated with only 30 percent indicating they joined because a brother or sister was in the gang while 46 percent joined because a friend was in the gang. This varied, however, from a low of 29 percent in Philadelphia to a high of 61 percent in Pocatello. Approximately 40 percent of the gang members in Phoenix, Orlando and Milwaukee joined because a sibling was in the gang while less than 20 percent of respondents in Philadelphia, Torrance, and Will County gave this as a reason.

Table 4. Reasons for Joining the Gang

Site	Forced to join	For money	For protection	Friend in gang	Sibling in gang	For respect
Kansas City	14%	55%	39%	41%	35%	39%
Las Cruces	6%	39%	46%	56%	25%	44%
Milwaukee	8%	57%	55%	51%	38%	48%
Omaha	7%	56%	60%	49%	34%	58%
Orlando	11%	42%	69%	49%	40%	60%
Philadelphia	0%	29%	37%	29%	15%	46%
Phoenix	7%	41%	44%	32%	41%	38%
Pocatello	8%	53%	64%	61%	25%	67%
Providence	0%	34%	44%	38%	22%	28%
Torrance	0%	29%	66%	51%	17%	44%
Will County	16%	65%	74%	55%	16%	68%
Total	**7%**	**47%**	**54%**	**46%**	**30%**	**49%**

Self- Reported Delinquency

Table 5 provides a summary of gang members' self-reported involvement in delinquent activities (ever prevalence). As has been reported in numerous publications, gang members are engaged in a number of criminal acts. Regardless of location, the results are remarkably similar. Approximately 75 percent of gang members reported that they had carried a hidden weapon. Half of them had attacked someone with a weapon, slightly fewer than 30 percent had robbed someone or shot at someone, over 80 percent had been involved in a gang fight, and almost 60 percent had sold marijuana at some time.

Table 5. Self-Reported Delinquency of Gang Members

	Percent of Gang Members Ever Committing Each Act					
Site	**Carried hidden weapon**	**Attacked someone**	**Robbed someone**	**Gang fight**	**Shot at someone**	**Sold marijuana**
Kansas City	75%	66%	41%	82%	32%	71%
Las Cruces	76%	41%	21%	85%	22%	62%
Milwaukee	76%	41%	23%	75%	38%	64%
Omaha	78%	47%	31%	87%	40%	55%
Orlando	78%	57%	33%	76%	33%	50%
Philadelphia	84%	52%	23%	77%	14%	36%
Phoenix	74%	56%	28%	88%	27%	72%
Pocatello	61%	44%	25%	83%	19%	58%
Providence	79%	46%	12%	76%	21%	49%
Torrance	78%	57%	29%	90%	26%	62%
Will County	75%	47%	38%	84%	28%	61%
Total	**76%**	**50%**	**28%**	**82%**	**29%**	**59%**

The gang members were also asked about their own victimization. Most of them had been hit by someone trying to hurt them, approximately 40 percent had been attacked by someone with a weapon, and one out of every four gang members had been victims of a robbery. Thus, while these gang members are perpetrators of a number of crimes, they also tend to be victims of crimes similar to those that they commit.

DISCUSSION

In this chapter our first objective was to explore the extent to which the gang image varies across eleven cities. While much prior gang research has focused on a single city, the current research project collected survey data from a sample of eighth grade public school students in 11 cities. This diverse sample allows us to combine responses from gang members across multiple social contexts. To what extent, however, does such aggregation mask local differences? The analyses reported here suggest that, depending upon site, slightly different images of youth gangs appear. Having said this, however, it is also necessary to highlight that there also exists a considerable degree of similarity of gang depictions across the eleven sites included in this study.

To highlight the differences, we will provide a general description of gang members in two different cities. The majority of Philadelphia gang youths reported living in single-parent homes (56%), were overwhelmingly male (75%), and African-American (51%). These gangs were characterized, relative to gang members in other sites, by both low levels of organization and illegal gang activity. Just over half (between 57% and 61%) of the gang members indicated that their gangs were involved in various illegal activities such as theft, robbery, vandalism, and drugs sales.

Contrary to this image, the majority of gang members in Pocatello, Idaho reported being male (58%), White (65%), and living in intact homes (58%). Their gangs tended to have a high degree of organization; the vast majority described their gangs as having initiation rites, established leaders, specific rules, symbols or colors, and holding regular meetings. Likewise, these gangs were described as being involved in a full range of illegal activities (see Table 3).

Gang youths in the other nine sites varied somewhat from these two extremes, but some similarities should be noted. With the exception of demographic characteristics, the picture of gang youths obtained from the aggregation of data from these eleven sites provides a composite from which most of the sites do not deviate substantially. Youth gangs are not uniformly organized entities, although approximately 75 percent of gang members in most of the sites indicated that their gangs had initiation rites, leaders, rules, and colors. There is also considerable similarity in gang members' perceptions of illegal activities in which the gang is involved. Likewise, the self-reported delinquent behavior of the gang members is remarkably consistent across the sites.

It is clear that the demographic characteristics of gang members are determined by the characteristics of the larger community. In cities with a large Hispanic population, gang members are likely to be Hispanic while in communities comprised mostly of Whites, the gang members will be representative of the larger community. This finding is neither new nor earth-shattering, but it does highlight the extent to which much prior research that has been restricted to single sites (primarily large urban areas with acknowledged gang problems) may have produced biased estimates of the demographic composition of gangs. It also highlights the problem confronting both field and survey researchers in identifying or sampling non-minority gang populations. Decker and Van Winkle (1996:57) commented on their inability to "recruit" White gang members in their St. Louis study: "The racial composition of our sample merits some comment. We are aware of white gangs in the city of St. Louis that have been in existence for several years. However, we were not able to gain access to members of these gangs through our street contacts." Surveys have also tended to over sample minority populations (e.g., Esbensen and Huizinga, 1993; Fagan, 1989; Thornberry et al., 1993). In their study of gang affiliation in "high-risk" Denver neighborhoods, for example, Esbensen and Huizinga (1993) had, at 90 percent, a disproportionate representation of minority youth. This kind of sample bias does not allow for a realistic assessment of the racial composition of gangs. The current research identifies a need for more surveys of the general adolescent population to clarify the extent of gang activity among different racial and ethnic groups.

SCHOOL SURVEYS AND GANG RESEARCH

School surveys provide one alternative to the sampling issues discussed above. While schools have rarely been viewed as the basis for a general study of gangs and gang prevention programs, the research reported here identifies the value of such an approach. School-based survey research is not, however, without limitations.

Surveys of public school students clearly restrict the surveys to students enrolled in public schools. Thus, students attending private or parochial schools, as well as those being home-schooled, are excluded from the sample. Likewise, chronic absentees, truants, the chronically ill, and dropouts will also be missed–the very youths who are likely to be involved in gang activity. The age or school level of study participants will clearly have an impact on the magnitude of the dropout problem, with relatively few students in this category in surveys of middle school students. As the targeted population ages, however, this non-representativeness of the sample becomes of greater concern. Non-participation due to absenteeism can be addressed, in part, by multiple visits to the schools. To assess the representativeness of the sample, the researcher can compare the entire school-level data relative to the sample data. Or, depending on schools, demographic data may be available for the non-respondents enabling the comparison of non-respondents to survey participants on key demographic variables.

In addition to sample representativeness, American researchers are confronted with two issues that affect sample representativeness: access to the schools and parental consent. Most large American school districts operate their own research offices that oversee all research conducted within their schools. Proposals stipulating the research purpose and design need to be reviewed by this office, often using their unique forms and/or format. Once permission has been granted, the researcher will need to secure the cooperation of each principal. While centralized, many school districts grant full autonomy to each school principal. So, even though central administration may approve the proposed research, this does not guarantee access to students.

Once entry has been achieved, another issue involves the informed consent process. Research involving minors requires not only child assent but also parental consent. Even if the funding agency and/or university institutional review board (IRB) has approved passive consent procedures (parents are required to exclude their child), a school district or an individual principal may impose additional requirements. Active parental consent (written permission is required to include a student in the study) introduces yet another series of questions about participation rates and sample representativeness. Participation rates will be substantially lower under active consent procedures, with a normal range of between 40% and 60%. Passive consent procedures, on the other hand, generally produce close to a full enumeration of students attending classes on the day of survey administration. In cases involving multiple sites, an additional problem arises when some schools or districts allow passive consent procedures while others in the sample request active consent. Under the more stringent level, not only will participation rates be lower, the sample will likely consist of fewer "high risk" youths. Parents who fail to return consent forms are more likely to be single parents, to be members of racial or ethnic minorities, and to have lower levels of education compared to the parents who provide active consent (Esbensen et al., 1999).

Several methodological issues also arise with the development of the research protocol. The group-administered questionnaire is the most likely method to be used in school-based surveys. Thus, questions should be relatively simple and straightforward, preferably close-ended in format. While some follow up or open-ended questions might be possible, by design, school-based surveys are intended for breadth of coverage, not depth. The questionnaire should include clear and concise instructions to the students. Also guiding the questionnaire development should be considerations of the age and reading level of the targeted youth–something that varies considerably by school and region. Another practical consideration is the length of the questionnaire. In schools, researchers are confronted with time limits associated with the length of class periods. Class periods range from less than 45 minutes to 90 minutes. Thought needs to be given to how many and what type of questions can be asked in the available time.

Of particular relevance for gang research is the fact that some school districts restrict the types of questions allowed and may request some questions be deleted from the research instrument. This should be addressed when obtaining district level approval from the research office. Many school districts, for example, consider questions about sexual activity and birth control to be taboo and will not allow such questions to be included. Other districts may also be reluctant to allow questions measuring illegal activity, clearly a problem for gang research!

One strategy to deal with differential reading levels is to read the questions out loud. This is most easily accomplished when more than one researcher is involved in the data collection in the classroom. Having multiple researchers in the classroom also serves as a "crowd control" factor and helps to enhance the level of confidentiality. By reading the questionnaire out loud, slow readers are also able to complete the questionnaire in the allotted time. In some instances, visual aids, such as response categories displayed on overheads, might also facilitate the administration process.

Another issue that appears in an increasing number of schools is the language ability of recent immigrants. Some schools have sizable non-English speaking minority populations, primarily Spanish speaking and Southeast Asian students. The researcher should consider the desirability or necessity of translating (a strategy that introduces additional problems concerning both validity and reliability) the questionnaire into the dominant languages at each school. Otherwise, external validity may be compromised.

One last issue in this section deals with the confidentiality of student responses. If the questionnaires are anonymous, their distribution and collection are relatively straightforward. If, however, confidentiality is required, then additional issues should be considered and questionnaire distribution and collection will be more time consuming. The traditional classroom setting is the preferred location for questionnaire administration. Large auditoriums, cafeterias, and gymnasiums increase management problems, decrease confidentiality, and negatively affect the quality of data collected. In prior research we found higher rates of incomplete questionnaires when administered in larger groups, especially in gymnasiums where students had to complete the instruments while seated on the floor.

Discussion until now has been limited to cross-sectional designs. Prospective longitudinal designs, whether panel or cohort, present additional methodological concerns. The most serious problem is one shared with all longitudinal research–subject retention. Conducting school-based research does have one advantage with regard to tracking subjects. Many larger districts have centralized data banks that allow researchers to locate study participants in other schools within the district. To take advantage of this system, however, it is generally necessary to have the student's identification number. While students might initially have been surveyed in particular classrooms, subsequent survey administration will not be so easy. Students participating will have changed class schedules, been promoted to the next grade, changed schools, or dropped out. For those students still in school, the researcher faces the task of administering surveys to a subset of students that will involve "pulling" students from class or surveying students during study hall or lunch. Such hurdles will increase administration costs (primarily in terms of staff time) and may contribute to lower retention rates. For students who have changed schools, contact must now be made with the principal of that school and arrangements made to survey the student. As the mobility rate increases, this aspect of following a school-based sample becomes increasingly problematic. One other solution might be to switch methods and send mail questionnaires to the students who have moved out of district or to those who are the only study participants at a particular school.

CONCLUSION

In this chapter, our objectives were to discuss the feasibility of using school surveys in gang research and to describe the gang picture produced by a school-based survey. As with other methodologies, school surveys may produce a potentially biased picture of youth gangs. We have attempted to identify potential pitfalls and methods for reducing their effects. With these caveats in mind, we have provided a glimpse of the youth gang situation in eleven different American cities. A number of similarities among gang members exist across these quite diverse settings. However, this multi-site research also highlights the extent to which the image of gangs can vary from one site to the next. It is our belief that school-based surveys, such as the one described in this chapter can provide a broad overview of gangs in a variety of settings. Clearly, in-depth interviews or field research can provide greater description and elaboration of gangs within more specific contexts. As we embark upon cross-cultural gang research, it becomes imperative that we incorporate methodologies that will allow for a breadth of coverage, as well as in-depth coverage, of the youth gang phenomenon in multiple nations.

To what degree is it feasible to conduct school-based gang research projects cross-nationally? Whereas school systems throughout the United States share a number of common characteristics that facilitate this methodology, the European situation raises more challenges. School organization, age of compulsory attendance, and language are among the additional issues to be addressed. Prior work on the International Self-Report Delinquency Study (Junger-Tas et al., 1994), however, provides evidence that this type of cross-national school-based research is possible. In that collaborative effort, school samples were utilized in Belgium, Finland, Italy, and the United States. In spite of associated obstacles, we contend that school-based surveys can be a useful tool in the study of youth gangs.

REFERENCES

Asbury, H. (1927). The Gangs of New York. New York: Capricorn.

Bjerregard, B. and C. Smith. (1993). Gender differences in gang participation, delinquency, and substance use. Journal of Quantitative Criminology 4:329-55.

Bursik, Jr., R. J. and H.G. Grasmick. (1995). The collection of data for gang research. In M.W. Klein, C.L. Maxson, and J.Miller (eds.), The Modern Gang Reader. Los Angeles, CA: Roxbury Press.

Campbell, A. (1991). The Girls in the Gang. 2nd. edition. Cambridge, MA: Basil Blackwell.

Cloward, R. and L.E. Ohlin. (1960). Delinquency and Opportunity. New York: Free Press.

Cohen, A. (1955). Delinquent Boys: The Culture of the Gang. Glencoe, IL: Free Press.

Cohen, M.I., K. Williams, A. M. Bekelman, and S. Crosse. (1995). Evaluation of the National Youth Gang Drug Prevention Program. In M.W. Klein, C.L. Maxson, and J. Miller (eds.), The Modern Gang Reader. Los Angeles, CA: Roxbury Press.

Curry, G. D., R.A. Ball, and S.H. Decker. (1996). Estimating the National Scope of Gang Crime from Law Enforcement Data. Research in Brief. Washington, DC: U.S. Department of Justice.

Curry, G. D., R.A. Ball, and R. J. Fox. (1994). Gang Crime and Law Enforcement Record Keeping. Research in Brief. Washington, DC: U.S. Department of Justice.

Decker, S.H., and B. Van Winkle. (1996). Life in the Gang: Family, Friends, and Violence. New York: Cambridge University Press.

Esbensen, F., M. H. Miller, T J. Taylor, N. He, and A. Freng. (1999). Differential attrition rates and active parental consent. Evaluation Review 23:316-335.

Esbensen, F., and E.P. Deschenes. (1998). A multisite examination of youth gang membership: Does gender matter? Criminology 36: 799-828.

Esbensen, F., and L, T. Winfree, Jr. (1998). Race and gender differences between gang and nongang youths: Results from a multisite survey. Justice Quarterly 15:505-525.

Esbensen, F., and D. Huizinga. (1993). Gangs, drugs, and delinquency in a survey of urban youth. Criminology 31:565-589.

Esbensen, F., D. Huizinga, and A.W. Weiher. (1993). Gang and non-gang youth: Differences in explanatory variables. Journal of Contemporary Criminal Justice 9:94-116.

Fagan, J. (1989). The social organization of drug use and drug dealing among urban gangs. Criminology 27:633-669.
Fishman, L.T. (1995). The Vice Queens: An ethnographic study of Black female gang behavior. In M.W. Klein, C. L. Maxson, and J. Miller (eds.), The Modern Gang Reader. Los Angeles, CA: Roxbury Publishing Company.
Fox, J.A. (1996). Trends in Juvenile Violence: A Report to the United States Attorney General on Current and Future Rates of Juvenile Offending. Washington, DC: U.S. Department of Justice.
Goldstein, A.P., and B. Glick. (1994). The Prosocial Gang: Implementing Aggression Replacement Training. Thousand Oaks, CA: Sage Publications.
Hagedorn, J.M. (1994). Homeboys, dope fiends, legits, and new jacks. Criminology 32:197-219.
Hagedorn, J.M. (1988). People and Folks: Gangs, Crime and the Underclass in a Rustbelt City. Chicago, IL: Lakeview Press.
Harris, M.C. (1994). Cholas, Mexican-American girls, and gangs. Sex Roles 30:289-301.
Harris, M.C. (1988). Cholas: Latino Girls and Gangs. New York: AMS Press.
Klein, M.W., and L.Y. Crawford. (1995). Groups, gangs, and cohesiveness. In M.W. Klein, C.L. Maxson, and J. Miller (eds.), The Modern Gang Reader. Los Angeles, CA: Roxbury Press.
Maxson, C.L., and M. Klein. (1990). Street gang violence: Twice as great or half as great? In C. R. Huff (ed.), Gangs in America, pp. 71-100. Newbury Park, CA: Sage Publications.
Miller, W.B. (1958). Lower class culture as a generating milieu for gang delinquency. Journal of Social Issues 14:5-19.
Moore, J.W. (1978). Homeboys: Gangs, Drugs, and Prison in the Barrios of Los Angeles. Philadelphia, PA: Temple University Press.
Moore, J.W. and J. M. Hagedorn. (1996). What happens to girls in the gang? In C. R. Huff (ed.), Gangs in America, 2nd edition. Thousand Oaks, CA: Sage Publications.
Puffer, J. A. (1912). The Boy and His Gang. Boston: Houghton Mifflin.
Short, J.F., and F. L. Strodbeck. (1965). Group Processes and Gang Delinquency. Chicago: University of Chicago Press.
Spergel, I.A. (1995). The Youth Gang Problem. New York: Oxford University Press.
Spergel, I.A. (1990). Youth gangs: Continuity and change. In N. Morris and M. Tonry (eds.), Crime and Justice: An Annual Review of Research, pp. 171--275. Chicago: University of Chicago Press.
Spergel, I. A. (1966). Street Gang Work: Theory and Practice. Reading, MA: Addison-Wesley.
Sullivan, M.L. (1989). Getting Paid: Youth Crime and Work in the Inner City. Ithaca, NY: Cornell University Press.
Thornberry, T.P., M.D. Krohn, A.J. Lizotte, and D. Chard-Wierschem. (1993). The role of juvenile gangs in facilitating delinquent behavior. Journal of Research in Crime and Delinquency 30:55-87.
Thrasher, F.M. (1927). The Gang: A Study of One Thousand Three Hundred Thirteen Gangs in Chicago. Chicago: University of Chicago Press.

Vigil, J.D. (1988). Barrio Gangs: Street Life and Identity in Southern California. Austin, TX: University of Texas Press.

Winfree, L.T., T.V. Backstrom, and G.L. Mays. (1994). Social learning theory, self-reported delinquency, and youth gangs: A new twist on a general theory of crime and delinquency. Youth and Society 26:147-177.

Chapter 7

YOUNG WOMEN'S INVOLVEMENT IN GANGS IN THE UNITED STATES: AN OVERVIEW

Jody Miller
University of Missouri at St. Louis

In the United States, the 1980s and 1990s have witnessed monumental national growth both in gangs and in the renewed academic study of gangs. Female gang involvement, which until recently was typically either stereotyped or ignored, has also garnered new interest among researchers, thanks in part to the work of feminist scholars, who have struggled to bring the study of women's lives more fully into the field of criminology.[1] One consequence of this renewed interest in gangs, and girls'[2] gang involvement in particular, has been much improved information about the topic, including a number of important questions: (1) how widespread is young women's gang involvement? (2) why do they join gangs? (3) what is the nature of their gang involvement? and finally, (4) what are the consequences of girls' participation in gangs? Here I will address each of these issues by reviewing recent research on young women's gang involvement in the United States.

HOW WIDESPREAD IS YOUNG WOMEN'S GANG INVOLVEMENT?

Recent estimates suggest that female gang participation is much more widespread than has typically been believed. On the one hand, data from official sources continue to underestimate the extent of girls' gang membership. For instance, Curry, Ball and Fox (1994) found that some law enforcement

M.W. Klein et al (eds.), The Eurogang Paradox, 115–132.

policies officially exclude female gang members from their counts. Excluding data from these cities, they still found that females were only 5.7 percent of gang members known to law enforcement agencies. Part of law enforcement's underestimation of girls' gang involvement is likely attributable to male gang members' greater likelihood of being involved in serious gang crimes (see below), as well as law enforcement's greater attention to older offenders (Curry, 1998). In contrast with law enforcement data, results from survey research with youths indicate that young women's gang involvement is much more extensive.

For instance, Esbensen and Deschenes (1998), based on a sample of eighth graders in eleven cities, report that the prevalence rate for gang membership is 14 percent for males and eight percent for females. Other studies examine the gender ratio within gangs; these studies estimate that young women approximate twenty to 46 percent of gang members (Esbensen and Huizinga, 1993; Esbensen and Winfree, 1998; Moore, 1991; Winfree et al., 1992). My own research, based on interviews with 48 female gang members, indicates that this varies considerably across gangs–girls were as few as seven percent or as many as 75 percent of the membership in mixed-gender gangs, and of course, 100 percent of the members in autonomous female gangs. Despite this variation, by and large girls were a numeric minority in their gangs; half (24 of 48) were in gangs with a third or fewer female members, and two-thirds (32 of 48) were in gangs in which females were less than half of the members (Miller, in press).

While my study included four girls from autonomous female gangs (approximately eight percent of the sample), other research has emphasized all-female gangs as a new and perhaps growing phenomenon (Lauderback et al., 1992; Taylor, 1993). However, survey research suggests that autonomous female gangs are far from the dominant form of young women's gang involvement. For example, from interviews with 110 female gang members in three sites (Boston, Massachusetts; Seattle, Washington; and Pueblo, Colorado), Curry (1997) found that only 6.4 percent described being in independent female gangs, while 57.3 percent described their gangs as mixed-gender, and another 36.4 percent said they were in female auxiliaries of male gangs.

In fact, while some researchers have suggested that female gang involvement is increasing (Fagan, 1990; Spergel and Curry, 1993; Taylor, 1993), it is difficult to discern whether these numbers reflect an actual increase in the rates of young women's participation in gangs, or simply better measurements (for an overview, see Curry, 1998b).[3] One critique of much traditional gang research is that it emphasized gangs as a principally male phenomenon (see for instance, Cloward and Ohlin, 1960; Cohen, 1995; Hagedorn, 1988; Jankowski, 1991; Short and Strodbeck, 1965; Vigil, 1988). In fact, until recently many gang scholars gained their information about girls' involvement from male gang members rather than the young women themselves (for an overview, see Campbell, 1984, 1990a, 1990b). Despite researchers' inattention to female gang involvement in earlier periods, both Klein's (1971) and Moore's (1991) research indicate that young women were between a quarter and a third of gang members in the middle part of the century. These studies suggest that young women's extensive involvement in gangs is not a new phenomenon. While the past remains sketchy, we have very good data today indicating that young women are participating in gangs in numbers large enough to cause concern.

WHY DO GIRLS JOIN GANGS?

There is a growing body of knowledge, including both qualitative and quantitative studies, which provides insight into the causes of girls' involvement in gangs in the United States. Addressing the question of why girls join gangs involves examining two interrelated issues–the background factors associated with girls' gang participation, and also the functions and meanings of gang involvement for girls, i.e., what they describe gaining from being in gangs. To examine these questions I will review the literature on four topics: structural and neighborhood conditions, the family, school factors, and the influence of peers. Understanding these life contexts provides insight into their decisions to join, as research suggests that gangs comprise an important element of the social support systems of their members (Soriano, 1993: 454; Vigil and Long, 1990), and likely meet specific needs for young women (Campbell, 1990a; Joe and Chesney-Lind, 1995).

To account for the proliferation of gangs in recent decades, many scholars have focused on compelling evidence that much, though not all, of this growth has been spurred by the deterioration in living conditions for many Americans. This has been caused by structural changes brought about by deindustrialization there (see Hagedorn, 1988, 1991; Huff, 1989; Klein, 1995). These structural changes have resulted in the growth of what scholars refer to as an urban "underclass"–disproportionately poor, African American and Latino individuals living in conditions of entrenched poverty in inner-city communities. These communities are characterized by intense racial and economic segregation and isolation, the outmigration of middle class families, and a precipitious decline in social services for those left behind (see Moore and Pinderhughes, 1993; Sampson and Wilson, 1995; Wilson, 1987, 1996). The resulting lack of alternatives and sense of hopelessness are believed to have contributed to the growth of gangs in many cities, as scholars point to the gang as a means for inner-city youths to adapt to oppressive living conditions imposed by their environments.

Though much of the focus of this research has been on gangs in general, or male gang members in particular, a few scholars have linked these conditions to female gang involvement as well. The characteristics of the neighborhoods from which the young women in my study were drawn were very much in keeping with the image of urban poverty and racial segregation described above. In addition, Campbell (1990a) notes that in addition to the limited opportunities and powerlessness of underclass membership shared with their male counterparts, young women in these communities also face the burden of childcare responsibilities and subordination to men. Joe and Chesney-Lind (1995: 411) argue that "the gang assists [both] young women and men in coping with their lives in chaotic, violence and economically marginalized communities." Moreover, because of the particular dangers young women face, Fishman (1995:87) argues that gangs may assist young women in protecting themselves by "provid[ing] opportunities to learn such traditional male skills as fighting skills and taking care of themselves on the streets." My research also provides evidence that young women believe the gang can offer protection and retaliation against the street predators prevalent in impoverished urban communities (Miller, 1998).

While this assessment appears to be accurate, it nonetheless remains only a partial answer to the question of why girls join gangs. Most research shows that fewer than one-quarter of youths living in high-risk neighborhoods claim gang membership (Bjerregaard and Smith, 1993; Winfree et al., 1992), and researchers have not found differences in perceived limited opportunities between gang and non-gang youths in these communities (Esbensen et al., 1993). Thus we need to look at what other factors might lead some girls into gang involvement, even while others within the same impoverished communities exercise other options.

A factor that has received quite a bit of attention is the family, which has long been considered crucial for understanding delinquency and gang behavior among girls (Canter, 1982; Cernkovich and Giordano, 1987; Hagan, et al., 1985; Moore, 1991; Smith and Paternoster, 1987). One set of family factors that has been considered includes the extent that youths are supervised by their caregivers, and by the strength of attachments within the family. Bjerregaard and Smith (1993) measured both parental supervision and parental attachment, and found neither to be significantly related to gang membership for girls. Esbensen and Deschenes (1998), in a multi-site study of risk factors for delinquency and gang behavior, found that lack of parental supervision was associated with gang membership for male and female gang members, but that maternal attachment was more predictive of gang membership for males than females.

Ethnographic and other qualitative studies are much more likely to suggest that serious family problems are major contributors to girls' gang involvement. With regard to the issues just noted, Joe and Chesney-Lind (1995) observe that the young women they spoke with sometimes had parents who worked long hours, or parents who were unemployed or underemployed–circumstances which they suggest affected the girls' supervision and the quality of their family relationships. Fleisher's (1998; see also Campbell, 1984) ethnographic study of gangs in Kansas City, Missouri documents intergenerational patterns of abuse and neglect, spawned by poverty and abject neighborhood conditions, which he suggests are at the heart of the gang problem.

Likewise, Moore (1991) documents a myriad of family problems that contribute to the likelihood of gang involvement for young women; childhood abuse and neglect, wife abuse, having alcohol or drug addicts in the family, witnessing the arrest of family members, having a family member who is chronically ill, and experiencing a death in the family during childhood. Her conclusion, based on comparisons of male and female gang members, is that young women in particular are likely to come from families that are troubled. My study offers a comparison of gang and non-gang girls from the same communities, and also suggests that gang girls are more likely to come from families with multiple problems, including violence, abuse, drug and alcohol addiction, and imprisonment (Miller, in press). Moore's research and my own also suggest that having close family members in gangs also increases the likelihood that young women will join.

Thus research suggests that "the gang can serve as a surrogate extended family for adolescents who do not see their own families as meeting their needs for belonging, nurturing, and acceptance" (Huff, 1993: 6; see also Brown, 1978; Campbell, 1990a; Joe and Chesney-Lind, 1995; but for opposing view see Decker and Van Winkle, 1996). Other gang members offer support, solidarity, and a network of friends for those girls whose parents are unable to provide stable family relations. Moreover, girls' friendships within the gang provide an outlet for members to deal with family problems and cope with abuse and other life problems (Joe and Chesney-Lind, 1995).

While qualitative studies are most likely to find family problems at the heart of girls' gang involvement, a number of studies based on surveys of juvenile populations note school-based problems. Bjerregaard and Smith (1993) found that low expectations for completing school were a significant predictor of gang membership for young women. Likewise, Bowker and Klein (1983) report that female gang members are less likely than non-members to intend to finish high school or attend college. More recently, Esbensen and Deschenes (1998) report that while boys who feel that educational success is unattainable are more likely to be gang members, this was not the case for girls. However, they did find school commitment or expectations to be uniquely associated with gang involvement for girls.

Finally, there is also strong evidence that peer influences are important for understanding gang participation among females, as well as males (Brown, 1978; Bowker and Klein, 1983; Campbell, 1990a, 1990b; Giordano, 1978; Morash, 1983). We know from much research that youths who participate in gangs often express the importance of the gang in their lives (Moore, 1991: 77). Esbensen and Deschenes (1998) found that although male and female gang members reported similar levels of commitment to negative peers, this was a stronger explanatory factor for gang involvement for females than males. In addition, they report that risk seeking was a predictor of female, but not male, gang membership. Short and Strodtbeck (1965) argue that the group meets self-esteem needs. The rewards provided by the gang–status, companionship, excitement, protection, and belonging–facilitate the building of esteem. Participation in the gang results from group dynamics that encourage member involvement through the provision of self-esteem and identity. Moreover, gang activities provide these youths with a way to alleviate the boredom of their daily lives, given the limited options for recreation and entertainment found in impoverished communities. Quicker (1983: 80) summarizes, "to be in a gang is to be part of something. It means having a place to go to, friends to talk with, and parties to attend. It means recognition and respected status." In addition, as the next section details, these peer factors also contribute to the gangs' facilitation of delinquency among its members, including its female members. It is to these issues–specifically the nature of girls' gang involvement–I now turn.

WHAT IS THE NATURE OF GIRLS' GANG INVOLVEMENT?

One reason gangs have received so much attention among criminologists is that we know from quite a bit of research that young people who are in gangs–male and female–are substantially more involved in delinquency than their non-gang counterparts. Research comparing gang and non-gang youths has consistently found that serious criminal involvement is a feature that distinguishes gangs from other groups of youths (Esbensen et al., 1993; Esbensen and Huizinga, 1993; Fagan, 1990; Klein, 1995; Thornberry et al., 1993; Winfree et al., 1992). This pattern holds for female gang members as well as their male counterparts (Bjerregaard and Smith, 1993; Esbensen and Winfree, 1998; Thornberry et al., 1993). The enhancement effect of gang membership is most noticeable for serious delinquency and marijuana use (Thornberry et al., 1993). Bjerregaard and Smith (1993: 346) summarize, "our study suggests that for females [as well as males], gangs are consistently associated with a greater prevalence and with higher rates of delinquency and substance abuse. Furthermore, the results suggest that for both sexes, gang membership has an approximately equal impact on a variety of measures of delinquent behavior."

Perhaps what is most significant about this research is the evidence that female gang members are more delinquent than their female non-gang counterparts, but also more so than their male non-gang counterparts. For instance, Fagan (1990) reports that "prevalence rates for female gang members exceeded the rates for non-gang males" for all the categories of delinquency he measured (see also Esbensen and Winfree, 1998). He summarizes his findings in relation to girls as follows:

> More than 40 percent of the female gang members were classified in the least serious category, a substantial difference from their male counterparts [15.5%]. Among female gang members, there was a bimodal distribution, with nearly as many multiple index offenders as petty delinquents. Evidently female gang members avoid more serious delinquent involvement than their male counterparts. *Yet their extensive involvement in serious delinquent behaviors well exceeds that of non-gang males or females* (Fagan, 1990: 201, my emphasis).

Despite these findings, there is also evidence of gender differences within gangs with regard to criminal involvement. Bowker et al. (1980: 516) suggests there is a "structural exclusion of young women from male delinquent activities" within gangs. Their (male) respondents suggested that not only were girls excluded from the planning of delinquent acts, that when girls inadvertently showed up at the location of a planned incident, it was frequently postponed or terminated. Likewise Fagan (1990: 196-197) reports greater gender differences in delinquency between gang members than between non-gang youth. Male gang members were significantly more involved in the most serious forms of delinquency, while for alcohol use, drug sales, extortion and property damage, gender differences were not significant.

Likewise, my research suggests that most gang girls do not routinely participate in the most serious forms of gang crime, such as drive-by shootings and drug sales, sometimes by choice but also as a result of being excluded by their male counterparts (Miller, 1998). Data from the St. Louis Homicide Project (Decker, et al., 1991) also offers support that female gang members are not nearly as involved in the most serious forms of gang violence as male gang members. From 1990 to 1995, there were 207 gang homicides within the study area of this project. Only seventeen of these (8 %) involved female victims, and in only one case was one of the suspects a female; she was reportedly not a gang member, but was protecting her children from local gang members who were harassing them.

It is likely that girls' participation in delinquency, and especially the extent that male gang members exclude them from activities, is shaped by the gender composition of their gangs. For instance, Lauderback and his colleagues (1992) describe an autonomous female gang in San Francisco, California–the Potrero Hill Posse (PHP)– whom they describe as "doin' it for themselves." PHP is heavily involved in drug sales, and the behavior and activities of the young women in this gang are very much in line with those typically attributed to male gang members. There is no "structural exclusion" of these young women from certain gang crimes, because they don't have any male members to behave in such a way. In fact, Lauderback et al. (1992: 62) suggest that PHP actually came about because these young women were dissatisfied with a "less than equitable...distribution of the labor and wealth" that had been part and parcel of their previous involvement selling drugs with males. Nonetheless, as noted above, research has shown that all-female gangs account for a very small percentage of girls' gang involvement.

In sum, it appears that when it comes to serious crime, male gang members are clearly more involved than their female counterparts. Nonetheless, all of this evidence does suggest that young women in gangs are more involved in serious criminal activities than non-gang youths–male or female. Although one of the reasons there is so much concern about gangs is their criminal involvement, it's important to recognize that not all of gang members' activities are delinquent. In fact, they spend much of their time involved in the same activities as other adolescents–hanging out, talking and laughing, playing games, listening to music or watching television. Gang members are more likely to drink and use marijuana than other youths are, but even these activities remain well within the purview of non-gang adolescent activities. One of the gang members in my study illustrates, "a typical day would be sittin' back at the park or somethin' like that or one of our friend's houses, or a gang member's house, gettin' drunk, gettin' high, and, you know, watchin' TV, listenin' to the radio."

This makes sense, given our discussion in the previous section about why young people join gangs–in part, because they believe the gang will provide a sense of belonging and support, status and identity, along with recreation and excitement. For some, delinquency is part of the allure, but evidence suggests that some gang members–particularly young women–are fairly ambivalent about their criminal involvement, even though they report finding it fun or exciting at times. On one hand, it brings them status and recognition within the group, as well as economic remuneration; on the other, it can get them into trouble with the law, or put them at greater risk for being victimized by rival gang members or others on the streets.

For girls in particular, many aspects of gang involvement, including delinquency, go against dominant notions of appropriate femininity. This shapes girls' experience within and outside of their gangs, often locking them into what Swart (1991) describes as a series of double binds. This point brings me to the last topic I want to touch on–the consequences of gang involvement for girls. Here I will focus on two points in time. First, what are the consequences of gang involvement for girls while they are active in gangs? Second, what evidence do we have about the long-term consequences of gang involvement for young women? Though young people often turn to gangs as a means of meeting a variety of needs within their lives, it is often the case that their gang affiliation does more harm than good, by increasing their likelihood of victimization, and decreasing their opportunities and life chances.

WHAT ARE THE CONSEQUENCES OF GIRLS' GANG INVOLVEMENT?

Girls' gang participation can be viewed as transgressing social norms concerning appropriate feminine behavior. I have also noted that young women are typically in gangs that are predominantly male, and that they are sometimes excluded by young men from activities, such as serious crime, that confer status within the gang. Leadership in these groups also typically is male (see Miller, 1998). Consequently, most gang girls are participating in what can aptly be described as gender-stratified groups. While some scholars would suggest that, because they are challenging traditional gender roles, girls' gang participation might be viewed as liberating, most researchers highlight what Curry (1998) refers to as the "social injury" associated with gang involvement. During the course of their gang involvement, girls face a number of risks and disadvantages associated with gender inequality (Campbell, 1984; Fleisher, 1998; Miller, 1998). Moreover, there is some evidence of long-term detrimental consequences for gang-involved young women (Moore, 1991; Moore and Hagedorn, 1996).

Research has shown that girls in gangs face social sanctions, both within and outside the gang, for not behaving in gender appropriate ways. For instance, Swart (1991) suggests that girls' experiences in gangs are complicated by the contradictions they face as they balance deviant and gender norm expectations. On the one hand, he argues, "the female gang member's behavior must be 'deviant' to those outside of the gang in order to ensure her place within the gang itself" (Swart, 1991: 45). On the other hand, if it is too deviant, it risks the danger of offending other gang members who maintain certain attitudes about appropriate female conduct when it comes to issues of sexual activity, drug use, violence, and motherhood.

These findings are complicated, as Curry (1998) notes, by evidence which also suggests that young women's gang involvement provides a means of resisting limitations placed on them by narrow social definitions of femininity, which they recognize as limiting their options in an environment in which they are already quite restricted. Campbell, for instance, found that "gang girls see themselves as different from their [female] peers. Their association with the gang is a public proclamation of their rejection of the lifestyle which the community expects from them" (1987: 463-464; see also Harris, 1988). Likewise, Taylor's (1993) study of female gang members in Detroit found young women highly critical of the entrenched misogyny on the streets and the difficulties females often face interacting in these environments.

Regardless of girls' awareness of gender inequality, it remains an inescapable element of their experiences within gangs, and brings with it particular sorts of consequences. For instance, there is a clear sexual double standard in operation within gangs, as in American society as a whole (Campbell, 1990a; Fishman, 1995; Fleisher, 1998; Horowitz, 1983; Miller, 1998, in press; Moore, 1991; Swart, 1991). In Moore's study, for example, many of the male gang members admitted that female members were "treated like a piece of ass" (1991: 52). Girls' dating options were narrowed as well. Being a Chola and having the look of a Chola was stigmatizing for girls, making them less attractive to boys outside the gang. On the other hand, male gang members frequently had girlfriends outside the gang who were "square"; these "respectable" girls were looked to by the boys as their future (Moore, 1991: 74-76; see also Fishman, 1995).

Moreover, research suggests that rather than challenging this sexual double standard, young women often reinforce it in their interactions with one another. Several studies reveal that gang girls create hierarchies among themselves, sanctioning other girls, both for being too "square" and for being too promiscuous. Typically, the sexual double standard is reinforced by girls as sanctions against those they perceive as too sexually active. Girls have not been found to gain status among their peers for sexual promiscuity (Campbell, 1990a; Horowitz, 1983; Miller, 1998, in press; Swart, 1991), rather they are expected to engage in serial monogamy. On the whole, the sexual double standard tends to disadvantage girls in their relationships with boys, but also interferes with the strength of their own friendship groups (Campbell, 1987).

My research suggests additional problems caused by gender inequality within gangs, specifically in relation to victimization risk. On the whole, gang participation is likely to involve high risks of victimization. We know, for instance, that delinquent lifestyles in general are associated with increased victimization risk (Lauritsen et al., 1991). As I have highlighted above, gangs are social groups organized around delinquency (see Klein, 1995), and participation in gangs escalates youths' involvement in crime, including violent crime. Moreover, research on gang violence indicates that the primary targets of this violence are other gang members (Block and Block, 1993; Decker, 1996; Klein and Maxson, 1989; Sanders, 1993). Gang members, then, are likely to be at greater victimization risk than youths not involved in gangs.

Since girls are less likely than their male counterparts to engage in serious forms of gang crime, they face less risk of victimization at the hands of rival gang members, because they are less likely to engage in those activities that would increase their exposure to violence. However, because leadership and status hierarchies in mixed-gender gangs are typically male-dominated, and because girls are less likely to engage in those activities that confer status within the gang (e.g., crime), they are often viewed as lesser members within their gangs. This devaluation of young women can lead to girls' mistreatment and victimization, especially by members of their own gang, because they aren't seen as deserving of the same respect (see Miller, 1998). These problems are further exacerbated by the sexual double standard described above.

Thus far I have discussed the impact of gang involvement for girls while they are in their gangs. What about after they leave? Few studies offer evidence of the long-term consequences of gang involvement for girls (see Moore, 1991; Moore and Hagedorn, 1996). However, the evidence that is available suggests that young women in gangs are at greater risk than others for a number of problems into and within their adult lives. Whereas many opportunities for legitimate success are gravely limited for young women living in impoverished communities, the negative consequences associated with gang membership can prove crippling. Gang membership exacerbates already troubled lives (Fleisher, 1998). Moore and Hagedorn note that while many young women turn to gangs as a means of dealing with multiple life problems, "for most women, being in a gang does have a real impact on later life" (1996: 215).

Moore's (1991) research on Chicano/a gang members in Los Angeles found that ex-gang members could be divided into three categories: tecatos, cholos, and squares. She reports that approximately a quarter of the males in her study, and "a much smaller proportion of the female sample" (1991: 125) were tecatos–heroin addicts involved in street life. About a third of the men but more of the women were cholos–persisting in gang and criminal involvement into adulthood. Women and men in this category typically had not held down regular jobs and had unstable marriage patterns, often characterized by early marriage and childbearing, followed by early divorce (1991: 125-127). Finally, she reports that while around 40 percent of the males in her sample went on to lead conventional lives ("squares"), this was the case for fewer of the women (1991: 127).[4]

While Moore's Los Angeles research was about individuals who had been in gangs in the 1950s and 1970s, her more recent work with Hagedorn (1996) compared these with contemporary African American and Latina gang members in Milwaukee, Wisconsin. They report that substantially fewer of these women continued their gang involvement into adulthood, concluding that "for women–but not for men–the gang was almost completely an adolescent experience" (1996: 209). Latinas were more likely to be involved in drug sales and use into adulthood, compared with African American women. Moore and Hagedorn (1996: 210) conclude:

> For Latinas in both cities, gang membership tended to have a significant influence on their later lives, but for African American women in Milwaukee, the gang tended to be an episode. There is much less sense in Milwaukee that gang girls of any ethnicity were as heavily labeled in their communities as were Chicana gang girls in Los Angeles.

It seems reasonable to suggest that the earlier a girl exits the gang, the greater her chances for a better life. Some evidence suggests that childbearing and the childcare responsibilities that result often facilitate young women's maturation out of gangs (Moore and Hagedorn, 1996). However, though having children may expedite girls' leaving their gangs, doing so does not necessarily increase their chances for successful lives. Partly this is because stable marriages and jobs are less available in the current socioeconomic climate in urban communities in the U.S. than in the past. Communities where many gangs are located have dwindling numbers of males in the marriage pool; moreover, skyrocketing rates of incarceration and lethal violence have greatly contributed to this shortage (Moore and Hagedorn, 1996; Wilson, 1987, 1996). Considering the high unemployment rates in most gang neighborhoods, many young men have few conventional opportunities and are increasingly likely to continue their gang and criminal involvement into adulthood (Hagedorn, 1994; Klein, 1995). The bleak futures that await the men in their communities often make marriage no longer a desirable component of gang-involved women lives (Moore and Hagedorn, 1996). The attacks on many social programs have also negatively affected women's lives after gang membership. Moore and Hagedorn (1996: 217) observe:

> Ironically, the most important influence on gang women's future may be the dismantling of the nations welfare system in the 1990s. This system has supported women with children who want to stay out of the drug marketing system and in addition has provided a significant amount of cash to their communities. Its disappearance will deepen poverty and make the fate of gang women ever more problematic.

CONCLUSION

This paper has addressed a number of issues concerning young women's involvement in gangs–the extent of their gang involvement, why they become involved, what their experiences in gangs are like, and the consequences of gang involvement. As I have shown, young women join gangs in response to a myriad of problems in their lives. Gang involvement, though, tends to exacerbate rather than improve their problems. Unfortunately, responses to gangs and gang members are primarily punitive in nature, disregarding the social, economic and personal contexts that cause gang participation. This punitive orientation toward gang members means that gang-involved youths are not seen as in need of assistance and protection, and this–coupled with the problems they face in their daily lives–has further detrimental effects on these young people (see Fleisher, 1998). Given the findings I have detailed above, the best course of action with regard to young women's gang involvement should involve policies that consider the social, economic and personal contexts that influence gang participation and gang crime. Initiatives that consider the best interest of youths are desperately needed in order to respond to gangs and young women's involvement in these groups effectively.

REFERENCES

Bjerregaard, B. and C. Smith (1993). Gender differences in gang participation, delinquency, and substance use. Journal of Quantitative Criminology 4: 329-355.

Block, C.R., and R. Block (1993). Street Gang Crime in Chicago. Research in Brief. Washington, DC: National Institute of Justice.

Bowker, L.H., H.S. Gross, and M.W. Klein (1980). Female participation in delinquent gang activities. Adolescence 15(59): 509-519.

Bowker, L.H. and M. Klein (1983). The etiology of female juvenile delinquency and gang membership: A test of psychological and social structural explanations. Adolescence 18(72): 739-51.

Brown, W.K (1978). Black female gangs in Philadelphia. International Journal of Offender Therapy and Comparative Criminology 21: 221-28.

Campbell, A. (1984). The Girls in the Gang. New York: Basil Blackwell.

Campbell, A. (1987). Self definition by rejection: The case of gang girls. Social Problems 34(5): 451-466.

Campbell, A. (1990a). Female participation in gangs. In C.R. Huff (ed.), Gangs in America, pp. 163-182. Newbury Park: Sage Publications.

Campbell, A. (1990b). On the invisibility of the female delinquent peer group. Women and Criminal Justice 2: 41-62.

Canter, R.J. (1982). Family correlates of male and female delinquency. Criminology 20: 149-167.

Cernkovich, S.A. and Giordano, P.C. (1987). Family relationships and delinquency. Criminology 25: 295-319.

Cloward, R., and L. Ohlin (1960). Delinquency and Opportunity. Glencoe, IL: Free Press.

Cohen, A. (1955). Delinquent Boys. Glencoe, IL: Free Press.

Curry, G. D. (1997). Selected Statistics on Female Gang Involvement. Paper presented at the Fifth Joint National Conference on Gangs, Schools, and Communities.

Curry, G. D. (1998). Female gang involvement. Journal of Research in Crime and Delinquency 35:100-118.

Curry, G. D., R.A. Ball, and R.J. Fox (1994). Gang Crime and Law Enforcement Recordkeeping. Research in Brief. Washington, DC: National Institute of Justice.

Decker, S.H. (1996). Collective and normative features of gang violence. Justice Quarterly 13(2): 243-264.

Decker, S., C. Kohfeld, R. Rosenfeld, and J. Sprague (1991). St. Louis Homicide Project: Local Responses to a National Problem. St. Louis, MO: University of Missouri-St. Louis.

Decker, S.H. and B. Van Winkle (1996). Life in the Gang. Cambridge: Cambridge University Press.

Esbensen, F., and E.P. Deschenes (1998). A multi-site examination of gang membership: Does gender matter? Criminology 36: 799-828.

Esbensen, F., and D. Huizinga (1993). Gangs, drugs, and delinquency in a survey of urban youth. Criminology 31: 565-589.

Esbensen, F., D. Huizinga, and A.W. Weiher (1993). Gang and non-gang youth: Differences in explanatory factors. Journal of Contemporary Criminal Justice 9: 94-116.

Esbensen, F., and L.T. Winfree (1998). Race and gender differences between gang and non-gang youth: Results from a multi-site survey. Justice Quarterly 15: 505-525.

Fagan, J. (1990). Social processes of delinquency and drug use among urban gangs. In C. R. Huff (ed.). Gangs in America, pp. 183-219. Newbury Park: Sage Publications.

Fishman, L. (1995). The Vice Queens: An ethnographic study of Black female gang behavior. In M.W. Klein, C. Maxson, and J. Miller, The Modern Gang Reader, pp. 83-92. Los Angeles: Roxbury Press.

Fleisher, M.S. (1998). Dead End Kids: Gang Girls and the Boys They Know. Madison: Wisconsin University Press.

Giordano, P.C. (1978). Girls, guys and gangs: The changing social context of female delinquency. Journal of Criminal Law and Criminology 69(1): 126-132.

Hagan, J., A.R. Gillis, and J. Simpson (1985). The class structure of gender and delinquency: Toward a power-control theory of common delinquent behavior. American Journal of Sociology 90:151-178.

Hagedorn, J.M. (1988). People and Folks: Gangs, Crime and The Underclass in a Rustbelt City. Chicago: Lake View Press.

Hagedorn, J.M. (1991). Gangs, neighborhoods and public policy. Social Problems 38: 529-542.

Hagedorn, J.M. (1994). Homeboys, dope fiends, legits and new jacks. Criminology 32: 197-219.

Harris, M.G. (1988). Cholas: Latino Girls and Gangs. New York: AMS.

Horowitz, R. (1983). Honor and the American Dream: Culture and Identity in a Chicano Community. New Brunswick, NJ: Rutgers University Press.

Huff, C. R. (1989). Youth gangs and public policy. Crime and Delinquency 35: 524-537.

Huff, C. R. (1993). Gangs in the United States. In A.P. Goldstein, and C.R. Huff (eds.), The Gang Intervention Handbook, pp. 3-20. Champaign, IL: Research Press.

Jankowski, M.S. (1991). Islands in the Streets: Gangs and American Urban Society. Berkeley: University of California Press.

Joe, K.A. and M. Chesney-Lind (1995). 'Just every mother's angel': An analysis of gender and ethnic variations in youth gang membership. Gender & Society 9: 408-430.

Klein, M.W. (1971). Street Gangs and Street Workers. Englewood Cliffs, NJ: Prentice-Hall.

Klein, M.W. (1995). The American Street Gang: Its Nature, Prevalence and Control. New York: Oxford University Press.

Klein, M.W., and C.L. Maxson (1989). Street gang violence. In N. Weiner and M. Wolfgang (eds.), Violent Crime, Violent Criminals, pp. 198-231. Newbury Park, CA: Sage Publications.

Lauderback, D., J. Hansen, and D. Waldorf (1992). 'Sisters are doin' it for themselves': A Black female gang in San Francisco. The Gang Journal 1(1): 57-70.

Lauritsen, J.L., R.J. Sampson, and J.H. Laub (1991). The link between offending and victimization among adolescents. Criminology 29(2): 265-292.

Maxson, C.L., K. Woods, and M.W. Klein (1996). Street gang migration. How big a threat? NIJ Journal, 230.

Miller, J. (1998). Gender and victimization risk among young women in gangs. Journal of Research in Crime and Delinquency 35(4):429-453.

Miller, J. (In press). One of the Guys: Girls, Gangs and Gender. New York: Oxford University Press.

Moore, J. (1991). Going Down to the Barrio: Homeboys and Homegirls in Change. Philadelphia: Temple University Press.

Moore, J.W., and J.M. Hagedorn (1996). What happens to girls in the gang? In C. R. Huff (ed.), Gangs in America, 2nd Edition, pp. 205-218. Thousand Oaks, CA: Sage Publications.

Moore, J., and R. Pinderhughes (1993). In the Barrios: Latinos and the Underclass Debate. New York: Russell Sage Foundation.

Morash, M. (1983). Gangs, groups and delinquency. British Journal of Criminology 23: 309-331.

Quicker, J.C (1983). Homegirls: Characterizing Chicana Gangs. San Pedro, CA: International University Press.

Sampson, R.J., and W.J. Wilson (1995). Toward a theory of race, crime and urban inequality. In J. Hagan and R.D. Peterson (eds.), Crime and Inequality, pp. 37-54. Stanford: Stanford University Press.

Sanders, W. (1993). Drive-Bys and Gang Bangs: Gangs and Grounded Culture. Chicago: Aldine.

Short, J.F. and F.L. Strodtbeck (1965). Group Process and Gang Delinquency. Chicago: University of Chicago Press.

Smith, D.A. and R. Paternoster (1987). The gender gap in theories of deviance: Issues and evidence. Journal of Research in Crime and Delinquency 24:140-172.

Soriano, F.I. (1993). Cultural sensitivity and gang intervention. In A.P. Goldstein and C.R. Huff (eds.), The Gang Intervention Handbook, pp. 441-461. Champaign, IL: Research Press.

Spergel, I.A., and G.D. Curry (1993). The National Youth Gang Survey: A research and developmental process. In A.P. Goldstein and C. R. Huff (eds.), The Gang Intervention Handbook, pp. 359-400. Champaign, IL: Research Press.

Swart, W.J. (1991). Female gang delinquency: A search for 'acceptably deviant behavior.' Mid-American Review of Sociology 15(1):43-52.

Taylor, C. (1993). Girls, Gangs, Women and Drugs. East Lansing: Michigan State University Press.

Thornberry, T.P., M.D. Krohn, A.J. Lizotte, and D. Chard-Wierschem (1993). The role of juvenile gangs in facilitating delinquent behavior. Journal of Research in Crime and Delinquency 30(1):75-85.

Vigil, J.D. (1988). Barrio Gangs: Street Life and Identity in Southern California. Austin: University of Texas Press.

Vigil, J.D., and J.M. Long (1990). Emic and etic perspectives on gang culture: The Chicano case. In C.R. Huff (ed.), Gangs in America, pp. 55-68. Newbury Park: Sage Publications.
Wilson, W.J. (1987). The Truly Disadvantaged: The Inner City, the Underclass, and Public Policy. Chicago: University of Chicago Press.
Wilson, W. J. (1996). When Work Disappears: The World of the New Urban Poor. New York: Alfred A. Knopf.
Winfree, Jr., L.T., K. Fuller, T. Vigil, and G. L. Mays (1992). The definition and measurement of 'gang status': Policy implications for juvenile justice. Juvenile and Family Court Journal 29-37.

ENDNOTES

1 This is not to suggest that all research on girls in gangs is from a feminist perspective. Rather my point is that attention to female offenders in general is largely a result of the emergence of feminist criminology, along with mainstream scholars' reactions to the U.S. women's movement of the late 1960s and early 1970s.

2 Because female gang involvement appears to be primarily an adolescent and, to a lesser extent, young adult phenomenon, I use the terms "young women" and "girls" interchangeably throughout the paper.

3 There is extensive evidence of the proliferation of gangs across the United States since the 1980s, including a tremendous increase in the number of gangs, gang members, and communities with gangs (see Klein, 1995; Maxson et al., 1996; Spergel and Curry, 1993). Of course this means that there are more female and male gang members than in the past. The question we cannot fully address is whether the ratio of female-to-male involvement has changed, though the few studies which addressed young women's gang involvement in earlier periods suggest that it has not.

4 Moore notes that this finding is partly an artifact of the under-representation of "square" women in her sample. She notes, "Some such women refused the interview because their husbands would not allow them to discuss their 'deviant' adolescence; others refused because they were afraid that they would be questioned about what they now define as 'deviance'– particularly about sexual activity" (1991: 130). Moore concludes, "These views offer a poignant confirmation of the stigma attached to women's gang membership" (1991: 130).

PART II

INTRODUCTION TO PART II

In this next section, the reader is introduced to street gangs in eight European cities: den Haag, Rotterdam, Manchester, Oslo, Copenhagen, Frankfurt, Kazan, and Paris. The chapter by Tertilt was available at the Workshop, although the author was unable to attend. The chapters by Mares and Lien were solicited after the Workshop as we became aware of these studies. The other chapters were all presented at the Workshop.

Although the original papers were written prior to the presentation of the American gang papers, some revisions have incorporated relevant aspects of the U.S. research. For example, either explicitly or implicitly, one can find here examples of the gang structures described in Chapter 1: specialty gangs in den Haag and Rotterdam; compressed gangs in Copenhagen, Frankfurt, Manchester and perhaps Oslo; neo-traditional gangs in Manchester; traditional gangs in Kazan. Only the description of gangs in Paris, and perhaps in Oslo, fail to yield reasonably clear parallels to those in the U.S. and these other European cities.

One should take note as well of the many ethnic and national minorities that comprise the vast majority of the gangs described. In four cases–England, Norway, Denmark, and Russia–indigenous or "native" gangs are reported. In most cases however, it is the refugee and immigrant populations, first as well as second generation, which are found in these gang structures. The list is very long: Afro-Caribbean, Algerian, Antillian, Croatian, Filipino, Iranian, Italian, Moroccan, Pakistani, Russian, Somali, Surinamese, Turkish, and Vietnamese. Such a list makes it abundantly clear no one ethnicity is more or less prone to gang formation. Rather, it is the status of being marginalized, alienated, or rejected that makes some groups more vulnerable to gang formation. This has been the picture historically in the U.S. as well, where the currently most visible black, Hispanic, and Asian gangs were preceded in the era of major patterns of immigration by gangs whose heritage was German, Italian, Jewish, Swedish, Irish, Polish, and so on. One is reminded, again, that gang problems cannot be resolved simply by attacking the gangs themselves; solutions are lodged in larger community and societal institutions.

The final brief chapter in Part II reminds us that the descriptions included in the eight chapters are not exhaustive of the gang situations in Europe, but rather are limited to those where research was known to be taking place. A thorough

M.W. Klein et al (eds.), The Eurogang Paradox, 135.

overview of European gangs would include other cities as well, and would also require research about those many cities that have not spawned gangs. Understanding comes from awareness of both positive and negative instances.

Chapter 8

TOWARDS A PROBLEM-ORIENTED APPROACH TO YOUTH GROUPS IN THE HAGUE

Paul Gruter and Peter Versteegh
Haaglanden Police Department, The Hague, The Netherlands

In the fall of 1993, the Haaglanden police in the Netherlands arrested a group of youngsters who had committed several violent crimes and intimidation. From the statements these youngsters made, it appeared that they were part of a group that called itself "Eight Tray Gangsters" like a gang operating in Los Angeles. In addition to the name, they had also adapted the clothing (blue), music (gangsta rap), hand gestures, and language from their American counterparts. At the same time newspapers and magazines published a series of alarming articles about more street gangs in The Hague.[1]

Because of these signals and because of the fact that two thirds of the crime committed by youngsters in The Netherlands is committed in groups, the The Hague police force decided to pay more structural attention to *problematic youth groups*. The first phase was to get a general insight into this problem. The major question in this phase was about the nature and size of these groups; the second question was the extent to which these groups were similar to the street gangs in the U.S. The second phase consisted of formulating and organizing a problem-oriented approach to the youth groups. Both phases will be described here briefly.

M.W. Klein et al (eds.), The Eurogang Paradox, 137–143.

GENERAL OVERVIEW OF GROUPS

In order to get a first rough impression of the youth groups, we chose the strategy of questioning the community policemen. In general these police officers are well acquainted with the people in their neighborhood and the specific (crime) problems therein.

The method used was a semi-structured questionnaire, which included themes such as:

location, nature and size of the group: age, sex, ethnic/racial composition, education, mobility, competition with other groups, leadership and organizational aspects;

problematic behavior: the kind of trouble these groups cause and youth culture.

The first time we applied this questionnaire was in 1995. About 95 percent of the community policemen (80 police officers) participated. In 1996, the questionnaire was applied a second time, but in a slightly different way.[2] Instead of sending the questionnaires by mail, we organized several meetings for the neighborhood police officers and told them what we had learned about problematic youth groups.

Next, the policemen were asked to write down any knowledge they had about the youth groups and their activities within their neighborhoods. The advantage of this data collection was that the researchers could gather the material within a couple of days. Furthermore, during the sessions the researchers could, where necessary, clarify questions; also, the police officers were able to compare–if necessary–their information directly with colleagues from neighboring districts.

Based on the data collected, a typology of problematic youth groups was developed. We differentiated four types, as follows:

(type 1) *troublesome behavior*: a group consisting of three or more youngsters who frequently meet, and by their presence, their appearance, or their behavior, irritate or annoy other people, like hindering other people, yelling and screaming in the streets, producing heavy noise (e.g., from ghetto blasters or motorcycles).

(type 2) *non-serious crime*: a group that, in addition to their troublesome behavior, commits non-serious forms of crime like shoplifting, stealing bicycles, graffiti, intimidation and threats and other forms of petty crime.

(type 3) *serious crime*: a group that, in addition to their troublesome behavior, commits non-serious but also serious forms of crime like car theft, burglary, drug abuse, stealing handbags, robbery and others kinds of violent property crime.

(type 4) *gang-related crime*: a self-formed association of three or more youngsters with identifiable leadership, who are bound together by race, culture or territory, and frequently meet with the purpose of committing mostly serious forms of property crime, often with violence like armed robbery, dealing drugs and prostitution.

NATURE AND SIZE OF THE GROUPS

In the first year, we found 98 groups within the region; in 1996:127 (Table 1). The difference between the two years is probably (partly) due to a higher reliability during the second measurement, especially when it concerns less serious forms of problematic group behavior.

Table 1. Number of Problematic Youth Groups in the Haaglanden Region

Type of group	**1995**	**1996**
Troublesome behavior	24	42
Non-serious crime	35	47
Serious crime	35	31
Gang-related crime	4	7
Total number	**98**	**127**

The majority of the problematic youth groups can be found The Hague. It is estimated that in 1996 about 2,500 youngsters (1.7 percent of all youngsters between 12-24 years) participated in one of these groups. The total number of participating girls is estimated around 400. More than half of the groups had more than twenty participants, predominantly in the age of fifteen to twenty years. Considerably over 500 of these youngsters can be seen as leaders within these groups.

Most of the youngsters taking part in the problematic youth groups are students, but about a quarter of them are truant on a regular basis. Moreover, our informants estimate that half of the criminal groups (types 3 and 4) consist of early school dropouts.

If we look at the ethnicity of the youth group population, we can conclude that about 70 percent of these youngsters have a Dutch background (Table 2). The number of groups that consist predominantly of Moroccan youngsters is relatively high.[3] Quite alarming is the fact that these youngsters can be found primarily within the more problematic groups. About twelve of the groups of which the members commit serious forms of crime consist principally of Moroccan boys. Also in the seven gangs we found that they seem to play an important part.

As for the motives for the youngsters to participate in these groups, recreation and prestige are mentioned most frequently. For the participants in the seven street gangs, financial gain seemed to be the major motive.

Table 2. Predominant Ethnic Background of Members in Problematic Youth Groups (1996)

Type of group	**Dutch**	**Suri-nam/ Antilles**	**Moroc-can**	**Turkish**	**Other**	**Un-known**	**Total number**
Trouble-some behavior	37	1	1	-	1	2	**42**
Non-serious crime	35	1	6	-	3	2	**47**
Serious crime	15	2	12	1	1	-	**31**
Gang-related crime	-	3	2	1	1	-	**7**
Total	**87**	7	**21**	**2**	6	**4**	**127**

COMPARISON WITH U.S. GANGS

When we compare the most criminal youth groups with gangs in the U.S., there seems to be less armed violence and no fighting with other gangs about their territory. On the basis of the two inventories, we also got no indications of strong organizational ties. What the respondents did report was imitative behavior. They knew quite a number of youngsters who were dressed in the blue outfit of the Crips and used gang language and hand gestures. When analyzing criminal activities of the groups these supposed Crips belong to, only some of the groups could be characterized as a criminal group or street gang. The fact that we encountered such activities in less problematic groups suggests that their Crip uniform seemed to be more connected with their wish to look like the boys in the daily MTV-clips. In fact from all of the four group types, the policemen reported examples of youngsters using the Crips' dress code.

THE GROUP INVENTORY AS A BASIS FOR A PROBLEM-ORIENTED APPROACH

The periodic inventory of problematic youth groups gave an indication of the severity of the problem concerning youth groups in the Haaglanden region. The results have several consequences for policy towards these groups as well as for a problem-oriented approach.

Consequences for General Youth Policy

The publication of the results of the two inventories appeared to be an eye-opener for several parties involved. They became aware of the shared responsibility concerning this problem. In order to tackle this phenomenon, real co-operation is a necessity. In the first place it means that the local administration must pay considerably more attention to the problems of the problematic youth groups, especially Moroccan youth. Second, the inventories were reason for the Public Prosecutor's Office to pay more attention to group criminality among youngsters, especially the criminal groups and youth gangs. Third, it established the view that in this respect there should a much more integrated co-operation, especially between the police, Public Prosecutor's

Office, local administration and local residents on the neighborhood level. An example of this co-operation is The Hague youth delinquency program with representatives from all the organizations concerned. In all this, special attention is given to the groups that turn out to be the most problematic (types 3 and 4).

Consequences for Police Policy

For the police, the inventories led to the idea of a problem-oriented approach. This approach consists–depending on the severity of the group activities–of finding the proper mixture of preventive and repressive measures within their mandate, and where necessary in co-operation with other parties involved. Figure 1 illustrates this.

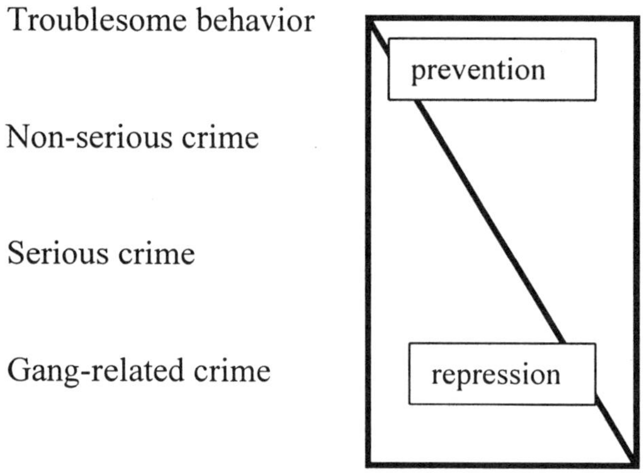

Figure 1. Forms of Intervention for Four Types of Groups

Once the group inventory for the whole region is made, the actual approach of the groups will be tailored to the neighborhood level. In order to take the necessary steps, additional data will be collected for a final problem analysis, which supports the organizations in selecting specific measures to tackle the concrete problematic youth group. This analysis is done by crime-analysts from each police station. In order to get this more detailed picture, they will verify the names of the participants within the group(s) and also examine the precise scale and severity of the activities of the group involved. This will be accomplished by interviewing several persons, like neighbors, schoolteachers, street-corner workers, but also youngsters and their parents as well. When all this work is done they will give their final advice concerning an appropriate and effective approach to each member of the group and to the group as a whole. Depending on the nature of the delinquent behavior of the juveniles, these will be repressive or preventive measures, or a combination of both.

ENDNOTES

1 The Haaglanden police operate in the Haaglanden region which has approximately 935,000 inhabitants; The Hague is the third largest city of the Netherlands and has 440,000 inhabitants.

2 In 1999 the inventory will be carried out again. The method used in Haaglanden will also be applied this year in five other cities in The Netherlands.

3 In the Haaglanden region there are approximately 6,000 Moroccans between the ages of 12 and 25.

Chapter 9

CRIPS IN ORANGE: GANGS AND GROUPS IN THE NETHERLANDS

Frank Van Gemert
Regioplan, Amsterdam, The Netherlands

INTRODUCTION

Gangs are a big and well-known problem in the United States. It is no accident that for quite some time now these gangs have occupied a prominent position in American criminological literature. Publications about Dutch juvenile gangs are still rare, however. What the Dutch know about this phenomenon is based on information from outside, for instance about gang wars like the one between the Crips and the Bloods in Los Angeles.

Whereas Americans appear to have primarily negative associations when thinking of juvenile gangs, this is not so in the Netherlands. In the past, the Dutch were interested in the music and romance of *West Side Story*. Over the past few years, Dutch youngsters have been attracted to video clips and compact discs with *gangsta rap*, in which the scene is set by young Afro-Americans with big cars and fat gold chains, and in the company of sensual ladies. The language of these youngsters is characterized by hyperbole and contains many references to competition and violence. The fact that famous rappers like Tupac Shakur, Notorious B.I.G., and Stretch not only talked about the hard life in the 'hoods, but actually were killed as gangsters in drive-by shootings, takes nothing away from their attraction. The youth style personified

M.W. Klein et al (eds.), The Eurogang Paradox, 145–152.

by these gangsters often refers to juvenile gangs. Such gangs are to be found at the other side of the ocean. But do they only exist over there?

In the summer of 1993, members of *Eight Tray Crips* were arrested in The Hague, and after some months youths from the *Eastside Crips* were also taken to the police station. One year later, in the summer of 1994, the Rotterdam *Southside First Tray Crips* were caught. The apprehension of these youngsters opened a new chapter for the Dutch police and justice. Investigations of groups like these are not an everyday phenomenon in the Netherlands, where offenders are regularly looked upon as individuals, not as group members. For this reason in both cities law enforcement activities were triggered, and special attention was paid to the investigations. As a result, the police reports on these groups were more extensive than usual.

These three Crips groups are central to this qualitative research (Van Gemert, 1998a). The data are extracted from court dossiers on these groups. The primary question addressed in this article is what kind of groups are these? In what activities do their members engage? To what extent are they influenced by the American examples?

THREE GANGS

The two groups from The Hague consist of adolescent males who know each other from the street. They sport together, and some of them are classmates. *The Eight Tray Crips* live in the Spoorwijk quarter, whereas the *Eastside Crips* stem from the City Centre and meet in Bakkerstraat. We are dealing with relatively small groups here: only ten youths from Eight Tray and seven Eastside members were arrested. They are almost exclusively black, but their national origin varies. They are mainly from Surinam and the Dutch Antilles, but there is also one member from Ghana, one from British Guyana, and one from Turkey. When they were arrested, they were a little over 15 years of age on average. Most of these boys were born in Holland, yet a history of migration plays an important role. Problems of adaptation and low socio-economic status result in difficulties that may increase the progression to law-breaking behavior.

Neither the *Eight Tray Crips* nor the *Eastside Crips* have a leader. Both groups have some members who are more daring than the others and who therefore stand out. But they do not derive any authority from this. The relationships among the boys are of an egalitarian nature. Especially in the *Eight Tray Crips* this can be observed quite clearly, as they use rules aimed at having all members commit about the same number of criminal offenses. For the *Eastside Crips* such behavior was not recorded. However, for both groups, new members are tested fighting to show that they are made of the "right stuff."

The members of the *Southside First Tray Crips* all live in the same neighborhood in the southern part of Rotterdam. They know one another from playing sports in the street, and some members are related. These youths are older, 18 years of age on average. The eleven males who were arrested form a group that consists almost exclusively of ethnic minorities. Apart from the street, the group often meets at the homes of two of the youths. According to police information, all members visibly carry a blue handkerchief in their hip pocket, and they use a kind of sign language that outsiders have difficulty deciphering. In several places in the Rotterdam neighborhoods, graffiti were found that originated from the Crips. This can be deducted from their so-called *tags*, the signatures they use, like "SSFTC." There are some indications of a hierarchy. Gang members speak of "OG's," original gangsters, when they are talking about the highest in rank. Members of the Rotterdam gang have a tattoo in the shape of a band around their arm. This band can be colored according to the rank of the member involved. New members are put to the test by committing a robbery.

Criminal activities

All three gangs involved in this research have one specific but different type of criminal offense in which their members mostly engage. The members of *Eight Tray Crips* have stolen bicycles and have beaten up former gang members, but their most common activities are "jackmoves" (street robberies). They have committed violent robberies eight times. These robberies are usually carried out by small groups of two to four members. The group involved goes to a certain spot where the boys select the victim. First the victim's way is barred, then he is grabbed and addressed in a threatening way. Sometimes considerable violence is used.

The *Eastside Crips* have dozens of violent thefts on their record. In most cases, girls are the victims of these thefts. One or two of the youth grab the girls while a third member body searches them and gropes in the pockets of their coats and trousers. Although the girls resist, they always have to yield to superior force. Mostly small sums of money are taken, but repeatedly the girls are also stripped of their jewelry or clothes (especially training jacks). A striking detail is that these girls are acquaintances of the perpetrators. Furthermore, several times the *Eastside Crips* have stolen mopeds from basement storage rooms, and they have repeatedly stolen goods by entering dwellings with stolen keys.

The members of the Rotterdam *Southside First Tray Crips* have six violent thefts in their history. However, they have attracted attention especially by robbing no less than fifteen shops in a period of only a couple of months. They have so much drive that a bakery, a video shop and a snack bar were even robbed twice during that period. Usually the perpetrators act in pairs, but sometimes they start out as a threesome or foursome. The first few times they threatened with a knife. Later they used firearms, but they did not shoot. They enter the shop and wait until the cash register is opened when a customer pays for what he or she has purchased. At that moment they draw out their gun, threaten the staff and the customers, and grab the money. Almost all of the criminal offenses of these youth are committed in, or in the immediate vicinity of, the main shopping street in their neighborhood. They know the surrounding area well, because they live there. They wear no masks, and they are observed when they flee into a dwelling after having committed an offense.

Group Processes

The members of all three gangs use violence, but they do not seem to need that to carry out their offenses. Their superior strength is such that as a rule the victims do not dare to react. Resistance is offered in only a few instances. Therefore, the thesis that the use of violence is instrumental seems unsupported. This becomes very clear from the example of a man in a park who was robbed of 25 guilders (12 dollars) by four youngsters. This man was taken completely by surprise and only stammered a few words. Still, he was beaten on the head with an iron bar and was severely injured.

Members of the *Eight Tray Crips* cannot avoid involvement in crime, because there are rules in which their participation is laid down. They all have to participate in the "jackmoves." These violent robberies are the criminal activity allowing the gang to "separate the men from the boys." Rotterdam youth that wish to become members of the *Southside First Tray Crips* also have to prove themselves by committing a robbery. In the latest robbery carried out by the gang it was decided that the newcomer was to use a gun and take the money. Should he fail, this failure would be unacceptable. The boy involved argued that he had already been taken to the police station many times, but this did not relieve him of his duties. The rules required his participation, and there was no getting around them.

The offenses presuppose direct contact. The boys are face to face with their victims, but there also are other members present. Apart from seizing the loot, having guts and the willingness to use violence are ever recurring ingredients. The offenses of these Crips gain importance when observed by other members of the gang.

The fact that there is loot to be hauled in plays a role in their motives. However, this is not a sufficient explanation for their behavior, because if it were they could also have focused on breaking and entering. The robberies are known to be not very lucrative, and the members of the two Hague gangs have certainly not become rich from them. However, they gain something else: they gain reputation. According to one gang member from The Hague: "Committing crimes makes you important in the group. A small crime, for instance, is stealing a moped. And a big crime is a jackmove, or a robbery. If one has committed some crime or other, this can be seen from small markings on the kerchief he carries in his hip pocket. Each marking represents one committed crime."

Reputation can only take shape in a social context; it presupposes the presence of others. How the perpetrators are looked upon by the other Crips is very important. A youth has to prove he has guts when he joins the gang, but once he is a member, he has to continue his efforts, or risk being surpassed by newcomers. This implies that a gang member constantly has to work hard at maintaining his reputation. It goes with the membership. It is important to do those things that carry weight within the group, and to do these things when others can see you doing them. Just boasting is not enough; you have to act the part, and you are carefully watched.

AMERICAN EXAMPLES

There is no denying that the three Crips groups are juvenile gangs. The members are regarded as a group, and that is also how they see themselves. Criminal activities are important to them and they get a negative response from the police and/or the people who live in the neighborhood (cf. Klein and Maxson, 1989:205). By focussing attention on the Crips groups, we cannot draw a clear picture of the whole range of Dutch juvenile groups and gangs. The Crips are juvenile gangs of a specific kind. Undoubtedly, the criminal gangs from the American West Coast have served as a model. This is underlined by the addition "Crips." *The Eight Tray Crips* have even taken on the name of an existing criminal gang. One of the members of the California gang was Cody Scott, also known as "Monster Cody." The members of the Dutch juvenile gangs know about this person and his criminal gang through his autobiography (Shakur, 1993). This book, together with the book *Do or Die* by the journalist Leon Bing (1992), was found in the homes of several members of these groups. Both books have been translated into Dutch. So, in addition to video clips and CDs, there are other channels through which knowledge about American gangs has reached the Netherlands.

The American examples have become entangled with a juvenile life style, and consequently spread gang music and the symbols all over the world. But this life style also encompasses attitudes and behavioral codes: boys have to be "tough," "cool," "bad," and "mean." Obviously, the mental baggage involved here differs, for example, from that of hippies. In the world of juvenile gangs, competition always plays an important role, and respect and reputation are key words here. The members do not want to rank second to anyone, and they can rise in the hierarchy by showing, face to face with others, that they do have guts and can be tough, and that they are able to deal with violence. This life style appeals to a broad juvenile audience, but in the Netherlands this especially attracts a specific category of youths–at least for the time being. The combination of elements of style, looks, and attitude, for now, seems to fit them best: Crips groups almost exclusively consist of black male adolescents.

CULTURE AND MOROCCAN GROUPS

Criminological theories relate the emergence of juvenile gangs primarily to structural and ecological factors. This account of Crips in the Netherlands illustrates that an international juvenile life style is influential, if only as a catalyst. Cultural factors should also be considered. The relevance of culture is clear in the case of Moroccan youth groups. Many of these, in contrast to the foregoing, are resistant to gang formation.

The Rif is an infertile and mountainous region in Northern Morocco. For a long time, Riffians have had a specific position in Morocco. The sultan (later the king) never fully managed to control these tribes. The Riffians had many conflicts among themselves, often resulting in blood feuds, but managed to unite against forces from outside. When Morocco was a protectorate, the Riffians, under Abdelkrim, were the only ones who managed to stand up to the foreign rulers (Gellner, 1973; Hart, 1976; Jamous, 1981).

Morocco became independent in 1956. At that time the Rif was poor and relatively densely populated. Many men left their households for a few months every year to work in Algeria. In 1961 this seasonal migration came to an end when upon the Algerian independence the eastern borders were closed. To avoid a situation where unsatisfied Riffians might become militant, the king cooperated and let them try their luck in Europe.

Since the end of the sixties, migrant workers in the Netherlands have been recruited from several countries in the Mediterranean area, including Morocco. About three-quarters of the Moroccans in the Netherlands originate from the Rif. Currently, except for people from the former Dutch colony of Surinam, Moroccans and Turks are the biggest ethnic groups. Economic depression has hit the Moroccans hard. Many have lost their jobs and are now dependent on the Dutch welfare system. Many migrants have sent for their families to come to the Netherlands. Unfortunately, research repeatedly has shown that Moroccan youths are over-represented in police statistics. Also, trouble with Moroccan youth groups is often mentioned.

These groups are sometimes referred to as "gangs." However, research based on participant observation over a period of three years has led to a different view (Van Gemert, 1998b). Following Islamic rules, the Moroccan girls mostly stay at home, while the boys participate in the outside world. Boys look for each other and come together on street corners. Outsiders often expect these groups to be cohesive, but the unwillingness of members to share and to collaborate for a common goal is notable. These youngsters are jealous and very competitive amongst themselves; distrust greatly influences their relations. It is everyone for his self, mitigating any pressure toward group cohesiveness.

The idea of a gang as a group that is more than the sum of its members does not seem to fit Moroccan youngsters. These groups are common in big Dutch cities, but symbols that distinguish one group from another are not used. There is no shared group identity. These findings show parallels with other phenomena, like the distance between children and elders or the poor level of organization among Moroccans in the Netherlands. Also similarities between Moroccan youngsters and their Riffian ancestors come to the fore. Distrust can be seen as a cultural element that is reproduced in different settings. For this generation of Riffians, at least, gang formation is unlikely, in contrast to the three groups described earlier. The study of gang formation, at least in the Netherlands, requires the study of culture as well.

REFERENCES

Bing, L. (1992). Gangs: Jeugdbendes in Los Angeles. Utrecht: Luitingh-Sijthoff (translation).

Gemert, F. van (1998a). Crips in Drievoud; Een Dossieronderzoek Naar Drie Jeugdbendes. Amsterdam: Regioplan.

Gemert, F. van (1998b). Ieder Voor Zich: Kansen, Cultuur en Criminaliteit van Marokkaanse Jongens. Amsterdam: Het Spinhuis, (thesis).

Gellner, E. (1973). Patterns of rural rebellion in Morocco during the early years of independence. In E. Gellner & C. Micaud (eds.), Arabs and Berbers: From Tribe to Nation in North Aftica, pp. 361-374. London: Duckworth.

Hart, D.M. (1976). The Aith Waryaghar of the Moroccan Rif. An Ethnography and History. Tucson: University of Arizona Press.

Jamous, R. (1981). Honneur et Baraka. Les Structures Sociales Traditionelles dans le Rif. Paris: Editions de la Maison des Sciences de l'Homme.

Klein, M.W. & C.L. Maxson (1989). Street gang violence. In N.A. Weiner and M.E. Wolfgang (eds.), Violent Crime, Violent Criminals, pp. 198-234. Newbury Park: Sage Publications.

Shakur, S. (1993). Monster: De Autobiografie van een Crips-leider. Amsterdam: Luitingh-Sijthoff (translation).

Chapter 10

GANGSTAS OR LAGER LOUTS? WORKING CLASS STREET GANGS IN MANCHESTER

Dennis Mares
Graduate Program, University of Missouri at St. Louis (Rotterdam, The Netherlands)

INTRODUCTION

Presently there is still little known about street gangs in Britain. The British do not perceive street gangs as part of their "civilized" society, which partly accounts for the lack of coherent research into this subject. Crime in general and gangs specifically are often associated with an alien "Other" (cf. Pearson, 1983). Not surprisingly, a few reports on street gangs in Britain point to ethnic youths in inner city slum areas.

During my research in Manchester I became aware of the extent to which gangs have become a constituting part of this society. In this chapter I will give a brief overview of several gangs that operate in the Greater Manchester area in north England. Furthermore, I will assess some of the recent changes that have been taken place among these gangs.

The data gathered during my research consist mainly of ethnographic data gathered between September 1997 and January 1998. In addition to conducting participant observation among several gangs, interviews were conducted with gang members, community workers and law enforcement personnel. Newspaper articles, literature and statistical data further supplemented these

M.W. Klein et al (eds.), The Eurogang Paradox, 153–164.

qualitative data. Unfortunately no statistical data on street gangs were available, as gangs do not yet comprise a distinct category within police statistics. The nature of the research itself was exploratory rather than in-depth, primarily because no previous research had been conducted in this city.

GANGS IN BRITAIN

The United Kingdom has been riddled by groups of youthful delinquents from at least the 17th century (cf. Pearson, 1983). The lack of coherent research on these street gangs meant that the names given to these groups were of a distinctly local character: *street Arabs*, *roughs*, *hooligans*. The gangs in question were often territorially distinct groups that emerged from the impoverished working class neighborhoods near the city center. They often engaged in violent clashes with neighboring gangs and used a wide array of weapons (ibid. 108 and 188). Even in the 20th century violent street gangs, commonly referred to as *mod* gangs after their stylistic features, were part of the urban scene (cf. Patrick, 1973). It is thus somewhat ambiguous to speak of a new development when addressing the gang problem in Britain. However, during the 1980s a new type of gang appeared to have emerged in several large metropolitan areas, most notably London, Liverpool, Birmingham and Manchester. These were mostly ethnic street gangs involved in the sale of drugs with strong intergang rivalry and high levels of violence. The British press heralded these gangs as "American style" gangs, modeling themselves after American West Coast gangs like the Bloods and Crips (cf. Silverman, 1994: 235 and 242; Thompson, 1995). Did the emergence of these ethnic gangs mean a clear break with the largely native street-gangs that prevailed in the United Kingdom until the 1980s, or is the present gang situation more subtle?

The Gooch and Doddington: Street Gangs in Britain's Bronx

Two of these newly emergent ethnic gangs are the Gooch and Doddington. Originally, the latter was the Pepperhill gang but several police raids broke this gang up and the remainder formed the Doddington. Both gangs are located in one of Manchester's most impoverished districts, Moss Side. During the 1980s members from both gangs became involved in the drug trade in hashish, heroine, cocaine and crack. With this involvement in the drug trade the levels of violence rose spectacularly, resulting in various gang-related homicides. In the last six months of 1992 no fewer than 100 shooting incidents had been reported to the police.

The gangs, however, are not drug-gangs principally organized around the distribution of drugs. Several of the gang members and drug dealers involved confided to me that the gangs and drugs were not "together"; drug dealing was carried out on an individual basis:

> Gooch, Doddington, Salford, I'm not part of any of them. Doing my own thing you know. Selling drugs and the gang are not together. Your own money is your own money. [Non-affiliated Moss Side drug dealer]

And although some gang members might work together, the gang as a whole was not an organization aimed at drug dealing but primarily existed as a social group (cf. Hagedorn, 1994). In fact, much of the violence attributed to "gang wars" was in reality clashes between members of the same gang.

According to gang members and police officials, both gangs have about 90 members in their ranks, although presently substantial sections of the gangs have been imprisoned. A number of 40 active gang members is therefore probably more correct. About 80 percent of the gang members are of ethnic descent, mostly Afro-Caribbean. There is however no reason to assume that either gang consciously decided to become an ethnically based street gang. The gangs are principally a reflection of the district's ethnic composition. The presence of substantial numbers of white and mixed-race gang members and the strong territorial nature of both gangs also suggest that the gangs are not primarily organized around ethnicity, but rather around turf.

Some subgroups have formed and are primarily oriented around age and friendship. The age range is substantial: the youngest members are around ten and the oldest members are sometimes in their early thirties. Apart from involvement in the drug trade Moss Side gang members commit a wide range of other offenses; car thefts, protection rackets and cash-point robberies to name but a few.

The Gooch and Doddington are not hierarchically organized gangs and there are no formal leaders:

> I can't see one person trying to lead all of them people. [Gang member in remand for murder]

> Our group's on equal terms. There's just members who've been there longer and got more money, but they don't give no orders. [Longsight Crew member]

Older members with a track record of criminal involvement do have a somewhat greater influence on the less experienced members, who are often used in the more risky operations. The most respected members are, in imitation of American gangs, designated as OG s (Original Gangsters).

During much of the 1980s and early 1990s both the Gooch and the Doddington firmly controlled their patches in the Alexandra Park estate in Moss Side. Presently many gang members have moved to nearby Longsight where again they assert their dominance over certain areas within that district. Drug dealing however mostly takes place on neutral ground in Moss Side.

Gang members stated that attaining respect was an important feature of being a member: "It's about power, nobody messing with ya," or as an ex-gang member stated: "Everybody else is doing it…it gives you power and that rush is good. Everybody is watching you, respecting you."

Having a reputation is a way of distinguishing between the haves and have-nots in gangs. It provides them with an alternative status system. Successful gang members in Moss Side were the ones with high priced designer clothing, sports cars and many women. Increasingly these "successful" gang members are becoming the role models for younger children, thereby replacing conventional role models within the area (cf. Anderson, 1991).

Both the Gooch and Doddington use stylistic features that are derived from popularized American gangs and Jamaican posses. In many ways the gangs are indistinguishable from their contemporaries in Los Angeles or for that matter Frankfurt or Rotterdam. The clothing style and musical preferences reinforce their *gangsta* style image (cf. Smith, 1995). Mostly they wear expensive designer clothes like Hilfiger, Versace and Armani. Many gang members also enjoy watching movies depicting gang life like *Menace II Society* and some even read popular books on street gangs and organized crime. Nevertheless the gang members rejected the idea that they were "American style" street gangs:

> We don't wear clothes like in America where the Crips and Bloods wear blue and red and all that. It's not like that. We like to look good, that's all really. [Incarcerated Gooch member]

The Moss Side gangs are not Crip or Blood style gangs in the strict sense. Although the levels of violence attributed to these gangs are high by British standards, they are low in comparison to the U.S. Colors and symbols are hardly if at all used and there are no initiation rites to name but a few dissimilarities.

While the Gooch and Doddington do use some popularized media images of gangs, this does not seem to have a large impact on the gangs. It is more likely that commodified gang images have provided them with stylistic features that are being used to express more located meanings, and therefore have an authenticity and directness of personal expression that are absent in the commodified forms (cf. Willis, 1977: 17).

In conclusion, both the Gooch and Doddington can be classified as having a neo-traditional structure (cf. Klein, 1996). They have developed too recently to give rise to an elaborate structure and subdivision but could evolve into a traditional structure over time.

Salford: Working Class Street Gangs

Salford is, like Moss Side, located near Manchester's city center. Unlike Moss Side the gangs in Salford are white, but apart from that there is in fact little to distinguish the street gangs in both districts from each other. Many respondents mentioned that the levels of violence associated with some of the Salford gangs are at least as high as in Moss Side. Although no statistical data on gang violence are available, crime in general in Salford is slightly higher than in southern Manchester, in which Moss Side is located. In the districts of Lower and Higher Broughton and Ordsall in particular, violent street gangs operate. Some of these became infamous during riots in 1992 when police vans were shot at (cf. Campbell, 1993).

At the close of the 19th century street gangs in Salford, who then were termed "scuttlers," were already being reported. As in many other areas of Manchester at the time, these gangs engaged in large street battles (sometimes as many as 500 youths were involved) and adorned themselves with a specific dress style (Pearson, 1983: 94-96).

Like the Gooch and Doddington gangs, some Salfordian gangs can be described as having a neo-traditional structure (Klein, 1996). The number of years that these gangs have been in existence is hard to trace, but most have been around for at least a decade.

In general the age range of most Salfordian gangs varies between ten and twenty-five, but the age range is widening:

> When you get older you start robbing, nicking cars and doing big stuff. I was about eleven. Now where I live the kids start robbing when they're eight and nine. [Young Firm gang member]

The gangs in Salford are somewhat smaller than the gangs in Moss Side, but usually somewhere between twenty-five and 60 gang members are present. This is most likely due to the impact of large criminal organizations in the area, which tend to incorporate some gang members as they reach their twenties. Linkages between criminal organizations and street gangs are not limited to a gradual transition from juvenile delinquency into "hard crime," but extend themselves throughout both groupings from an early stage:

> Say we do one shop, yeah [ram raid, also known as a 'Crash and Carry'] take all the clothes and we can sell 'em within the hour, anything. Even if we've got fuckin' two quid pyjamas we can sell 'em in bulk. We sell our stuff to people, older ones who got loads of money. [Young Firm member]

When it comes to subgroups the picture is less clear. The overall group size is too small to give rise to an elaborate set of subgroups, but the youngsters do have a general instrumental attitude towards the number of people involved in specific activities, which might point to the development of subgroups:

> When you go out robbin' and all that you only have about four mates, and when you go to a fight, you take a lot. Get in a car and sort it out. [Young Firm member]

The Salfordian gangs are involved in a variety of crimes, but concentrate mostly on car thefts, ram raids, robberies and the sales of party drugs. Like many other Manchester gangs, the lads in Salford are very territorial, and, therefore, gangs form on specific streets or in certain neighborhoods. They also adopt the name of the main street in which they operate. Gang fights are often related to gang members trespassing on the territory of other gangs. Occasionally alliances are formed to fight larger gangs, but these are short-lived and unstable. The degree of organization is low and there does not appear to be any structural role division: "Ye don't say, 'You're the boss.'...We're just boys, go out robbing, making money, getting a buzz, beating people up."

Some gang members are involved in the sales of the drugs, although unlike their counterparts in Moss Side who primarily sell heroine and cocaine, the lads in Salford largely deal in "clean drugs" like xtc and speed. Given the distribution channels of the criminal organizations operating in Salford, which extend themselves through many parts of Manchester's extensive club scene, this is not very surprising.

Having a rough reputation, like proving oneself in fights and delinquency, is in these gangs an essential requisite to become an established gang member. This harks back to the district's history as a residence for Salford dock workers that were reputed for their toughness and overt masculine behavior.

Salford gang members dress, talk and walk gang, just as in Moss Side. They favor expensive clothing, *jungle* music and *gangsta* rap and enjoy watching gang films. It seems that the largely ethnic gangs in Moss Side have much in common with their white peers in Salford. Furthermore the few differences–drug sales and gang size–are most likely attributable to local factors, for example, the impact of adult criminal organizations in Salford.

Wythenshawe: Suburban Street Gangs

Unlike the neo-traditional street gangs that can be found in central areas of the metropolitan area, many other districts in Manchester have gang structures that can be described as compressed (Klein, 1996). Often located in impoverished council estates, the British form of high-rise and low-rise public housing, cliques of youth have formed street gangs that are often short-lived and whose members seldom exceed thirty.

Wythenshawe in that respect is probably the most obvious example. This district in south Manchester has about 75,000 inhabitants and is located near the city's airport. The area, originally designated to become a "garden city," is primarily inhabited by working class families. Wythenshawe has a reputation for being a rough area, because many residents formerly inhabited slum areas in the central districts of the city which since have been cleared.

Although there is a relatively large variety between different gangs, most gangs have about twenty-five members, usually supplemented by five or six females. Well over 90 percent of the gang members are white, and the remaining ten percent are mostly black or mixed descent. The life span of these gangs is fairly limited, usually about five to ten years. Most gang members are between the age of fourteen and eighteen but sometimes younger as well as older youths are present. Gang members mature out of this life style once they are in their early twenties.

There are no subgroups, which can be attributed to the gangs' small size. Gangs may however form alliances to fight other gangs. Furthermore, the gangs lack any form of organization and there are no established leaders. Individual gang members nevertheless can build up a reputation by showing their skills in fights or delinquency.

Each gang controls its turf, usually a main traffic artery with some shops. Their names are most often derived from the streets in which they hang out. Gang fights, most often caused by youngsters, exemplify this as they wittingly or unwittingly end up in another gang's patch. In fights, weapons are seldom used and serious woundings are therefore rare.

Their criminal patterns are versatile, ranging from shoplifting and joyriding to extortion of local shopkeepers. Most gangs do not display a major involvement in serious delinquency and the gang members in this area are only marginally involved in the sale of drugs and the use of extreme forms of violence. Most of their criminal behavior consists of petty crime and minor law infractions like alcohol and drug abuse. Furthermore, Wythenshawe gangs are not linked to criminal organizations operating in the area.

The gangs in the Wythenshawe district displayed similar stylistic features as in the other gang areas. Especially during the 1980s gang fashion became important identity markers for the youths. However, it prompted no Americanization of the gangs and they are principally symbols of cultural capital signifying a break with middle class values.

"Being Hard": Street Gang Attitude in Britain

Compared to Manchester gangs in the late 19th century, the current gangs are small and are probably less delinquent. Major alliances like some gangs formed in Glasgow in the 1960s (cf. Patrick, 1973) are not to be found. This suggests that the gang problem in this northern city is fairly limited. Since the 1980s, however, violence and delinquency among inner city gangs has been on the rise once more. Unlike the ethnic based gangs that can be found in Germany and the Netherlands, street gangs in Manchester are predominantly white and there are no ethnically "pure" gangs (cf. Tertilt, 1996; van Gemert, 1995a, 1995b, 1998; Stelfox, 1996). This suggests that the British experience is slightly different than the continental and is intimately linked to historical class antagonisms.

The gangs found in Manchester can thus only be properly described by looking into historical class relations and the contemporary difficulties faced by urban youths. One clear aspect that can be found in all the gangs studied is their attitudes towards the working class notion of "being hard," which primarily hark back to working class assumptions of labor (for a further discussion see Mares, 1997, 1998 and 1999). By being hard, gang members can demonstrate their cultural capital, which does not rest on formal educational skills but on working class street values. It refers to both physical strength and masculine power, which gang members use in acquiring status. In the gangs it is a way of coming to terms with, not necessarily a conscious rebellion against, structural class differences, but at the same time reproducing and mocking these legitimized dissimilarities on a more localized scale. Being hard can be seen as a *habitus* which provides them with a plan of action, a plan which redefines the notion itself (cf. Bourdieu, 1977:72; Bourdieu, 1990:53). In general the more hardness the gang members display the more status is acquired. But the actions that are associated with being hard vary to a large extent, depending largely on the external constraints that operate in the different districts in Manchester.

To explain why gangs in Moss Side and Salford have developed a neo-traditional structure during the 1980s while most other street gangs retained their compressed structure, it is necessary to take a closer look at the impact of the process of de-industrialization that has hit Manchester since the 1970s. The unprecedented scale of industrial reform that has hit Britain has had profoundly different effects on different areas (cf. Taylor et al., 1996; Champion and Townsend, 1990). Much as in the U.S., inner city areas in Britain have been more affected by these structural changes. Districts like Salford and Moss Side have seen an accumulation of social problems or *concentration effects* (cf. Wilson, 1987). Apart from being geographically located, these economic changes also had a greater impact on youths than on adults, as youngsters became more excluded from economic participation because of the declining demand for industrial laborers (cf. Roberts, 1995).

Not surprisingly youth unemployment in Moss Side and Salford is extremely high, with unofficial figures running as high as 70 percent. Most of the jobs that are available to youngsters in these areas are low paying, insecure jobs in the service industries. This labor places them between their sense of cultural dignity (being hard) and the humiliating interpersonal subordination of service work. Working class values do not coincide with the "feminine" nature of these jobs, thereby propelling large batches of youngsters permanently out of the formal labor market, into the underground economy (cf. Bourgois, 1995: 141).

The proximity to the city center and its large drug market, coupled with the existence of distribution channels of drugs, further adds to development of drug dealing and very violent gang members in Salford and Moss Side. More isolated areas like Wythenshawe are not so profoundly affected by these processes, explaining why the gangs in those districts remain short-lived groups of delinquent adolescents.

CONCLUDING REMARKS

It is quite hard to predict what the future will hold for the gangs in Manchester. It is not likely that gangs will evolve into traditional gang structures in the foreseeable future as consistent intervention from law enforcement agencies puts tremendous strain on the gangs' structure. Furthermore, poverty and deprivation have not yet reached the levels of some American inner city neighborhoods and even the most impoverished districts recently have shown some signs of improvement.

The Manchester case however also reveals that gangs are not a new development in Europe but a clear continuation and redevelopment of already existing gang structures. It further illustrates the predicaments of gangs that are swept up in the contemporary turmoil and which are being shaped by the interplay of historical, local and contemporary forces. Nevertheless there is much work to be done on gangs in Britain, as this limited case study may or may not represent gangs throughout the U.K.

REFERENCES

Anderson, E. (1991). Streetwise: Race, Class, and Change in an Urban Community. Chicago: University of Chicago Press.

Bourdieu, P. (1977). Outline of a Theory of Practice. Cambridge: Polity Press.
Bourdieu, P. (1990). The Logic of Practice. Cambridge: Polity Press.
Bourgois, P. (1995). In Search of Respect: Selling Crack in El Barrio. Cambridge: Cambridge University Press.
Campbell, B. (1993). Goliath: Britain's Dangerous Places. London: Methuen.
Champion, A.G. and A.R. Townsend (1990). Contemporary Britain: A Geographical Perspective. London: Edward Arnold.
Davies, N. (1997). Dark Heart: The Shocking Truth about Hidden Britain. London: Chatto and Windus.
Gemert, F. van (1995a). Amerikaanse gangs en Nederlandse jeugdbendes. In Rood-Pijpers, E. (ed.), Preventie van Jeugdcriminaliteit in een Ggrote Sstad. Gouda: Quint.
Gemert, F. van (1995b). Gangs in Amerika en Nederland. Justitiële Verkenningen. Jrg. 21(9): 68-83.
Gemert, F. van (1998). Crips in de polder. Facta 1998-7: 18-20.
Hagedorn, J.M. (1994). Neigborhoods, markets and gang drug organization. Journal of Research in Crime and Delinquency 31(3): 264-294.
Klein, M.W. (1996). Gangs in the United States and Europe. European Journal on Criminal Policy and Research 4(2):63-80.
Mares, D. (1997). Gangs, Gangculturen en Modernisering. Utrecht: Utrecht University (unpublished paper).
Mares, D. (1998). Gangchester: Youth Gangs-Cultures in Manchester. Utrecht: Utrecht University (unpublished MA thesis).
Mares, D. (1999). Globalization and gangs: The Manchester case. Focaal 34.
Patrick, J. (1973). A Glasgow Gang Observed. London: Eyre Methuen.
Pearson, G. (1983). Hooligan: A History of Respectable Fears. London: MacMillan.
Roberts, K. (1995). Youth and Unemployment in Modern Britain. Oxford: Oxford University Press.
Silverman, J. (1994). Crack of Doom: The Extraordinary True Story Behind Crack-Cocaine. London: Headline.
Smith, K. (1995). Moss Side Massive. London: X-Press.
Spergel, I. (1994). The Youth Gang Problem: A Community Approach. Oxford: Oxford University Press.
Stelfox, P. (1996). Gang Violence: Strategic and Tactical Options. Manchester: Greater Manchester Police.
Taylor, I., K. Evans, and P. Fraser (1996). A Tale of Two Cities: Global Change, Local Feeling and Everyday Life in the North of England: A Study in Manchester and Sheffield. London: Routledge.
Tertilt, H. (1996). Turkish Power Boys: Ethnographie einer Jugendbande. Frankfurt am Main: Suhrkamp Verlag.
Thompson, T. (1995). Gangland Britain: Inside Britain's Most Dangerous Gangs. London: Hodder and Stoughton.
Willis, P. (1977). Learning To Labor: How Working Class Kids Get Working Class Jobs. New York: Columbia University Press.

Wilson, W. J. (1987). The Truly Disadvantaged: The Inner City, the Underclass, and Public Policy. Chicago: University of Chicago Press.

Chapter 11

THE CONCEPT OF HONOR, CONFLICT AND VIOLENT BEHAVIOR AMONG YOUTHS IN OSLO

Inger-Lise Lien
The Norwegian Institute of Urban and Rural Research (NIBR), Oslo, Norway

In a recent study of gang behavior in Oslo (Lien and Haaland, 1998, a project undertaken in collaboration with the organization Youth Against Violence), we found that the center of Oslo has become an arena for new groups of youth operating on the streets. Some of these groups are multicultural and have a high level of crime. They have links with Norwegian and foreign criminal environments. As part of the project, we conducted fieldwork among youth that were members of and in other ways connected to Youth Against Violence. We also distributed a questionnaire to a *strategic sample* of 85 informants, aged 13 to 18. The results of the study showed a significant correlation between criminality and gang membership.

In our study we define a gang as a collective with a name and a minimum level of organization. Of our informants who are members of gangs, 53 percent admit to having robbed someone, 60 percent say they possess weapons, and of these, 28 percent say they possess a gun. Gang members owe a great deal of money to "the street boys." The debts average about 8000 Norwegian kroner (roughly $1,100) and range from $20 to $5,400. Only a minority of the informants said that they intended to repay their debts with money obtained from legitimate sources.

These groups also maintain a high level of conflict preparedness. They report having many enemies whom they hate and they are often involved in fights with other groups. Their feelings of antagonism create a climate in

M.W. Klein et al (eds.), The Eurogang Paradox, 165–174.

which hostilities can be triggered by the merest trifle. They are fearful of losing face and self-esteem and, therefore, easily hurt. Ideals of masculinity based on physical strength are values that rank high; the creation and spread of fear are the instruments they use to attain respect and recognition from their enemies and others.

There is hardly a day when the Oslo newspapers do not write about this new violent gang phenomenon. Youths have been seriously hurt and even killed in the ongoing fights between the various groups. There are the Vietnamese against the Filipinos, Vietnamese against Pakistanis, Somalis against Iranians, and so on. The neo-Nazi gang "Viking" was formed after a fight with a Vietnamese gang at Manglerud, an Oslo suburb. Added to this background of antagonism and young multicultural groups fighting among each other are the skinhead groups such as the Boot Boys and Ariske Brødre (Aryan Brotherhood) whose main targets are the antiracist groups, especially members of the so-called Blitz group (Bjørgo, 1997).

It appears that the racist gangs, the immigrant gangs, the multicultural gangs, and the antiracist gangs all have certain traits in common. There are both structural and cultural traits. Before we take a closer look at these traits, it is necessary to give a short description of the history and the development of multicultural gangs in Oslo.

GANG DEVELOPMENT IN OSLO

Fights between youths belonging to different streets and areas in Oslo have been a well-known phenomenon for many years and are well-documented in research and the media. Two of the most famous of these gangs in the fifties were the "Frognerbanden" (the Frogner gang, Frogner being a middle-class area in Oslo) and the Blackie gang. They fought with their fists and robbed people on the street. They received a lot of attention in the press. The city was struck with moral panic and the female members of the Storting, the Norwegian parliament, declared in the house that they were afraid to go home after work in the evenings. Then followed the Punks and the Rockers in Youngstorget–one of Oslo's central squares–in the sixties and seventies (von der Lippe, 1993). This was before Norway became a popular target for immigration from the

Third World, so all of these gangs were, ethnically speaking, home grown Norwegians.

However, a recent report by Anders Bakken (1998) finds that the youth of Oslo have become more law-abiding than earlier studies have shown. A questionnaire was given to 11,500 school children from 14 to 17 years of age. This self-report study also reveals that immigrant children are even more law-abiding than Norwegian children, but there is a sharp distinction between the very well behaved– who have become even more well behaved since 1992–on the one hand, and the 5 percent who are the least well-behaved. The latter committed a greater amount of criminal and violent behavior than in previous years. In Oslo, 550 boys reported that during 1996 they had taken part in fights that included weapons. There are as many immigrant youths in this category as there are Norwegians and the immigrant boys are more violent than Norwegian youths are even though they use fewer drugs and less alcohol than do the Norwegians.

The groups of youths, which give rise to terror and insecurity in the city of Oslo, are comparatively small in numbers. But their acts of violence can have a great effect on the welfare and feeling of security of the majority. A case from our material (Lien and Haaland, 1998) illustrates this: A single member of Tøyen Black Gangsters had 37 charges of violent behavior in 1996.

Immigrant gangs, both homogeneous and multiethnic, represent a new phenomenon that has emerged during the eighties. The most famous of these is a gang composed of Pakistani youths called the Young Guns, named after an American movie of the same name. The Young Guns came to the attention of the media during the eighties through a series of fights with other gangs, among them a Pakistani group called the "Killers," a Filipino gang called the "Outsiders," and a group named the "Rebels." The level of violence increased to such a degree that in 1988 it ended in the terrible axe-murder of an innocent young Pakistani boy, a brother of one of the members of the "Killers." Thirteen twenty-year-old Pakistani boys, members of Young Guns, were arrested for the murder.

Young Guns can be described as a group that carved out a career path for other groups to follow. They became famous heroes, and many other Pakistani youths wanted to become members of the gang. They are not second-generation immigrants, but half-generation. They were all between 10 and 12 years of age when they came to Norway. Their friendship and gang-related behavior "*developed through strife and nourished on conflict*" (see Thrasher's classic description of 1927 on the development of gangs in the U.S.).

Through clashes and fights with rival groups they were drawn more and more into criminal activities. It started with antagonism and with fights between rival groups. Crime has been a secondary effect of this development. The pattern bears comparison with patterns of development found in the motorcycle clubs, Hell's Angels and Bandidos. From simple antagonism a transition has taken place to a combination of crime and antagonism. Two of the members of Young Guns were real brothers belonging to a jat-biraderi, but the rest came from raja and gujr families, all three of these being ethnic Pakistani groups or agricultural castes. But the biraderi metaphor was used as a symbol of internal loyalty. They called themselves "bai" (brothers) and were constantly guarding the honor (izzet) of the group. They constituted "a closed and bounded group" (Bjørgo, 1997).

After serving their prison sentences, several of the boys became law-abiding citizens and respectable members of both the Norwegian and Pakistani communities, but a few members of the group continued their careers into serious crime. Some became involved in the sale of heavy drugs while others threatened Pakistani shopkeepers demanding protection money from them. What remains of the gang now consists of adult family fathers. New people have been recruited and the gang is now called the A-gang and consists of about 40 members. They have developed an international network with connections in Denmark and England and they collaborate with Turkish and Moroccan criminal gangs. Several Young Pakistani youths have tried to become members, and some have developed supporter gangs such as the "Young Force" and the "Little A." The B-gang is a group that consolidated itself after disagreements with the A-gang. The two gangs compete against one another and often fight. The B-gang seems to be a group of 50 Pakistanis ranging in age between 20 and 40. They collaborate with Hell's Angels and other gangs from various ethnic groups settled in Oslo. They have a small supporter gang of brothers and relatives who call themselves the "Little B."

Together with motorcycle gangs, A and B gangs are among the most famous in Oslo. They have been interviewed on television and by the major newspapers. Journalists have followed them around in the streets of Oslo, reporting their fights and presenting their justification: "I have balls. People without balls can stay away" (uttered by a member of the B-gang to *Aftenposten* 13/3-98).

These famous veteran gangs have their young followers. We may call them the C generation (Lien and Haaland, 1998). They are much younger, from 12 to 16. They form groups with minimal organization. They watch American gangster movies and give themselves gangster names like Cash Money Brothers, Black Mafia Society, Mafia Sisters, Cats and Tøyen Svarte Gangstere (Tøyen Black Gangsters).

Some of the gangs do not have an identifying name of their own, they are labelled the "Somali gang" or the "Vietnamese gang." Some are purely ethnic, but several of them, such as the Tøyen Black Gangsters (TSG in the following), consist of several nationalities. In 1996 the TSG numbered more than 30 members and the core consisted of six Somalis, four Pakistanis, two Moroccans, two Turks, two Vietnamese, and a couple of Norwegian boys. They were most active in 1996 when they threatened and stole from children of the same age as themselves. Five or six of them would walk together, pick out a weak victim and then attack him and take his jacket or money. Then they would threaten him so that he would not dare to go to the police. They operated both within and beyond the city. They tagged their initials "TSG" on different places in the center to mark their area, but they would travel all over the city to fight. "We wanted to be respected and protect our honor. If anybody wanted to mess with us, we would fight." Very often they fought over minor issues, but if somebody insulted their girlfriends, a fight would be inevitable. In cases like this they would mobilize and agree on a place to fight. A minor insult could result in a fight with more than 100 participants. They would mobilize widely. They were nomads and moved around across city and municipality borders. In the course of a single evening a group could be found first in the city center, then in different city districts, and even in neighboring municipalities, all of which could host fights and violent behavior. "We met at different places in town and outside. We fought racists. We wanted to get the Nazis and the racists. That's why we went where they were." They could move unimpeded from place to place in a virtual free zone across municipal borders because the various decentralized local authorities with their geographically fixed areas of responsibilities where unable to decide "whose problem" it was, and were therefore unwilling to take responsibility. Most of the gang members either had a cellular phone or a pager. The transfer of information was swift and permitted rapid mobilization, often on the basis of fragmented and uncontrollable rumors.

The violence found its justification in the demonization of others and by claiming to represent the position of the antiracist, i.e., by moral arguments. It was all for a good cause. The enemy deserved to be beaten, as either they were racist, Ku Klux Klaners, whores, or homos. Because the enemy was thought of as evil and bad, the fight was conceived as a fight in self-defense, even though the "enemy" had not made the first move. Physical violence was often used as a communicative tool that took the place of verbal communication. A verbal insult was not always met with a verbal response, as was expected by the opposite group, but with violence. Violence was, therefore, in many circumstances, a very powerful communicative tool that could instantly reverse a position from inferiority to superiority, thus stopping any further verbal discussion. When the enemy lies on the ground there is a feeling that the game has been won. Violence has the effect of "tactical pre-emption" (Riches, 1986) by reducing the opportunity to retaliate by diminishing the power of the victim. Violence is a tool to generate respect by creating fear in the victim that violence will be repeated. Violence is also regarded as fun by many of our informants, generating meaning in an otherwise dull everyday life.

These multicultural gangs are different from the Norwegian gangs that used to find refuge in the center of Oslo, the drug addicts in conflict with their parents. The boys in the multicultural gangs are gymnasts, who train in the arts of self-defense. They invest a lot of energy building up what they perceive as their masculinity. Their role as males is very important to them. Conflicts with their parents usually take indirect forms. They play the respect game: "At home we behave like angels because we respect our father. We say, yes, yes. But outside in the streets, we demand the respect and fear of others. We are angels no more." They wear two faces: at home subordinate, outside high and mighty. In these gangs the boys with immigrant backgrounds and boys with a Norwegian background talk constantly about their honor and about respect. Some of the Norwegian boys often play the role of warmonger. The general image among immigrant boys of Norwegian boys is that they are cowards and usually not willing to fight. Norwegians who want to join a multicultural gang have to prove their masculinity and courage by any means to deserve a place. They regard themselves, and are regarded by others, as "white-blacks," and they are ready to fight for their honor at any time, to prove that they are not "chicken" and not as cowardly as other Norwegian boys. In the newspaper *Dagsavisen* (1/18/98) the journalist Tuva Gry Øyan reflected on a conversation that she had with her sixteen-year-old Norwegian son. They live in Grunerløkka in what is in the eastern (less prosperous) area of Oslo where more than 60 percent of the pupils at the local school are immigrant children with non-western backgrounds. She writes: "The most important thing is honor," says the sixteen-year-old, "honor and respect. We have started to talk about values round our kitchen table at Grunerløkka. A new phenomenon is emerging in the melting pot of east Oslo. A new and pluralistic shared culture is sprouting, created by young people with family background in Norway, Pakistan, Morocco, Vietnam and other countries. This common culture influences also its Norwegian members, and will, I think, change Norway forever."

THE "RATE" AND THE "INCIDENT" OF GANGS AND HYPER-HONOR

In the book *Suicide*, Durkheim (1979:277ff, 297ff) distinguishes between the factors that can explain the rate and the general pattern of a phenomenon, such as suicide, and the various specific individually motivated factors that can cause an incident. Durkheim argues that the variations and incidents of a phenomenon are influenced by factors explaining the general pattern, but a distinction between factors explaining "the rate" and "the incident" can be useful for our purpose of understanding the development of gangs and the occurrence of hyper-honor.

Structural and Cultural Factors

Economic and structural conditions seem to be important for the development of gangs and hyper-honor. "If a community's economy is not based solidly on wages and salaries, other economies will begin to develop. Welfare, bartering, informal economic arrangements, and illegal economies become substitutes–simply because people must find a way to live. Young people growing up in these communities have little to look forward to" (Moore, 1990:172). Klein (1995) claims that when gangs arise in a neighborhood, it is because the environment has not been able to integrate and socialize parts of the youth population. The gang is a side effect of a local community that does not work the way it should.

Gangs operate mostly in the eastern areas of Oslo. From 1987 until 1997 the proportion of children aged 7–15 in the Grünerløkka/Sofienberg area increased by 80 percent. As Heidi Gautun (1996) has documented, youths in these areas more often than in other places are victims of violence and threats, and they carry weapons more often as a preparedness measure against violence. The rate of unemployment has decreased dramatically in Oslo (it is now at about 2–3 percent), but in Grünerløkka/Sofienberg and Old Oslo there is an unemployment rate of 10 percent, and 20 percent of the population receives social welfare benefits. In our study we found that boys in gangs often played truant from school, and did not believe that they would land a proper job. They expected to be victims of discrimination. They had no trust in adults–neither their parents nor their teachers.

They were very pessimistic about the options for the future, and as they did not think that they would get a proper job through legal channels, their pessimism about the future was turned into gangster dreams:

> I was a member of a gang called Gangster Brothers–GB. We were inspired by American gangster movies. We bought rings with dollar signs on them and used sixpence caps. We wore Levi shirts and had golden chains around our necks and fixed our hair with hair gel. We sprayed the whole area with GB graffiti. We listened to rap. A gangster is very tough. But to be O.G. is also tough. Now I want to be O.G., and I will stop being a full-time gangster. In spite of everything we live in Norway and not in Chicago. But there are too many of the boys who believe that they live in America. They have seen too many American films.

Nisbett and Cohen (1996) have shown that there is a significant correlation between what they conceive of as a culture of honor and the rate of violence. This implies that conceptions of honor are connected with hyper-vigilance for potential insults, which can lead to a greater preparedness to use violence. These cultural representations can spread and be internalized when conditions create susceptibility to them. With a high unemployment rate and relative poverty there is nothing to which to attach the feeling of self esteem, so that the need for respect must be based on something else, that is, the creation of fear. The image of the self as dangerous, with a temper that can kill, with brothers who will always support you, with the power for destruction, is the image that is chosen when few other alternative ways to obtain recognition and respect exist. Many immigrants have brought with them ideas of honor from their home countries, ideas that are transmitted from parents to children. But these ideas can take hyper-forms under conditions where there is a lot of pessimism for the future created by structural factors. Norwegian boys harboring a lot of pessimism can also feel attracted to this idea of honor based on fear, and they will use violence to obtain a position in a local community. Through violent behavior they compensate for their lack of influence and recognition unavailable through other means.

The "Incident"–Why Become a Member of a Gang?

There are many factors that may explain the incident. Bjørgo (1997) has shown that several of the Norwegian boys who later became skinheads usually had experienced a period where they were harassed by fellow pupils and excluded from friendships. This motivated them to seek friendships in an environment that would accept them. Their new "family" demands total loyalty, and the code is "one for all, all for one." It gives them strength, a sense of belonging, and recognition. When they dressed up in uniform together and experienced the fear that this created in others, they felt good, and their sense of self was heightened when they saw the fear in the eyes of the old tormentor. To build an identity on creating fear and toughness can represent an alternative for young boys from different cultural backgrounds. Creating fear becomes part of a prestige game and a gender identity game. It works as a protection. Those who seek membership in a gang may be motivated, by low self esteem, harassment, and isolation. As a member of Young Guns once said:

> We were poor, and we were newcomers to Norway. We found each other and made a family. We were all brothers, and we protected our honor. The boys in the Killers were second-generation immigrants. They drove around in BMWs and Mercedes. They thought they were better than us (*sic*), but we wanted to show them who we were, and put them in their place. This is how all this gang business started. We taught them how to respect us, and when they saw us they would tremble. We were happy.

In conclusion we can say that for many individuals who seek membership in violent gangs, pessimism about the future and the lack of legal career alternatives play an important role in explaining both the creation of gangster-dreams and the rate of memberships in gangs. Hyper-honor seems to become an attractive value for gang members and the generation of fear seems equally to be an important instrument to build up and to protect this hyper-honor. It can be motivated by low self esteem and fear of shame. This seems to hold true both for racist gangs and multicultural criminal and violent gangs. At the same time there may be large differences between gangs–their activities, their organization, and ideology among other things–but a discussion of these differences must be the focus of another paper.

REFERENCES

Bakken, A. (1998). Ungdomstid i Storbyen, NOVA-Rapport 7/98.

Bjørgo, T. (1997). Racist and Right Wing Violence in Scandinavia, Tano Aschehoug.

Durkheim, E. (1979). Suicide: A Study in Sociology. London: Routledge and Kegan Paul.

Gautun, H. (1996). Voldens Ansikt. Ungdoms Erfaring Med Vold i Oslo og Landkommuner, FAFO-rapport 189.

Klein, M. (1995). The American Street Gang. Its Nature, Prevalence and Control. New York: Oxford University Press.

Lien, I., and Haaland, T. (1998). Vold og gjengatferd. En pilotstudie av et ungdomsmiljø. NIBR/UMV-samarbeidsrapport.

Lippe, H. von der (1993). Strategiker i forhold til gjengdannelser og vold ved skolene og i enkelte fritidsmiljøer i Oslo. Foredrag, Barne og Familiedepartementet.

Moore, J.W. (1990). Gangs, drugs and violence. In M. de la Rosa, E.Y. Lambert and B. Gropper (eds.), Drugs, and Violence: Causes, Correlates, and Consequences. NIDA Research Monograph 103:160-176.

Nisbett, R.E., and Cohen, D. (1996). The Culture of Honor. The Psychology of Violence in the South. Boulder, CO: Westview Press.

Riches, D. (1986). The phenomenon of violence. In D. Riches (ed.), The Anthropology of Violence, pp. 1-27. Oxford: Basil Blackwell.

Thrasher, F. (1927). The Gang. Chicago: University of Chicago Press.

Chapter 12

STREET GANGS AND CRIME PREVENTION IN COPENHAGEN

Arne Stevns
Copenhagen Police Department, Copenhagen, Denmark

DEFINITION AND CHARACTERISTICS

In the fall of 1998, a committee under the Danish National Police commissioner issued a report on street gangs in Denmark. In its report, the committee defined a street gang as a group of youngsters who commit crimes and/or violate the peace by intimidation and aggressive behavior in public areas. This rather broad definition helps to describe a phenomenon that has given rise to growing public concern and fear.

The gangs in question normally do not have any fixed organization, hierarchy or membership ties, but can be characterized as having situational leadership, floating "membership" and reasonably good solidarity, allowing them to generate fear in the neighborhoods and city centers. The types of crime include street robberies, violence, threats, malicious damage, attacks on police officers, thefts and extortion.

There are about 15–20 street gangs in Copenhagen, consisting typically of 5–20 members between the ages of 15 and 20 years. The majority of the youngsters have ethnic minority background. They come from families that are poorly integrated. They generally lack education and jobs and feel marginalized and discriminated against. A typical street gang consists of **key members** who act as leaders in the instigation of crimes; **members** who are active in crime

M.W. Klein et al (eds.), The Eurogang Paradox, 175–179.

and benefit from the solidarity in the peer group and their status as gang members; and **hang-arounds** that often take part in confrontations with the police.

STRATEGY AND APPROACH OF THE COPENHAGEN POLICE

Investigation and prosecution of crimes committed by street gangs has high priority, but it is recognized that this approach alone cannot solve the problem. In order to establish better knowledge, understanding and rapport with the youngsters in the threatened neighborhoods, problem-oriented community policing has been strengthened. In close co-operation with local social authorities and schools that normally have good knowledge of the youngsters, their families and their social-economic situation, the police determine if a crime prevention initiative should be established. Such initiatives should aim at socially stabilizing the youngsters in order to help them through a realistic education program with good job prospects.

A major problem has been that the authorities could not exchange confidential personal information. This has been resolved by an addition to the Administration of Justice Act, whereby such information can be given if it is necessary for crime prevention purposes under the condition that information received by the police must never be used for investigation purposes.

EFFECT

After several years of increase in crimes committed by youngsters with ethnic minority background, 1998 saw a change in this trend. The crime rate among these youngsters dropped by 16%. Whether this can be ascribed to our crime prevention initiatives, prosecution, the lower unemployment rate or the drop in the number of teenagers is hard to tell, and few external evaluations have been attempted on the effect of crime prevention.

One highly resource-intensive crime prevention project in Copenhagen has been evaluated by external evaluators Annette Leleur and Frank Robert Frank Pedersen. Another project is currently being evaluated. Since both programs seem to deal effectively with street gangs, a short description will be given of the Dog Sledge Project and the Jobmotivating SSP (school, social authorities and police) Project.

THE DOG SLEDGE PROJECT

The Dog Sledge Project was initiated on September 1, 1993, as an interdisciplinary project between social and school authorities and the police. It was targeted against a street gang of 40–60 youngsters of Danish origin between 13 to 21 years of age. The gang had American street gangs as role models and was called "Raiders." The project was divided into four phases.

1. The starting point was to introduce the whole gang into the project, since the gang supplied the youngsters with their most important social network. Rather than trying to destroy this network it was decided to build on it and change its negative aspects to positive behaviors. After 3–4 home visits to their families, 47 youngsters joined the project. Many explained that the big attraction was that it involved the youngsters that they already associated with. When the first were recruited the rest followed easily. The youngsters were divided into groups of 5–7. Each group was supplied with a "Bonus Pater," a personal adviser, who was to act as a "good parent" on a 24-hour basis. The Bonus Paters, who were working in their spare time, came from the police, school, and social authorities, and had agreed to stay with the project until the end. The Police Youth Club, of which I am chairman, paid them. The evaluation showed that the police officers were extremely well suited for this role. Every effort was made to provide concrete services to the youngsters and their families in connection with job hunting, education, housing, etc.
2. The second phase, after trust had been established between the Bonus Paters and the youngsters, was the signing of a contract by the parties and the parents. The purpose was to make the demands and expectations of the youngster visible, such as staying away from crime and attending school/other education.

   The sanction for committing crimes was exclusion from the project. This sanction was modified during the project. Exclusion was not always necessary as the close contact between Bonus Pater and the local police station gave the Bonus Pater the possibility of confronting the youngster with criminal or unacceptable behavior immediately after the incident. The confrontation between Bonus Pater and the youngster had the necessary effect since it was accepted as a breach of trust and the youngster was genuinely embarrassed.

The contracts also held out the prospect of a trip to Greenland in connection with concluding the project. This phase focused on co-operation, competition, team building, attitudes and developing the skills and knowledge necessary for embarking on a Greenland tour.

3. Phase 3 was the Greenland expedition. Evaluation has shown that this was a rather expensive and unnecessary part of the project. The purpose had been to attract the youngsters to the project and give it a clear ultimate purpose, but it was later established that the tour was not a motivating factor of any significance.
4. Phase 4 was the termination of the project in the summer of 1995 and the transfer of the youngsters as a group to the established youth clubs. This part was not planned nor executed well enough.

RESULTS

There was a dramatic drop (more than 60%) in criminality among children and youngsters in the neighborhood. Of the 47 youngsters from the project, 34 got jobs or attended school. Eight were still unemployed and five have disappeared. Fifteen of the 47 later committed crimes but not of the same serious nature as before the project.

The evaluator recommended:

- group therapy
- the Bonus Pater component
- the use of police officers as Bonus Pater
- the recruitment method and
- the activity program.

These recommendations have been used in the current program targeted against a street gang of youngsters of ethnic minority background.

THE JOB MOTIVATING PROGRAM

This program, which is a joint venture between schools, social services and police (SSP) has targeted a group of approximately 30 youngsters with Muslim backgrounds coming from families that are generally poorly integrated into Danish society. They live under difficult socio-economic conditions with unemployment, lack of education, and unrealistic expectations. Some of the youngsters are heavily involved in serious crime and drug abuse.

The aim of this project is to prevent crime. The method is to stabilize the youngsters socially and secure them education, jobs and self-esteem. As in the Dog Sledge Project, the group has been divided into smaller groups of 5–7 youngsters supplied with a Bonus Pater.

The Bonus Paters are all police officers who use 20 hours a week of their work time on the group. It was decided that working hours should be used since the Dog Sledge Project demonstrated that the Bonus Pater role was so demanding that it was not reasonable to make it a spare time function. Based on mutual trust and confidence, the Bonus Paters are to motivate, help and support the youngsters' social stabilization and education. They ensure that the educational program corresponds with the skills and interests of the youngsters who often have difficulties with theoretical education.

Cooperation with the families is of vital importance, but experience has shown that this can be difficult since these parents, out of pride, often refused to admit that their children are criminal. For this reason, an ethnic minority teacher who had primary knowledge of the families and their attitudes introduced the Bonus Paters. It has been possible for the Bonus Paters to establish good relations with the families and win the confidence of most of the youngsters.

As in the Dog Sledge Project, the police officer effect has been beneficial and a notable decline in the antisocial and criminal behavior has been seen. Based on interviews with the local police, schools and youth clubs the neighborhood has become considerably more peaceful. The project will finish at the end of August 1999, at which time an external evaluation report will be made by the same team that evaluated the Dog Sledge Program. The social authorities in Copenhagen are presently planning a similar program targeting approximately 200 youngsters in Copenhagen who seem to have turned their back on schools, education, work and society.

Chapter 13

PATTERNS OF ETHNIC VIOLENCE IN A FRANKFURT STREET GANG[1]

Hermann Tertilt
Dresden Bank, Frankfurt, Germany

Abstract: This paper analyzes the relationship between ethnic violence and the social position of those belonging to a Turkish street gang in Frankfurt. The relationship is examined through a discussion of the cultural values that inform the gang's thefts of leather jackets worn by young Germans and the explanations provided by the gang members for their aggressive acts. Their violence is a response to the segregation, degradation and humiliation that these young Turks experience as "foreigners" in Germany. Their rationalization can be understood as attempts to justify their violence and to ignore the viewpoints of their victims.

I have my own rights my own rules
I have my own fights my own fools
I know my friends and my enemies
I know who I am and how to be

If you punch me I'll punch you back
Punching you I'll swing my flag
I'm a warrior against the time
My weapon is my lyric and my power is my rhyme

There are some, they don't understand me
They think I'm running for money
But I won't cry when I am sad
And I won't run when I'm afraid

M.W. Klein et al (eds.), The Eurogang Paradox, 181–193.

I'm not the black man
I'm not the white man
I'm just the type between them
I'm a Turkish man in a foreign land

INTRODUCTION

This rap was originally written in English by a sixteen-year-old Turkish boy, Hayrettin, who lives in Frankfurt. He was a member of the Turkish Power Boys, a street gang formed at the beginning of the 1990s. His group became known more for violent attacks than for raps or lyrics. The best example of such violence was a series of muggings in the autumn of 1990. In more than 40 cases, the police at this time accused the members of the gang of brutally beating up German youths and of stealing their jackets.

Since the end of the 1980s, gangs such as the Turkish Power Boys have appeared in almost all the big German cities. They are characterized by brutality and street crimes. What is new about this gang phenomenon in the German Republic is that the gang recruits sons of immigrant families and proclaim to the world their ethnic identity. At the beginning of 1990, only five such groups existed in Frankfurt. During that year, this number increased to 25. The police estimated that by the end of that year some 500 youths had organized themselves into violent cliques in the city. Some of these gangs used the names of their parents' home countries and identified themselves in nationalist terms (Croatia boys, Italy boys, Russ boys, Turkish Power Boys). Other gangs reflected local Frankfurt districts in their names (Ring Boys, Ginnheimer Posse, Süd Boys, Ahorn Boys, Sinai Boys). Yet others formed their gang names without reference to any territorial origin (Le Mur, La Mina, Los Desperados, Los Lobos, Bomber Boys or Club 77). In all these gangs male youths of the second immigrant generation are represented, occasionally in a multi-ethnic composition. The majority of members were Turkish youths, with Germans playing, according to the police, "an absolutely unimportant role." It is clear from the contemporary context that the Turkish Power Boys did not originate as an isolated phenomenon but were part of a whole immigrant subculture dominated by Turkish youths.

The German public reacted to the phenomenon of gang violence with shock, incomprehension and disdain. Police controls were strengthened within the city, and the deportation of "criminal foreigners" became not only the subject of political debate but also a reality.

I examined the Turkish Power Boys and their acts of violence over a course of a two-year field study and have presented my conclusions in an ethnography. From early 1991 until the break-up of the gang in autumn 1992 (and after that, in further contact with single youths until 1994), I made very detailed observations of this gang, took part in their daily lives and interviewed them personally or as a group. I spent almost every afternoon with the boys, met them in bars, ate and drank with them, played table football and billiards with them, went where they went, attended their parties, visited their families, their court trials, etc. My interest in the Turkish Power Boys had nothing to do with criminology in the sense of solving their crimes: my goal was to interpret the phenomenon of violence from the subjective perspectives of the youths. I tried to understand how ethnically motivated violence correlates with the social circumstances of the second immigrant generation in Germany.

The first part of this article portrays briefly the two-year history of the gang. It sets the background for an understanding of the second part, in which I deal extensively with the stealing of jackets as an example of ethnically motivated violence. The third part interprets these violent acts. I see in these acts the attempt of immigrant youths to free themselves from the low levels of self-esteem that have been forced upon them by German society.

THE TURKISH POWER BOYS GANG

In the summer of 1990, four schoolboys from a Frankfurt secondary modern school founded the Turkish Power Boys gang. In the course of time, about 50 boys aged between 13 and 18 years joined this gang. The group came into being through a loose network of Turkish friendships, to which a few members of other immigrant groups also belonged–but never Germans! The most striking aspect of the gang's composition was the very different educational backgrounds of the members. One-third of the members attended intermediate school, a third attended secondary modern school, and the rest went to grammar and vocational schools. The last third also included two boys who went to a "special school." The deciding basis for the strength of the relationships among the members was the common experience of growing up as immigrant children in an urban neighborhood, and not, as is usual for other peer groups, educational standards. Their parents occupied the lowest paid trades as unqualified workers (such as refuse disposal, cleaning crew, factory).

The boys did not see their future in Germany as permanent. Through brotherhood within the gang, the youths could face up to, often aggressively, their status as "illegitimate children"[2] in society. Some of the Turkish Power Boys were strongly delinquent, some only occasionally, and yet others not at all. All of them, however, identified with the violence and crimes carried out by the other gang members. The spectrum of delinquencies ranged from petty crime such as shoplifting, truancy, and rowdy behavior to drug abuse and grievous bodily harm, as well as car theft, kiosk robberies, muggings, and other offenses connected with the acquisition of money. However, crime only represented a small portion of the gang's activities. Friendship and solidarity, respect and recognition, masculinity and courage, girls, music, football and billiards were significant to the everyday life of the group, as well as unbearable boredom. During the initial phases of the group's development, there was no apparent hierarchical structure. They collectively practiced jacket theft as important. Bomber jackets with prestigious designer names were much sought after objects. These were held as status symbols by the youths, and were stolen more for personal reputation than for financial gain. Even months after their "infamous" deeds, the boys raved to me about them:

> Ismail: In half a year we made more hits than other gangs made in one whole year. We did that within one month–took so many jackets, took money, beat up guys...
>
> *Why did you do this?*
>
> Ismail: Just for fun. It used to be "in." Everybody did it.
>
> Veli: It shows power, man.
>
> *And from whom do you take the jackets?*
>
> Muzaffer: Above all from Germans.

What types of jackets? A certain kind?

Ismail: Bomber jackets, Chevignons, leathers, we don't care...

Veli: The main thing is the jacket.

Muzaffer: But it has to be a good jacket!

In their crimes the boys followed the overall rule: "Only from Germans! We have always ripped it off the Germans." Opportunities for stealing jackets were offered in public parks or on fairgrounds, though jackets were also stolen in the Frankfurt underground or on streets where the gang had their hangouts, looking for trouble with Germans.

At the end of the first phase of its existence, the gang was shaken by a wave of arrests. Consequently, the gang reorganized by establishing a leadership of four members resulting in the replacement of its initial egalitarian structure by a type of oligarchy. At the same time, the gang's meeting point moved away from the streets to a public youth club.

This second phase of the gang's existence, from spring to autumn 1991, was marked by the leadership's decision to stop the thefts. Instead, the gang started to exchange blows (usually on an "athletic" level) with rival gangs. When "their" youth club closed down that autumn, the gang's meeting point went again somewhere else. They established their hangout at the local community center where they also were no longer under social workers' care. At that stage the gang showed obvious signs of dissolution; the leaders distanced themselves from the others and some members started to consume hard drugs, such as heroin. The drug abuse split the gang into two parties: one that smoked or snorted heroin regularly, the other that rejected drugs.

The ones who became addicted had to face a series of severe personal and social changes. The drug consumption had to be kept secret from family and, in part, even from friends due to a feeling of disgrace. When the parents found out about their child's addiction, out of shame and dishonor the boys often fled their homes. Some would spend days away from home, sleep at their friends' houses or in cheap hotels in the city center. Others had to repeat one class because of regular truancy; again others were suspended from school completely. The drug-taking boys more increasingly had to face the daily burden of addicts, finding themselves in a vicious circle: the need for the drug and the difficulty of financing it. Consequently, the problem of heroin purchase led to drug-related crimes and theft became a part of everyday life again. The consumption of heroin and the drug-related crimes resulted in police investigations, further arrests and court trials. Within the gang, conflicts also arose between the heroin consumers and those who kept their distance from drugs. The addicted among the friends had offended the sense of solidarity by becoming disloyal and unreliable; their appointments and promises did not count anymore. In autumn 1992, the final dissolution of the Turkish Power Boys took place.

My short summary of the gang history shows the interdependence of violence and the structure of the group. Violence had had at first a ritualistic character, but then the behavior very much shifted in connection with the structural transformation of the gang on the whole. With the increase of drug abuse the attacks on Germans served primarily the acquisition of money than–as originally–a humiliation in public.

MAKING *TOKAT*

Initially the Turkish Power Boys had become known for their attacks on German youths; their name even reached beyond the city limits. By using the example of jacket *tokat*, as the boys called the thefts, I would like to discuss the direction which ethnic violence took in practice and the rules that it followed.[3] The expression *tokat* is borrowed from the Turkish and means "slap in the face." In their jargon, however, the boys changed its meaning into "theft of jackets" which they obviously used as a slander against Germans. "Making *tokat*" referred not only to the stealing of jackets but also of other items such as Walkmans, hats, neck chains, wallets, or even bikes.

The leaders of the gang explained to me how they usually proceeded in a *tokat*: generally as a group, or at least in pairs, but never alone. Also characteristic of a *tokat* was its spontaneity. "With me it was like this," illustrated Yildirim. "When I took a jacket I didn't leave the house thinking, 'Okay, today I'm gonna take a jacket.' It was more like; I walk around and somebody walks by and I look at him–that's it, we're gonna take his jacket." The victims of these thefts were nearly always German boys who "could afford expensive jackets." "Especially when it's a German and he's got a little bit shorter hair, like skinheads, then he's worse off than us and so we take his jacket away," emphasized Veli. In the Turkish Power Boys' perception, the roles of victim and perpetrator were clearly assigned according to national origin. Only "Germans" could be victims, only "foreigners" could be perpetrators.

> Hayrettin: The people who make jacket *tokat,* that's always foreigners. And I mean which one of us looks like a German? Nobody! I've been wearing my bomber jacket for six or seven years. And nobody's ever said: "Hey, how come you've gotta bomber jacket...!" Probably because I'm a Turk and nobody gets on my nerves 'cause I'm Turkish.

The provoking of a potential victim always preceded the *tokat.* Veli describes a typical scene:

> Veli: It depends on our mood, you know. If we want to take a jacket then we always act cool and walk on normally, you know. And then when we see a good jacket, a really good one, then we'll go up to you and talk to you. And I say, "Hey, don't I know you from somewhere?" I've done that before. "Aren't you so and so?" and stuff. And then: "Take your jacket off, you asshole!" If he doesn't do it, then we beat him up a bit. And then he has to take it off. That's how it goes.

If the victims were intimidated by such provocations, and reacted with anxiety, they would be forced by further threats to hand over their jackets. "Then you say, 'Take off your jacket!' And if he doesn't do it you punch him, and then he takes if off anyway. So it would be cleverer for him if he took his jacket off straight away before he gets punched." To enforce the intimidation, the boys also used weapons, such as knives or pistols, or they simply grouped around and administered fear by simply outnumbering their victims.

Whoever tried defending himself and refused to take off his jacket straight away had to count on a beating up. "We even like it when somebody tries to defend himself," emphasized Muzaffer and justified this by saying, "When we take the jacket and the guy doesn't defend himself, then we don't have fun. It's more fun when you get a punch yourself. Then you get aggressive quicker and punch back."

Without doubt, the boys' accounts were not at all exaggerated; they tell of petty theft true to reality from the perpetrator's point of view. In the court trials, the witnesses' statements and confessions gave similar impressions of these violations. I would like to quote from one of the recorded jacket thefts reported in a ruling against one of the gang members:

On the evening of the 15th of August 1990, the accused Dogan, in accompaniment of further members of the Turkish Power Boys, (one of which, Biçakçi, was tried separately) demanded the surrendering of jackets from witnesses Krüger, Weiß, and Kopp at about 20.15 during the journey from Festplatz to City Centre on the tram line 18. Biçakçi knocked witness Weiß's baseball cap off his head and asked the witnesses Krüger and Kopp whether their baseball jackets were authentic. As he pulled the witness Krüger's jacket from behind to look at the label, the witness stood up, upon which Biçakçi hit him twice flat-handedly on the right cheek. Then Biçakçi pulled the right sleeve of the witness' jacket while two accomplices standing behind the witness pulled the witness's arm up behind his back. All participants tore the jacket from the witness's body and left the tram at the next stop.[4]

The victims, according to the boys, normally reacted defensively and tried to calm them down in order to avoid a conflict. "Most of them are shit-scared," described Arif as the usual pattern of reaction. The German youths tried to prevent a clash by saying, "Hey, knock it off, hey stop it, quit it." The boys were very well aware of the humiliation they imposed on their victims. Their motives for the *tokat* seemed trivial. "We only do it to have fun," reasoned Veli. "We go out, see the guy with the jacket, take the jacket, and are happy, you know." The act of taking the jacket must have been especially satisfying. "That was the greatest. Everybody did it," Safir described the situation, "because those rich Germans, they had the Chevignon-jackets."

I asked the boys whether they could justify their actions. On the one hand their motto was: "I don't give a shit if a German gets his jacket stolen or not." On the other hand, however, some of the boys had a guilty conscience and showed sympathy towards their victims.

> Muzzafer: Like I took a jacket and at night–I swear to God–sometime I couldn't sleep, you know, 'cause I took the jacket. I always said to myself, "Hey, how would it be if somebody came up to you and wanted your jacket, you know? How would you feel?" Sometimes I thought about that in the early morning. I couldn't sleep on the nights when I ripped someone off.

To identify with the victim was obviously one of the largest psychological hindrances to being violent. However, Hayettin and Ismail did not agree with Musaffer's account. They tried to provide a moral justification for the *tokat* and created from their point of view the social context in which they seemed to justify their violence.

Hayettin: I never have a guilty conscience. I mean, that's life, c'est la vie. Every guy in Frankfurt knows that if he buys a Chevignon-jacket it might get stolen. You shouldn't buy a jacket if you don't have the right friends. That's life: You've gotta look at it like that. Some are born as Turks in a dangerous neighborhood, in a bad area. Someone else is born a German. That's why! Look. I have my friends. I make jacket *tokat*. And people are scared of me. That's life. One guy is born a black and is called a "nigger," but he beats up whites. And the whites are scared of him. But they say "fucking nigger" anyway.

Ismail: And they say "fucking Turk" to us. Okay, they're right–we are bad. But there are other guys too who are really nice. And they say "fucking Turk" to them too 'cause other Turks do bad things. When they say "fucking Turk" then they mean every Turk, you know. But there are Turks who are okay. They don't do bad stuff, they go to work, go to school, have their own friends. And they say "fucking Turk," "wog," "get out of Germany," "we don't want to have you here!" That's how the whole crap started, you know.

Hayrettin: I wouldn't say that. I say the Germans started it. Say, ten years ago the Germans started it. "Turks take away our jobs, our houses..."Not because of the beating-up, making *tokat*–that didn't exist back then. This is how they started: "fucking Turks." They made that up. And then the Turks answered: "You say fucking Turks to us so then we start fucking you: take your jacket off!" That's how it started. Now of course the Turks are worse because they exaggerated it all. I have to admit it even thought I'm a Turk. But when someone says "fucking Turk" to me then I really feel like going and beating him up.

What is remarkable about this discussion is the concept of social reality behind *tokat* which Hayrettin and Ismail evoke. It is based on the construction of two classes whose respective affiliation is determined by birth. Both classes struggle against each other. Xenophobia on the one hand and ethnic violence on the other characterize the two fronts. Ethnic violence appears to be a legitimate way of self-maintenance in this scenario; it is one way of dealing with conflicts by answering to humiliation with humiliating aggressiveness. The evocation of two antagonistic classes is indicative of the social situation in which the boys are part of an ethnic minority. In the same way, this construction also neutralizes the scruples of being violent and helps the boys to ignore the victim's point of view.

DISCUSSION

At the beginning of my field study, long before I gained a comprehensive impression of the extent of the delinquency and whilst trying to get close contact to the gang, I was frequently confronted with violence myself. My first contact with the Turkish Power Boys took place in January 1991 in a youth club where the boys used to meet. At this first occasion I was threatened and attacked without having delivered any appropriate motive. I could not explain to myself why I had become a target to their verbal and physical attacks. The boys' violent provocation remained a mystery to me and I could only put it down to pure bloodthirstiness. Naturally, I had tried to explain it to myself by thinking that the boys wanted to test the water with me to determine what my reaction as an outsider would be. However, these rationalizations were anything but satisfactory given the great number of attacks.

Only the method of participant observation and dialogue with the boys allowed me more and more to gain an understanding of their violence. The process of establishing such a dialogue was difficult due to distrust and hostility. Later, in a conversation with one of my attackers, it became clear to me why I had been violated. He justified it by pointing out that Germans were treated in Turkey "like kings," whereas the Turks were treated "like niggers" in Germany. It was made apparent that his aggression was not addressed to my own behavior, but to my status as a German, a representative of the ethnic majority.

Before I was able to consider the relationship of dominance and subordination between the German majority and the Turkish minority, I followed up one other approach. The correlation of foreign behavioral patterns with "cultural values" might be a prejudice of my profession: cultural anthropology. I myself tended to apply this type of interpretation. While I was gaining more and more security within the gang, I got to know the masculine bearings of the boys; the challenging, boastful *machismo* with which they carried out conflicts. I was sure I could find a connection between their virile *habitus* determined by their Turkish background and the group's violence. The strongly developed consciousness of *machismo* on the Turkish part and the weak one on the part of German youths seemed to me to cry out for disaster. This cultural (mis)interpretation prevented me from discovering the other side of the already sovereign and seemingly superior gang members. Not until one year later, when we were sitting over our fourth beer, did I learn how the status "foreigner" damaged their self-esteem. It seemed to me that the boys had incorporated the degrading picture of themselves with which they were confronted in German society. However, the boys could not admit to this, neither in the gang's daily life nor in front of my microphone. On the contrary, they told anecdotes about their violence with an attitude of detachment. To them brutality was a matter of course and hardly questioned in respect of the victim.

The court and police records make evident the considerable brutality with which the boys committed their crimes. The following case is an excerpt from a police record and documents the progress of a conflict:

> Around 18.40 the accused, Koca, situated himself in the path of witness Neumann, who was riding along Burgstraße on his mountain bike. As the witness got off his bike the accomplices of the accused circled the witness. One of the unknown assailants [not all perpetrators were identified–H.T.] pressed a knife against the victim's thigh and another held a pistol in his hand. The accused, Koca, took the victim's walkman, gold chain with pendant, as well as a ring. Then the accused, Karadeniz, hit the witness Neumann in the face, pulled him off his mountain bike and grabbed the bike. The unknown assailant with the pistol grabbed the victim by the T-shirt. The accused Çevik kicked the victim karate-style once in the nose and once in the back. He also "head-butted" the victim, breaking his nose.[5]

In many instances it was characteristic that the progress of punishable acts did not follow the pattern of challenge and reaction, i.e., this was not a defense of one's honor. Violence was rather targeted at the humiliation of the victim. The victim was brutally "head-butted" after he had been robbed. If the attack had purely been instrumental in getting their "loot" it would have been enough to leave the boy alone.

The gang members repeatedly used the "crooked" glance from the Germans as a motive for an act of violence. From this glance they automatically inferred a contemptuous image of themselves. Striking out meant a legitimated striking back at the Germans. At least, some of their accounts indicated this. With phrases like "I'm gonna give it to him now" or "got no respect for the Germans," "don't talk, just punch him in the face, just punch" they projected their own humiliation onto their victims. The Germans were faced forcefully with the same degradation with which the boys associated their own low self-esteem. Thus the stare of Germans remains significant as a banal trigger for violence. "Then they all look at us as if we are the biggest thieves," Muzaffer claims as he describes the start of a violent conflict between Germans and gang members. He continues by saying, "So I went up to him and said, 'What are you staring at? Something up, or what?'"

I consider the violence resulting from such situations as an attempt by the Turkish Power Boys to become liberated from a damaged self-image. The idea of revenge is expressed here–a type of equalized injustice–namely the experience of injustice is rewarded with injustice. My interpretation of this violence phenomenon is based on a notion of normal migrant youths that in their violence, react to an abnormal cultural situation. So the German manner of dealing with foreigners by segregation, degradation and humiliation is one of the main factors to consider when explaining the violence of the Turkish Power Boys and other migrant gangs.

REFERENCES

Hermann, L. (1991). Straßenraub in Frankfurt am Main–Gewöhnung an ein versbrechen? ["Street robbery in Frankfurt–Getting used to a crime"] In: Hessische Polizeinundschau, Heft 3/1991, S.9.

Tertilt, H. (1995). Turkish Power Boys. Ethnographic einer Jugendbande [An Ethnography of a Street Gang]. Frankfurt: Shurkamp.

ENDNOTES

1. Reprinted with permission from International Journal on Minority and Group Rights (1997) 4: 341-352. Kluwer Law International. Translated by Léonie G. Avery.

2. In German cities like Frankfurt, nearly half of the juvenile population has a German passport. Thus most of the members of the Turkish Power Boys were born and brought up in Germany but still hold the status of a "foreigner" which is passed on from generation to generation. This systematic form of discrimination and the withholding of rights (such as the right to vote) are based on a social consensus that still clings to the picture of an ethnically homogeneous German volksgemeinschaft.
3. I only witnessed the crimes committed by the gang on exceptional occasions. I gained a great portion of my information through the boys' accounts, newspaper articles, and the court trials that I visited. The boys also allowed me to study their various criminal records. A systematic insight into the complete court trial files was not possible for confidentiality reasons.
4. All information that could lead to a positive identification of any person has been changed.
5. All information that could lead to a positive identification of any person has been changed.

Chapter 14

EVOLUTION OF DELINQUENT GANGS IN RUSSIA

Alexander Salagaev
Kazan State Technological University, Kazan, Tatarstan, Russia

The first time delinquent gangs appeared in Russia was during the Civil War (1918-1921). These gangs were formed by homeless children left without parental care. This kind of gang gradually disappeared with the liquidation of child homelessness in the mid-1920s. In general, the crime rate in the former Soviet Union had been decreasing with some fluctuations since the 1920s up to the mid 1960s.

The economic reform that took place in 1965 gave some independence from the state to the business enterprises in solving internal problems. This situation led to the appearance of unregistered goods production in illegal (or even legal) shops in 1970-1975. Such an activity became a substantial profit source in many regions. A special social group called "cekhoviki" (illegal shop managers) was formed. These criminals had a wide economic network, corrupted connections and special security groups. Physically trained young people of proven ability were needed for these groups. In fact it was a kind of demand formulated by a social class for juvenile gangs. Toward the end of the 1980s, this situation occurred in approximately 40 cities of the former Soviet Union. We would like to examine the phenomenon using the research study in Kazan. Journalists labeled such a situation in Kazan as the "Kazan Phenomenon." Since 1982, the research headed by the author was regularly carried out in the laboratory of Sociology at Kazan State University and was one of the first projects conducted in the former Soviet Union. Kazan was one of the first cities where the phenomenon appeared as well.

M.W. Klein et al (eds.), The Eurogang Paradox, 195–202.

The first gang whose activities were registered by the Kazan police in the first half of the 1970s was called "Tyap-Lyap." Thirty-four volumes of the Tyap-Lyap case were investigated by the Supreme Court of Tatarstan in 1978. Unfortunately, only judicial aspects (i.e. proof of guilt) of the gang activities were stressed during this investigation. I would like to give a sociological interpretation of the case.

The organization developed from neighborhood ties of the youth. Workers made up the majority of inhabitants of these neighborhoods. We can add some statistical evidence from the prosecution report to illustrate the range of the gang's criminal activity. This gang committed more than 60 crimes that were brought to evidence in trial including robbery, armed robbery, extortion, racketeering, fights, beatings, murders and so on. On the other hand, the major victims of robberies and rackets were criminals themselves: the black marketers, cheats, shop assistants who broke the law, and other persons who rarely turn to the police for help. But even those crimes that were known to the Ministry of Internal Affairs and to the Office of Public Prosecutor were unopposed by law enforcement. During the period of the gang's activity, thirty-six criminal cases were concealed by the officials of the Kazan Police Department.

In the beginning, Sergey Antipov (gang leader) organized a boxing club in a specially equipped gym, and soon developed a devoted following of younger boys (generally two or three years younger than he). Soon his group had, as a witness reported, 30-40 members. Gradually, Sergey drew a great number of teenagers into criminal activities and started organizing the gang.

With the gang developing and with the growth of its power and influence in the city, the leaders of Tyap-Lyap began to pursue a policy of usurpation of new territories. Widening of the gang borders occurred: some neighborhood youth groups who enjoyed authority in their region were joined (peacefully or by force) to the major gang as one of its branches in the new territory.

To resist the Tyap-Lyap a gang needs to have a sufficient number of "fighters," have a system of involving teenagers in criminal activities, and have a large-scale organization with strong discipline. So the phenomenon–well organized street gangs, formed on the territorial principle, united in the alliances that came up against each other–remained and began taking on a life of its own.

It is useful to compare and examine the difference between gangs and traditional, "old" neighborhood youth groups. The traditional neighborhood youth groups may be recognized as informal youth peer groups. We know that these unions fulfill a very useful social function. The majority of teenagers are socialized in such peer groups. We also can find a subculture that is more or less common for such neighborhood peer groups. It implies that there are some natural forms of behavior, such as principles of conflict resolution.

We find a different situation among the gangs. A gang in Kazan is not an informal union of teenagers, but an organization with strict norms and a hierarchical structure of administration. The perspective of a gang member does not depend on his personal qualities but it corresponds with his position in the hierarchy:

- "sheluha," "scorlupa" (slang, word for word translation–husk, peel, shell)–15-16 years old;
- "molodiye" (slang, close to "bridegrooms")–17-18 years old;
- "stariki" (slang, close to "old man")–older members.

A teenager's life in a gang is, in many respects, precisely assigned (e.g., as at a factory). He has to know his role exactly and fulfill the functions that conform to his position. Such functional structure provides the inclusion of a teenager in the numerous processes that determine a gang's life. For instance, taking part in the group fights, guarding (patrolling) the territory, providing efficient communications, organizing the meetings of gang members, collecting the "taxes" and so on.

For further understanding of these juvenile gangs it is useful to investigate group warfare. This is one of the key elements of gang life.

Fights with other peer groups played a large role in the lives of the old neighborhood youth. The teenagers built their relationships through these fights, they cleared up "who is who." The fights were conducted under certain norms: only one-on-one, don't beat a guy who is on the ground, fight only to the first drop of blood, don't use any weapons. The group fights were transformed in the following way: from the rituals of the traditional peer groups, to warfare between gangs, to a means for reproduction of the forms of gang organization. The honor code was forgotten; all means to success were suitable. They began to use weapons in the fights and these fights were finally simply turned into group exchanges of gunfire. This model demonstrates the mechanism of the gangs' formation and development to where a gang is considered as a particular form of youth association. Towards the mid-1980s, about 100 juvenile gangs had formed in Kazan. Their relationships were characterized by permanent warfare. During the first half of 1988, for example, five teenagers were murdered in the fights between delinquent gangs. In 1989, there were three more deaths, and two more occurred in 1992. Additionally, there were many more teenagers hospitalized with serious injuries.

In September 1992, a law "not to divide the asphalt" was made. Since this time the wars between gangs have stopped. All the gangs began occupying themselves with some commercial activities and pooling their money in the "obchak" (slang for common money fund).

Nowadays, Kazan has over 20 more or less considerably large gangs. The number of members in these gangs varies from 50 to 200. The majority of gangs are named according to the territories of their activity.

The internal structure of the gangs is constantly changing. Today, the almost army-like system of names (i.e., "scorlupa," "molodiye") that existed 5-6 years ago has stopped being used. Functioning and reproduction of contemporary juvenile gangs are provided by their organizational structure that has a well-defined system of responsibilities and, accordingly, levels of social hierarchy. The relations inside the gangs were changed with the transition from ideology to commercial activity. Every gang consists of the separate "brigades" that have their own specific business. Today nobody is pressed to enter the gang, but far from everybody will be accepted. Every brigade has its reserve of 15-20 juveniles; however, only 3-4 of them will enter the gang in the future. "Nobody comes from outside. All are friends, classmates, or relatives and live side by side. We look at the intellectual and business abilities. But all new members first of all should, of course, be tested..." (according to an authoritative member of one of the Privolzhskiy County gangs).

Discipline in the gangs remains strict. Everybody has to gather at the meeting promptly at the appointed time. If somebody cannot come in time, he must let others know beforehand. Cafes, restaurants and car parks owned by the gang serve as locations for such meetings.

In every organized criminal gang, irrespective of the number of its members, region of activity and type of business, four stable categories can be singled out: leaders, "avtoritety" (members with authority), "razvodyashie" (slang, similar to a person who decides cases, solves different problems, etc.), and "infantry."

Infantry. This stratum consists of the youngest or the strongest guys with dull wits. If the members of other strata get some money from the obshak (common money fund), the infantry has no access to it. Some of these juveniles get money for guarding car parks owned by the gang or fulfilling various commissions: racketeering businessmen, burning a mini-market of a competitor, etc. Besides robberies, brigandages and engaging in drug retail trade could be another financial source. Infantry, as a rule, don't have cars (only the most gifted may "inherit" a broken Lada car from the older gang members).

Razvodyashie. The major business of all the gangs is "razvodit" (slang for problem solving) for various firms that are situated inside (or, if it is possible, outside) their territory. Many businessmen themselves ask gangs for defense or help in the solution of some disputable problem (i.e., claiming a debt, solving a traffic incident). To solve problems is one of the "krisha's" (slang, meaning "a cover") functions. Krisha means gang patronage and defense of the specific business. Subsequently, no more or less serious bargain is concluded without involving krisha. Moreover, big businessmen pay for their own guard or krisha in the person of police.

According to Mr. Nafiev, public prosecutor of the Tatarstan Republic: "A considerable part of state enterprises and 9 out of 10 private businesses, to some extent, are under the influence of organized crime." Often even strong firms are controlled by juvenile gangs.

All small shops and mini-markets pay to one or another juvenile gangs, or belong to them. Thus, street traders pay about $50 per month; small shops and mini-markets pay $150-200 per month. Special attention is paid to those economic spheres where the "black (unregistered) cash" is used (i.e., casinos and marketplaces).

Banks are the major objects of gang activity. The machinery of interaction is very simple: a gang has a credit on preferential terms and invests it in Moscow. If a gang makes up its mind to proceed with the relations, the credit will be returned. If not, which happens much more often, the credit will not be returned. According to bankers, a half of the hopeless debts belong to the gangs.

The majority of Kazan gangs have branches in Moscow, and some have branches even in St. Petersburg. Apart from functioning as krisha, these branches control the investing of gang money. Some gang members settled in these cities; some go from city to city.

Many of the "razvodyashie" have businesses of their own. First, capital can always be taken from the obshak. However, every businessman of this kind pays a definite percent of the profit to his gang.

Members with authority ("avtoritety") constitute the next stratum of a gang. As a rule, these people are 25-30 years old. They enjoy an undoubted respect from every gang member. Every brigade has several (not more than six) members with authority. Together they form the council of a gang. This council discusses the problems that cannot be solved by the leader alone. The key persons in every gang–the "cashier" and the "armourer"–are elected or appointed by the members with authority.

The cashier controls the common money fund of a gang–obshak. Besides the invested money, obshak contains some cash reserves (usually several tens of thousands of dollars) used for urgent needs like bribes and financial support for those who go to prison and so on. Name and nickname of the cashier are kept secret. Money is stored, as a rule, by a cashier's mother, wife, or friends. Besides the cashier, only the leader knows where the obshak is situated.

The armourer manages weapons and ammunition that are not in the hands of other gang members. He is responsible not only for technical conditions of available arms but also for buying new ones.

Leader. All the gangs are characterized by the authoritarian style of management, so a leader is respected, feared, and all his orders are obeyed. One can become a leader only after changing (often murdering) the previous one or creating his own gang. Modern leaders differ from those that existed only ten years ago. Earlier, strengthened prison experience was rated highly. Nowadays the abilities of organizer and businessman are appreciated. The leader's aim is not only to organize people around him, but also to give all these people an opportunity to earn money. A leader draws up a strategy for the gang's activity, solves problems with friendly gangs, and, concurrently, controls the obshak. He also gets the greatest reward.

Personal qualities of these people are as follows: they are not stupid (though the majority have at best secondary technical education), they are energetic, and have the ability to subordinate people. Today, where the generation in the majority of gangs is naturally changed, even leaders are not convicted. Not even occasionally, because no leader commits any offenses. They can only be caught red-handed after carrying unregistered arms or committing an accidental hooliganism, although, according to the new Criminal Code, creating an organized juvenile gang is considered a grave crime.

CONCLUSION

It is clear that the roots of this phenomenon, the great development of youth delinquency, originated from the results of an economic stagnation that occurred in the Soviet Union. Economic stagnation also led to the formation of illegal economic structures that needed people in order to function. This situation had the effect of creating a crisis among the youth toward socialist ideals; especially the youth felt that the system limited individual activities. The reason for the stagnation was the strong control by the Communist Party on all social institutions. This control similarly caused crises in other social institutions, such as the family and the educational system, which added to the development of delinquent gangs.

A gang provides a teenager with the possibility for self-affirmation and self-expression, and this cannot be found as a possibility either at school or in the family and legal economic enterprises. Joining the gang gives a teenager the feeling of a defense. If he is not a member of one or another gang he always lives under the threat of beating, extortion and mockery. But the main cause, in our opinion, is that in many regions the majority of teenagers cannot choose to be or not to be a member of a gang but they naturally find themselves in a gang and they also naturally become accustomed and keep on with it. Today, a whole system of gang regeneration has been formed.

In the past, there was a definite bond between the street world and groups of criminals, but only a few teenagers had been accustomed to the criminal life. This process was conducted through direct personal involvement and with concrete, vital consequences. The evolution of street gangs in the majority of Russian regions went through three main stages: 1) neighborhood peer groups; 2) juvenile gangs with age stratification and fighting for territories; 3) youth gangs with functional stratification that controls specific economic spheres. Nowadays, the gangs control the majority of small, medium and even large businesses. During the last 10-15 years, the personnel of the gangs have remained almost stable, but all the members have become much older. Therefore new generations of juveniles occupy a subordinate position and serve as a reserve for criminal activities of youth gangs.

It is appropriate to consider some peculiarities of the Kazan gangs in a broader context of similar phenomena. For instance, the following are typical characteristics of American street gangs offered by Malcolm W. Klein in his book *The American Street Gang*:

1. they are territorial;
2. they acknowledge themselves as criminally oriented groups;
3. they manifest cafeteria-style crime patterns rather than crime-specific focuses;
4. their structures are moderately cohesive, neither very tight and structured nor quite amorphous;
5. seemingly, they are the products of current or growing inner city areas of poverty, alienation, and discrimination; they display the cultural signs that provide special identification.

As can be seen from the case study of the Tyap-Lyap gang, the majority of these characteristics also apply to the gangs in Kazan. However, discrimination in America is connected with such ethnic minorities as African-Americans, Latinos, Asians, etc. This situation is not so true for Kazan. The "moderately cohesive" structure of a typical American gang is also different from the Kazan gang structure. This latter is characterized by strict norms, clear roles, and hierarchical structure. According to Klein, Tyap-Lyap as well as more than twenty gangs in Kazan could best be compared with the "supergangs" of Chicago–El Ruk'n, Latin Kings, Gangster Disciples–which are seldom found elsewhere.

Chapter 15

YOUTH GANGS IN FRANCE: A SOCIO-ETHNOGRAPHIC APPROACH

Maryse Esterle-Hedibel
CESOIP, Guyancourt, France

Pervasive within the analyses about gangs in France is the question: do gangs *really* exist? The issue is not about adult criminal gangs but about youth groups, what we call in French *bandes.* The confusion is fed by two problems. The first of these is the political use of the concept. The presence of a "gang" in an area is equated with a highly dangerous situation that calls for repressive measures. Regular mass media campaigns insist that youth are manifesting increasing violence.

Conversely, the theories of teenage gangs linked to industrial society imply that in a period of post-industrial society, the most vulnerable youngsters are unable to form organized groups. They are in an anomic situation, so they suffer from *disorganization, exclusion and rage* (Dubet, 1987). The myth of the teenage gang as a very strongly organized group overshadowed the nature of the 1980s-90s gangs as well. In France there is also a tendency to idealize the past, even among scholars, so that the *blouson noirs* (in the 1960s) were analyzed in the 1990s as "real gangs," while in their time they were not considered highly structured groups (Monod, 1968).

However, in the beginning of the 1990s, the supposed disappearance of bands was contradicted by other analyses that discovered gangs in the same places where they were not supposed to exist anymore. Some peer groups, called *posses*, appeared in the cities and suburbs, and were known by several street fights. They originated principally among young Antillians and Africans. The journalists wrote sensational articles about these groups. The phenomenon

M.W. Klein et al (eds.), The Eurogang Paradox, 203–207.

has apparently been exaggerated: I conducted a study in a suburban city where there was supposed to be a gang called "Vicious Sharks," but I did not find one real member. Yet some gangs exist and their reality should not be denied.

As a matter of fact, a movement existed called "Zulus," with some simple rules such as respect for authority of the Queen Candy (Louis and Prinaz, 1990), no stealing or use of violence. This movement did not attain its goal due to the behavior of the youth groups, which were unable to federate and respect the collective discipline of the association. In particular, these groups were attached to their own territories, and the perspective of a sort of suburban federation was not realistic to them.

The ethnographic approach linked to data collected from the police and justice services is certainly an appropriate method for studying juvenile gangs, but few scholars have recently undertaken such studies. Data reported in this chapter were collected from two bands living in two housing projects in the Paris suburbs. The first had forty members, and the second about thirty. Open-ended interviews were conducted, notes were taken following informal exchanges, and participant observation was conducted during the many real-life situations encountered. Drug trafficking gangs exist also, and sometimes become visible because of other crimes and murders committed in retaliation, but we have little socio-ethnographic data on them.

First, we need to have a definition of what a youth gang is. It would be what we call bands (close to what Klein (1996) calls *compressed gangs*). They differ from organized groups, spontaneous groups that evolve out of the latter, crowds and *traditional gangs* as those found in the US. We find them in the lower class, localized in suburbs or cities. They principally gather young boys who all share ethnic discrimination and scholastic failure. When committing offenses, they are amateurish and poorly organized, and they rarely participate in formal trafficking networks. They are characterized by a youth group structure devoid of any adult intervention: group cohesiveness in opposition to the outside world; by delineation of a territory of action–the neighborhood in which they live–and by a definite series of values and norms that vary from those of the rest of society.

The band lives in the present, a present that it stretches to fit the contours of its accession to the mythical attributes of adulthood without going through the phases proposed by society at large. It turns inward to weather the period of crisis that brought it into being. In this sense, it does not help its members to achieve adulthood, but relegates them to a vague future.

It is grounded in the rule of mutual segregation; contacts with the outside world (adults, institutions, and other youth groups) are based on the logic of verbal or physical struggles for power. It is a form of organization that arises in response to the absence of socialization provided for that portion of the lower class youth with the least educational and cultural capital.

In the gangs we observed closely, most of the young people are of Maghrebine, essentially Algerian in origin. In other districts, it is possible to observe various ethnic origin groups. It depends on each peculiar area history, and on similar socio-economic conditions, scholastic failure, and discrimination (both real and perceived). Gang members are bound by a shared history that took shape at the same time as their particular neighborhood. This form of gang organization is only found in a small minority of young people born to immigrants, but its visibility is enormous. Many members come from problem families (marital difficulties, violence, etc.), a fact that partially accounts for their presence in the gang.

Their subculture consists of bits and pieces of their culture of origin and from the culture in which their parents came to live, patched together in a specific type of acculturation. The fact that their family had migrated caused cultural rigidity in the parents, who attempted to enforce a lifestyle that was not operative in their society of adoption: great freedom given to boys and strict control of girls, respect for tradition, and predominance of primary relations over secondary relations. The young people found themselves faced with a paradox: the injunction to conform to a tradition in which the group prevails over the individual, while simultaneously climbing the social ladder following the wishes of their parents. In so doing, they have opted for a strategy of individual social achievement requiring autonomy and independence.

In addition, there was the awareness of the stigma placed on them by their ethnic origins. The gang was formed in reaction to and in defense against the outside world, with a sign reversal of the stigma, making it a part of its identity. Members of the gang had experienced this stigmatization since childhood, concentrated in the formula "young-Arab-delinquent." The forming of gangs by those groups least able to withstand the negative way their reference group is marked may be viewed as a warrior-like expression of the diffuse but not explicit demand for a place in society.

The band subculture emphasizes male values: power, potency, speed, and prestige. To make its values visible, it advances a normative system different from that of the rest of society, which accounts for and justifies the deviant behavior. By enforcing its segregation, the band reifies the outside world. Only when it falls apart can some of its members succeed in communicating and empathizing with that world.

Juveniles in bands are restricted to their territory, which they reconstitute through the accentuation of their distinctive signs when they leave it. They use their vehicles, mostly cars, for short excursions elsewhere (for war expeditions or joyriding) in order to reinforce the group and its virile values. Theft for immediate use corresponds to this objective. The mobility afforded by a car enables them to leave the scene rapidly following a physical or verbal aggression, and to avoid prolonged confrontation.

These gangs take passing possession of the presumed attributes of power and wealth. To do so, they steal for display. Their delinquency is not specialized due to lack of organization of the group. Criminal adult organizations are contemptuous of youth gangs because of this amateurism. This fleeting appropriation maintains the cohesion of the group and does not challenge the overall functioning of society. It also enables these adolescents to ward off the feeling of social uselessness aroused by confrontations with members of the established society.

Cars are instruments for settling scores, symbols of in-group and external power relations, and the expression of sexual potency. The fact that their parents' culture demands that women be respected makes it possible to tolerate the presence of some girls, provided they accept male supremacy. Others may be the object of aggression when the band or a small group is on the town. Girls practice a specific and discreet form of delinquency: theft in supermarkets, falsification of official papers or checks. They don't take part in violent fights.

Recently, some very young teenage gangs have become known for assaults they have committed against other teenagers. Does this represent a new wave of gangs, characterized by a high level of violence and the young age of the participant (13 to 18 years) as well as the presence of very young female gangs? Does this represent a new, increasing phenomenon, or is it only the result of a trend toward repressive actions against deviant youngsters, a trend which would be supported in a journalistic treatment of the problem, by systematically emphasizing the incidents implicating very young boys and girls? The media amplification is certainly a factor to consider, but some data we collected (directly and by local testimonies) seem to confirm the existence of new forms of "mini-gangs" that escape from adult control. These gangs are very young

(13-18 years, some of them girls), with few members, and a tendency to commit physical violence against isolated persons (often as young as they are) or other groups. Understanding these "new gangs" would be a very interesting focus for further research.

REFERENCES

Dubet, F. (1987). La Galere Jeunes en Survie. Paris: Fayard.
Klein, M.W. (1996). Gangs in the United States and Europe. European Journal of Criminal Policy and Research, 4(2).
Louis, P., and L. Prinaz (1990). Skinheads, taggers, zoulous and co. Eds la table ronde.
Monod, J. (1968). Les Barjots. Paris: Julliard.

Chapter 16

OTHER GANG SITUATIONS IN EUROPE

Malcolm W. Klein
Social Science Research Institute, University of Southern California, Los Angeles, California

Street gangs are not common to most European cities, and clearly they do not mirror the stereotypical and uncommon American gangs such as the Crips and Bloods of Los Angeles or the Latin Kings and Black Gangster Disciples of Chicago. Nonetheless, the previous chapters demonstrate the existence of street gangs in various European settings. To deny the existence of such groups is to engage in the behavior of the ostrich, not the owl. Indeed, to illustrate the virtue of not overlooking the obvious, one of the Workshop participants, John Hagedorn, reported the following story, as taken from the Internet. It seems that Sherlock Holmes and his companion Dr. Watson decided to visit the U.S., and in particular the vast reaches of the Western plains, to which they went with full camping gear. On one particularly clear, star-filled night, they awoke to see the great dome of twinkling lights above them. Holmes turned in his bedroll and said,

"Watson, what do you make of this magnificent view above us?"

"Well, speaking philosophically," replied Watson, "I realize how vast the cosmos is, and how miniscule we beings are amidst all this."

"Hmmm," muttered Holmes, "and what else does it make you think?"

"Well, speaking theologically," he replied, "I realize how fortunate we are to be a part of God's great scheme."

M.W. Klein et al (eds.), The Eurogang Paradox, 209–213.

"Anything else, Watson?" Asked Holmes.

"Yes, speaking meteorologically, I can predict that we will have a clear day for our hike tomorrow."

There was a pause, and then Watson asked, "And what does all this above us mean to you, Holmes?"

My dear Watson," came the reply, "Someone has stolen our tent."

Van Gemert's description of the Crips in den Haag and Rotterdam reveals small, specialty gangs among marginalized minorities (some minorities in Holland are neither marginalized nor gang-prone). Gruter's description clarifies that gangs in den Haag contribute a very small portion of the law-violating youth groups and thus draws attention to their special nature. Lien's description of both native and immigrant gangs in Oslo is complemented by Mares' description of white and minority gangs in Manchester, reminding us that class as well as ethnicity needs consideration. Stevns notes some fifteen gangs in Copenhagen, of which one or two are native Danish but most of which are drawn from the immigrant population of that city.

In Germany, Tertilt's Turkish gang in Frankfurt resembles compressed street gangs in the U.S., different from the Bremen situation offered by Schumann and Huizinga as a counterpoint to Denver gangs. Esterle-Hedibel's description of "amateurish" Algerian youth gangs in Paris, heavily status-oriented and rebellious, remind one of the early descriptions of U.S. street gangs by Thrasher, Miller, and Cohen. They contrast remarkably with the gangster groups offered by Salagaev in Kazan, groups that have evolved out of more traditional gang structures of the prior decade.

These gang depictions do not, however, exhaust the street gang situations in Europe. In an earlier paper (Klein, 1996), I noted other locations where expert opinion claimed the existence of gangs in the years around 1990, and in several instances I made personal observations of these. Kazan, for instance, is not alone in having a youthful street gang history, as other Russian writers have listed eight additional Volga region locations. In London there are and have been gangs of Indian, Pakistani, Chinese, and Afro-Caribbean origins. Hans Werdmölder (1997) has provided a close-in view of a mixed Dutch and Moroccan street gang in Amsterdam, following them over a period of several years. In Stuttgart, and even Zurich, small street gangs have appeared, including young apprentice groups labeled "Toy Gangsters" by the police there. In Berlin, the police gang intelligence unit and a gang worker social agency in the Kreuzberg area alerted me to several Turkish gangs whose structure strongly resembled that of traditional American gangs. One Workshop participant confirmed the existence of such gangs as the Bombers and the Thirty-Sixers (whose graffiti I observed) but noted they had faded away in the mid-'90s. I have since been informed of other currently active gangs in Berlin.

In Stockholm, as I noted in Chapter One of this volume, clear evidence of street gangs emerged in the early 1990s, most of them of mixed immigrant ethnicity, but including a few native Swedish groups as well. The descriptions suggested variations around the compressed and specialty structures seen in the U.S. Whether they have now melted away or are simply not the focus of attention is not clear.

Finally, during Workshop discussions it was suggested, albeit with minimal research evidence, that one might currently find gang-like structures in Munich, Liverpool, Budapest, Warsaw, St. Petersburg, and Athens. Badly needed at this point is some sense of the economic, geographic, and demographic parameters of European cities that might make them more and less vulnerable to street gang formation. What are the ingredients that, unhindered by public policy or unanticipated good fortune, would more likely lead to a gang-spawning city, or section of a city to be more exact?

American gang theorists have suggested such parameters: interstitial or transitional urban areas, marginalized minority populations, radically declining legitimate economic resources for young people, disorganized communities, especially with entrenched adult criminal systems. In *The American Street Gang* (1995), I suggested two broad causal complexes to explain the enormous proliferation of gang-involved cities in the U.S.

The first of these was a set of structural factors as suggested by William Julius Wilson's (1987) description of the urban underclass. As these impinge on a neighborhood, they create mediating variables that eventually yield the proximal requirements of gang formation–"sufficient numbers of lower class, minority males, aged 10 to 30, hard to employ, in an area featured by high crime, absence of social controls, and absence of alternative activities" (Klein, 1995:198). Added to these were reinforcing or maintenance variables such as oppositional structures (e.g., hard-nosed police and school systems), group rivalries, perceptions of barriers to social advantages, and misguided gang intervention programs. Are there European cities that fit such a pattern? Some Workshop participants thought so, while others were skeptical. This question assumes major focus in plans for future European gang research.

The second causal complex is what I have loosely referred to as the diffusion of gang culture, a pattern that increasingly becomes confused with or even incorporated into modern youth culture. Thanks to media portrayals–movies, television, and news stories as well as "gangsta rap" music–it is said that almost any child in America knows how to walk, dress, and talk like a gang member. "He walks the walk and talks the talk," as the saying goes. The result is that many youth try on the mantle of gang member, and many groups toy with gang-like behaviors. Many find the fit uncomfortable and desist. Others, however, find rewards in gang activity and adopt its style and, eventually, the reality.

Can this happen in European cities? Yes, it can. In Stockholm and in Berlin, American style gang graffiti are easily observed. Van Gemert's Dutch Crips read American gang biographies and offer photos of themselves looking like typical show-off Los Angeles Crips, tattoos and hand signs and all.

In noting these potentials for gang formation, I am not suggesting that I want to find gangs in Europe (as was suggested by one or two Workshop participants). What I want to do is to demonstrate that they have emerged here and there, and may well continue to do so. I believe Europe, with due care, and should move beyond the denial stage because we may now know enough to identify gangs that do exist (as differentiated from other youth groups). Further, we may now know enough to anticipate where they may emerge in the years ahead and to take precautionary counter-measures to minimize their growth and effect. Housing and employment patterns for marginalized populations can be planned; employment opportunities for youth can be manipulated; media portrayals can–voluntarily–be limited and adjusted so as to minimize the glorification of street gang styles. Well-intentioned, but misguided intervention practices, both by law enforcement and social welfare services, can be informed by the unhappy experiences in the U.S., and carefully planned research into these issues can be implemented without calling undue attention to it in the media.

REFERENCES

Klein, M.W. (1995). The American Street Gang: Its Nature, Prevalence, and Control. New York: Oxford University Press.

Klein, M.W. (1996). Gangs in the United States and Europe. European Journal on Criminal Policy and Research 4(2):63-80.

Werdmölder, H. (1997). A Generation Adrift: An Ethnography of a Criminal Moroccan Gang in the Netherlands. The Hague: Kluwer Law International.

Wilson, W.J. (1987). The Truly Disadvantaged. Chicago: University of Chicago Press.

PART III

INTRODUCTION TO PART III

In the following chapters, we deal more directly with the puzzle of fitting street gangs into a broader group context. It is an issue we will address in Part IV as well.

The final chapters by editors Maxson and Weitekamp are summative, suggesting patterns and implications for the study of gangs emerging from both parts II and III. The preceding chapters engage the gang versus youth group distinction in three ways. Both Hakkert et al. for the Netherlands and Sarnecki and Pettersson for Sweden look at group-related crime patterns. Neither chapter considers the gang issue, except that the Swedish paper is explicit in noting that network analysis of group-related criminal arrests gives no hint of gang relationships. For the editors, both papers inadvertently clarify that to study co-offending or group patterns of crime may have little to do with the study of gangs; as we have noted elsewhere, we take street gangs to be quite a special topic.

Two of the papers, those by Kersten on German groups and Dekleva on Slovenian groups, remind us that there is an even broader but still relevant context, one of youth cultures. Kersten points out that soccer hooligans (almost unknown in the U.S.) and neo-Nazi groups are as different from each other as each is from those he terms neighborhood cliques (some of which take on street gang attributes). The most shared characteristic Kersten finds, beyond the age factor, is the emphasis on masculinity. For Dekleva, the Slovenian situation is subtler, as indigenous and immigrant cultures co-exist in part through the medium of a general youth culture and its musical and stylistic facets. The ambiguity of the "Chefoors" as an emerging group or subculture and as a pre-gang phenomenon captured special attention at the European Workshop. Some participants were later heard to call out to one another, "Hey, Chefoor," much as our American gang member might call to his peer, "What's up, Cuz?"

The other two chapters raise the same sorts of questions, but from situations in which gangs might indeed seem to exist. In Bremen, Schumann and Huizinga describe groups of youth that, using identical methodologies, would be acknowledged to be gang members in Denver. Differences in crime seriousness and drug involvement are carefully noted. The similarities are such that, given the authors' own hesitation to apply the gang label, we invite the reader to conclude whether or not the Bremen schools contain street gangs.

M.W. Klein et al (eds.), The Eurogang Paradox, 217.

Similarly, Vercaigne is very cautious in applying the gang label in Brussels, and describes the patterns of gang reportage by the local media. At the same time, she notes that the law enforcement community has developed a gang typology that her data suggest is rather unstable over time. Does Brussels have gangs, or groups that are learning to be gang-like, or groups that are gangs only in the minds of enforcement officials and the media? This concern, one of what has been called a possible "moral panic," will be addressed in Part IV.

This would seem to be a good time, then, to amplify what we believe is implied by the term, street gang. Definitions continue to fail; for each one proposed, exceptions are found. Narrow conceptions ignore relevant counterparts, while broad conceptions become too inclusive. Street gangs are, after all, **informal** youth groups in large part self-formed and self-defined as well as defined by different elements of their communities. Most have no constitutions and by-laws, no rosters of dues-paying members, no organizational charts, no archived histories.

Still, we can get a reasonable handle on the large majority of street gangs by adding to their placement on structural dimensions as described in Chapter 1. We can characterize the usual–but not a universal–street gang by reference to common research data.

Street gangs are:

- mostly male, but usually with female members
- mostly minority by race, nationality, or ethnicity (and almost always comprised of alienated or marginalized youth in any case)
- mostly youthful (ages are reported between pre-teens to forty or more, but typically in the adolescent and early adult years)
- often territorial and street-oriented
- mostly self-recognized as a group, even as a special group
- mostly oriented toward criminal activity, but with considerable variation in the level of such activity
- somewhat stable over time, generally from one to many years.

These characteristics, at least, receive wide consensus among gang researchers. Many would add the existence of special names, clothing, signs, and other symbols of membership. Some would add the importance of inter-group rivalry. Together, these attributes of street gangs also allow us to exclude from their category certain other groups: prison gangs, terrorist groups, motorcycle gangs, music-driven groups such as rockers, stoners, and so forth. Finally, we can exclude that vast majority of youthful groups–some of them addressed in the chapters of Part III–that certainly are peer groups, clubs, cliques, pick-up and formal teams and the like. These latter groups seem inherent in youth culture–often with some anti-social involvement–but do not measure up to the combination of characteristics listed above and in Chapter 1. With all this, we turn the reader loose on Part III to make his or her own judgment about Kersten's skinheads, Schumann's and Huizinga's Bremen school groups, Dekleva's Chefoors, and Vercaigne's groups in Brussels.

The final two chapters by the editors are provided as guideposts for such judgments. Maxson's plea for more informed approaches to comparative research should help if undertaken seriously. The three-stage approach she recommends can provide a solid foundation missing in much American work on gangs and other youth groups. The Weitekamp chapter specifies the indicators of possible gang-like groups in various European settings–places where such comparative research might prove useful. Further, it places all this in the context of social changes in Europe that might well make such research even more necessary in the near future.

Chapter 17

GROUP CRIMINALITY [1]

Alfred Hakkert, Anton van Wijk, Henk Ferwerda, and Ton Eijken
Ministry of Justice, The Hague, The Netherlands

SUMMARY

A great deal of youth crime is committed in groups, which has been proven empirically for quite some time now. Nevertheless, the group aspect is still paid relatively little attention by the criminal justice system and in the field of criminology. This may be based on the fact that group behavior is more difficult to describe than the nature and characteristics of individual persons.

In its report about the approach to youth crime, written a number of years ago, the Van Montfrans commission also ascertained that the group aspect is often paid too little attention in the approach to this phenomenon. It is only recently that various municipalities have begun to chart the groups of young people held responsible for the majority of crimes committed, this within the framework of the policy on the "hard core" of juvenile delinquents.

There has been relatively little research into the subject of group crime in the Netherlands. Despite a certain common sense about the influence of the group in committing crimes, there is little systematic data on the subject itself. The Stafbureau Informatie, Voorlichting en Publiciteit of the Prevention, Youth and Sanctions Policy Department has now co-operated with Advies- en Onderzoeksgroep Beke to map out this area in more detail. This was based on results from existing research in the Netherlands and further afield, a re-analysis of a self-report study among young people, and a limited number of

M.W. Klein et al (eds.), The Eurogang Paradox, 221–229.

interviews with relevant key experts and young people who are members of groups.

RESEARCH INTO GROUP CRIME

The inventory of the research into group crime shows that such research goes back many years. The fact that most youth crime is generally committed in the company of other people became particularly known from the report by Shaw and McKay in 1931. In the 1960s, the most popular theoretical studies into youth crime concerned delinquent behavior in groups and delinquent sub-cultures. From the 1960s onwards, the attention shifted from a study of the gangs, groups and sub-cultures to the study of (individual) delinquent behavior.

The inventory also shows that it is not simple to identify criminal youth groups. Not every youth group is necessarily a delinquent group. Young people have many different reasons for forming a group. Moreover, not every delinquent youth group is a gang.

DEFINITION OF YOUTH GROUPS

The establishment of an (operational) definition of groups or gangs has proven to be difficult. The definition of gangs takes into account the fact of whether: (a) the young people see themselves as a separate group; (b) whether other people see them that way (e.g. people living in the neighborhood); (c) as well as whether there is an orientation towards anti-social or criminal behavior which is accepted by the group. This need not be directly related to a great degree of violent crime, a fact that often plays an important role in the popular image of youth gangs.

The studies carried out so far clearly show that it is better to pay attention to the (wider) concept of group crime than exclusively to gang crime. On the one hand, namely, there is little consensus on the definition of a gang, while on the other hand, there is agreement on the fact that gangs only constitute a fraction of delinquent groups.

Currently in the United States efforts are being made to distinguish gangs from other law-violating youth groups. In the Netherlands, we see such a distinction in the Haaglanden police force, which sub-divides the youth groups into various types: nuisance groups, trouble making groups, criminal groups and youth gangs. A group is taken to mean three or more young people who regularly associate with one another. The differences between the types of groups concerns the fact of whether the group members cause nuisance or trouble, or develop criminal activities. However, this distinction is not as simple as it would seem. Behavior such as hanging around the streets in a group and causing trouble for people on the streets is often associated with groups of young people who are not further particularly involved in crime, but criminal groups demonstrate this same behavior.

GROUPS OR NETWORKS

The literature also shows that a study of group crime cannot be limited to youth groups. In committing crimes together, the groups are not essentially large or well structured. The majority of youth crime is committed by two or three persons who have little mutual alliance with their accomplices. A large majority of the young people who are criminally most active, can often be associated with a large-scale network of criminal relations, however. Loosely structured groups can then be distinguished within such a network, in which groups of young people become briefly involved. Another important matter is to trace the central figures in the network, as they are often the leaders who recruit other members and keep the network together.

NUISANCE AND TROUBLE

In the phenomenon of group crime, the nuisance and trouble caused by groups of young people or street loitering plays an important role, and is also the most visible manifestation of group behavior. Figures from the Police Monitor show a slight increase in the number of Dutch people who believe that trouble caused by groups of young people is a common problem. Twelve percent of the population was of this opinion in 1997, compared with 9 percent in 1993. The degree to which this is experienced by the general public varies greatly depending on the area, of course. As one might expect, it is more common in, but not exclusive to, large urban areas. The police in smaller municipalities also regularly receive complaints about troublesome young people, according to police information. Nuisance and trouble making by groups of young people is certainly not a problem for large urban areas alone.

CO-OFFENDERS

On the basis of police figures and analysis of self-report studies among young people, an inventory was made of the extent to which young people committed offenses together with other young people, and which offenses were committed in this manner. This showed that youth crime is often committed in groups but that this does not apply to all types of crimes. Co-offending scores highest in vandalism, drug-related offenses, intimidation, arson and participation in riots, according to the Dutch self-report study among young people. The Dutch research material gives less precise findings on this subject than its foreign counterparts. In the self-report studies in our country, for example, young people were only asked whether they committed an offense alone or with others, while the foreign studies applied a more finely tuned distinction between "always" or "sometimes" alone or with other people. Figures on the size of groups show that offenses are often committed in small groups, often limited to one or two persons. The exception to this rule is the participation in riots or destructiveness, which is characterized by large groups.

SCOPE AND NATURE

It is no simple feat to gain insight into the existence, the scope and the nature of problematic or criminal youth groups. Dutch research in that field often deploys the knowledge gained from key informants. This has shown that a number of medium-to-large municipalities do indeed have insight into the existence of youth groups. However, other municipalities have inadequate knowledge of such groups. Such a lack of knowledge would suggest that group crime is not paid structural attention by the various authorities. Because of this it can as yet not be ascertained to what extent there are youth groups in the Netherlands. This demands further research.

The knowledge that is available from key experts often concerns groups which cause incidents in terms of trouble making, in other words the most visible groups. There is little insight into groups which are less long-lasting in character and less tangible. Key experts also indicate a great variation in the types of groups and their scope. The average scope is between 15-20 persons, but there are also groups of 40 or even 70 persons. Experts indicate that the composition of the groups can change continuously but that there is often a permanent leader or hard core. Interviews with young people confirm this. A small core group ensures the continuity of the group that may be liable to change in terms of scope or composition. Young persons on the outskirts of these groups in particular may well belong to other groups as well. Another striking feature is that young people who are part of a group do not consider themselves to be group members but are certainly seen as being such by the outside world.

Another method of gaining insight into youth groups is by means of further analysis of police files or information from the computerized police information system HKS (recognition service system). Such data can be used to construe networks or circuits of young people who cooperate with one another. Geographic analysis can then be applied to determine whether the networks or circuits are limited to a certain area or whether they have a larger geographic spread over various areas.

In studying group crime, it is important to consult with both key experts and police data. The knowledge held by key experts on criminal young people could be an aid to the analysis of criminal relationships on the basis of police data. The police do not have information on all young people involved in networks or groups, and key experts may well supplement the information not otherwise available.

CHARACTERISTICS AND BACKGROUNDS

An important conclusion on the characteristics and backgrounds of young people who commit offenses in groups is that solo offending increases with age. Also, the mean number of offenders declines with age. In youth groups, the average age is 15-20, with the youth who are members of nuisance groups being younger than those in trouble making or criminal groups.

There are more boys involved in youth crime than there are girls, but if girls commit offenses, they are more likely to do so together with others, preferably in a small group of 2 to 3 persons. Girls are clearly under-represented in youth groups however, and are on average younger than the boys.

There is not yet clarity on whether non-Dutch nationals commit more group offenses than the Dutch youth. They do however work in larger groups on average. Groups that include non-Dutch nationals are usually relatively large, and are also characteristic in that they commit more serious crimes and use violence more frequently.

As regards the general composition of groups, such groups are not exclusively non-Dutch nationals: the information from the Haaglanden police shows that approximately three-quarters of the groups there is of Dutch origin. However, the share of non-Dutch nationals is very high among the criminal groups and youth gangs.[2]

Serious criminal youths, also known as hard core youth, commit offenses more often in cooperation with others than other young people would, and the average group size is larger. Furthermore, it becomes apparent that the young people who commit offenses together with others are more likely to be in trouble with the police than the solo offenders. The reason for this is possibly that group behavior is more noticeable than solo behavior, or there is an increased risk of "shopping" one another.

In the situation in which offenses are committed with other people, these are often "friends." Neighborhood youths are also important to the boys, classmates to the girls and family members to the non-Dutch nationals. However, acquaintances from sports clubs or youth clubs have little influence on the composition of the group. This is also in keeping with the recreational activities of the young people. Loitering is the main activity and is often the result of the lack of alternative recreational options, such as group sports or attendance at a youth center.

It has also been shown that young people who commit offenses together with others are not distinctive from the other young people in their alcohol consumption, but there are differences in drug use. It would seem that the group or the group process not only influences the criminal behavior but also the use of substances. The use of soft/smart drugs is an ideal group activity.

GROUP PROCESSES

Youth crime is often a direct consequence of processes that occur in a group, where the quest for sensation and impulsive behavior is more easily manifested. Young people can also encourage each other and cross certain thresholds. What may begin as an insignificant incident can get out of hand in a group or can suddenly erupt. In a group, one can hide behind others, blaming them for the behavior.

Interviews with young people show that the development of a group is often more of a coincidence than a purposeful act. Initiation ceremonies are scarce or non-existent at most in groups which are systematically involved in crime. The motives behind membership are status and prestige, while the age phase also plays an important role. Belonging to a group allows young people to rebel or be different, but on the other hand offers security and structure. The young people themselves are not so explicit about their motives. They apparently find it important to maintain friendships and enjoy a common recreational activity (loitering).

Departure from a group is mainly related to reaching a certain age. This is particularly true of those groups that cause trouble. This type of group in particular ceases to exist after a while, with only a small portion of such groups surviving. These are mainly the groups involved in serious forms of crime.

In some cases, groups have a **group name**, which functions as a collective identity on the one hand, and distinguishes this group from other groups on the other hand. The police regularly also play a major role in the creation of group names. The reaction by police and society towards young people who are believed to belong to a group works as a stigma and can even reinforce criminal behavior.

Girls are under-represented in groups and generally fulfill a marginal role when it comes to actual criminal behavior. The girls who do belong to groups often provoke the boys and act as catalysts to the boys' behavior (acting tough).

Key experts indicate that there are informal leaders when it comes to decision making and **leadership** within the groups. However, the young people themselves deny that there are leaders. Research into youth groups has shown that in some groups, i.e. in the groups that commit the more serious offenses, there are "instigators." They are often older, male, and have more criminal experience. Incidentally, they do not fulfill such a role permanently. Their role varies per type of offense or per group.

Parents are apparently often not aware of the fact that their child belongs to a group. The main reason is that the group behavior is inherent to the recreational activities of the young people, in which the parents may not be involved, as a matter of principle, at least in the perception of the young people. With due caution, one could suggest that pedagogic powerlessness or indifference by the parents can promote the joining of groups. After all, young people from such families spend more time on the street, so that there is more chance of them joining a group.

The group process can also have an effect on the criminal behavior. It can go from bad to worse. The longer a group exists and becomes closer, the greater the chance of an (autonomous) development in the severity of the criminal acts.

TACKLING GROUP CRIME

Based on the facts that the group and the group process play a very prominent role in committing offenses, it is an obvious conclusion that various organizations that are involved with young people and the maintenance of public order are taking (or beginning to take) the phenomenon of group crime seriously. The charting of this area has shown that there is insufficient local knowledge on existing groups. The acquisition and particularly the updating of this knowledge is an essential precondition for a better understanding of the scope and development of the phenomenon and for a more direct approach to the problem. It is also important that more information be gathered on the composition of the various groups. For that matter, identification of a group is no easy feat, as groups are often of a short-lived nature and the composition is by no means always the same. Key experts also often lack insight into this.

A collective approach to a group is apparently not always the best approach, as this can lead to a group manifesting itself as such in the future. This actually creates a group. A better approach is to tackle group members individually. This brings them out of the shadows of anonymity and deals with their individual responsibility. It is particularly important to pay attention to the central figures (leaders, instigators) in groups or networks.

In terms of a preventive approach, one could think of the deployment of youth work, the organization of activities for at-risk youth or the arrangement of meetings with residents in a neighborhood. The creation of their own place in the neighborhood (to hang around, youth center) where the young people are given a high degree of responsibility for the location allocated to them is certainly also an option. Some experience has already been gained in this matter in the Netherlands. A group approach has also been implemented within a youth prevention project, group learning projects by the probation service, and experimental treatment for young criminals in the youth care system. The experience gained so far in such group-based projects has varied, being both positive and negative.

Another possible approach is to inform the parents of the criminal behavior of their children and the fact that they are group members. A confrontation between victims and perpetrators can also be useful. After all, young people who commit crimes in a group feel less responsible because they can hide behind the group identity. Besides the preventive approach, a repressive approach is also important. This should particularly be aimed at the central persons within groups or networks.

Finally, we must ascertain that not all questions regarding the theme of group crime can be answered as yet, as this report has been mainly compiled on the basis of existing research material. Further research is required, not only at the national level but also locally. It is also recommended to combine various sources of information; the young people must themselves be involved in the research, alongside the information gained from key experts and the police.

ENDNOTES

1 This is the summary from a longer report by the authors, Group Delinquency in the Netherlands, published by the Ministry of Justice, 1998.

2 See the chapter in this volume by Gruter and Versteegh (editors).

Chapter 18

GANG MEMBERSHIP IN BREMEN AND DENVER: COMPARATIVE LONGITUDINAL DATA

David Huizinga and Karl F.Schumann[1]
University of Colorado, Boulder and Bremen University, Bremen, Germany

"BANDE" = GANG?

Are there gangs in Germany? The word "gang" is not used in Germany, but some German words may refer to similar groups of delinquents. For example, the term *Bande* is often used in connection with kids (*Kinderbande, Jugendbande*). However the term *Bande* is also used in the German criminal code to refer to offenses committed by a group of criminals.[2] Apparently this meaning led Webster's German-English dictionary to translate "gang" as "Bande," describing it as an organized group of thieves, thugs, and hoodlums. The penal code of Germany considers a criminal act committed by an organized group of criminals a reason to increase the punishment. If the "Bande" can be called *kriminelle Vereinigung* (criminal organization) the very membership in such a group is punishable. However, these provisions of the penal code are rarely used for prosecution. The use of the words "gang" and "criminal organization" is similar in the U.S., where "gang" may refer to either juveniles or adults, but the most frequent connotation of the word "gang" is probably of a delinquent juvenile gang. Thus, there is some similarity in the connotations of the terms "Bande" and "gang" and reported membership by juveniles in a *Bande* or in a gang may imply involvement in a particular kind of a delinquent group.

M.W. Klein et al (eds.), The Eurogang Paradox, 231–246.

Beyond the semantic analysis it should also be pointed out that there is certainly no gang problem in Germany sufficient to cause fear among the public. However, there are disturbances by youth groups. From time to time police in Frankfurt, Berlin or other metropolitan areas inform the press that gangs have formed, in most cases by immigrant youths, and are causing trouble. However, they rarely persist for a substantial time. Also other features of gangs seem to be missing in those cases, notably territoriality or hierarchical leadership. But then, those features also seem to be lacking in many gangs existing in American cities (cf Klein, 1996:67).

In this paper we address the question of whether there are gangs in Germany by asking: What percentage of young persons in a German metropolitan area report membership in groups they call *Bande*? Are those who do report such membership similar in important respects to those young persons who call themselves gang members in a metropolitan area in the U.S.? Thus we talk about gang membership based on the self-reports of youths rather than by referring to the judgement of police. If a person claims to be member of a gang, or *Bande*, the meaning of this statement is an open question. The person may refer to distinctive features of the particular group to which he or she belongs, e.g., more commitment to delinquent acts, and thus point to major criteria for gangs. The statement may be based on the views of outsiders, parents or police on the particular youth group. It may even verbalize an ideal, based on the myths of the American gang, toward which the group the youth belongs to is striving but has not yet attained. Whatever the basis of this judgement, any group referred to as gang or *Bande* must be at least somewhat different from regular youth groups.

We try to answer the question regarding the presence of gangs in Germany by comparing youths in Denver who identify themselves as members of a gang with youths in Bremen who identify themselves as members of a *Bande,* in two respects. First, does a similar proportion of youths of the same age group and in equivalent risk situations in Germany and the U.S. report that they are members of gangs or *Banden*? Second, do those who call themselves members of Banden or gangs account for a similarly high proportion of the delinquency of the total cohort to which they belong? If such is the case, we would be tempted to conclude that youth in Germany and the U.S. entertain a somewhat similar type of group membership. This type may be called gang or–as many Europeans would prefer–gang-like youth group.[3] To understand this type of group in Germany better, we also present very preliminary descriptive data for gang and

Banden members regarding their group activities in general. Before we report on the findings, we describe the empirical basis of our effort.

METHODS OF THE COMPARATIVE LONGITUDINAL STUDY

The findings are based on a comparative data set derived from two ongoing prospective longitudinal studies in the U.S. and in Germany: the Denver Youth Survey and the Bremen School-to-Work-Cohort Study.

The Denver Youth Survey (DYS) is based on a probability sample of households in a wide range of high-risk neighborhoods in Denver, Colorado. The neighborhoods were selected on the basis of a social ecology analysis of population and housing characteristics associated with delinquency and higher-than-average crime rates. The survey respondents include approximately equal numbers of boys and girls–who were 7, 9, 11, 13, and 15 years old in 1987–and one parent of each of them, who lived in one of the more than 20,000 randomly selected households.

Each child or youth was interviewed annually over a period from 1988 to 1992 and 1995 to 1998. Respondents who moved anywhere in the United States continued to be included in the survey. Each interview was conducted in a private setting and lasted one to two hours. For the purpose of comparison with German data, however, only the two oldest sub-samples are used (ages 13 and 15 in 1987). There are 570 youth in these two DYS subsamples.

The Bremen Cohort Study (BCS) is a longitudinal study of youths that left school at the legally earliest possible time after having completed the compulsory number of nine years of schooling. The cohort consists of all students who left the *Hauptschule* or *Sonderschule* that is from the lowest educational level, in 1989 in the city of Bremen. The mean age of the cohort was 16.6 years (in 1989 at the time of the first wave). Leaving school at this early age and on the lowest educational status poses a particular risk for youths in a "credential society" (Collins, 1979) and is–according to criminological literature on dropouts–correlated with delinquency. The Bremen cohort is thus based on a selection of youths in a high-risk situation. The Bremen cohort has been interviewed four times (in 1989, 1993, 1995 and 1997). The age of the respondents at wave 1 of the study ranged from 15-18 years, at wave 4 (collected in 1997) the age ranges were 24-27 years. The current size of the cohort is about 380 male and female youths.

The comparative dataset includes questions that refer to standard variables in criminological research and are equivalently measured in both sites, as well as variables that have been specifically added to each questionnaire to make the studies more similar. Starting with the third wave of the Bremen study, items from the DYS-questionnaire have been included and vice versa (starting with the 6th wave of DYS). Variables which are measured or recoded to allow direct comparisons include relationship to family (e.g., living at the parental home, relationship to mother and father, control by parents, trouble at home, and attachment to parents), school experiences (e.g., highest grade completed, trouble in school, attachment to school, and negative school experiences), peer groups (e.g., delinquency of peers, gang membership, and time spent with peers), being married, health status, time spent watching TV, life plans, and attitudes towards the future. Both DYS and the BCS use self-reports of delinquency as a dependent variable.

The similarity of both studies (e.g., longitudinal design, sample of youths in a high risk situation, a substantial overlap of equivalent variables on the life-course and its context), has led us to conduct various comparative analyses. Besides the topic of this paper, gang membership, we have looked into the impact of differences in the school-to-work-transition in the U.S. and Germany and are planning a study on the impact of differences in police and court reactions towards delinquency in both countries on secondary deviance. For that purpose we have developed indexes for property offenses, violence, and drug-related offenses as well as a total delinquency index, each of which consists of exactly the same types of deviant behavior.

The two cohorts used in these analyses are similar in age structure and have an almost equal distribution of the sexes (DYS: 50:50; BCS: 55% males: 45% females). They differ, however, on the proportion of minority youth, roughly 90 percent in the DYS and only 17 percent in the Bremen cohort (predominantly immigrants). Also, as already mentioned, the sampling strategy of problem youths was slightly different at the two sites; the DYS is based on high-risk-neighborhoods while the Bremen cohort is based on low educational status. However, even with these differences both samples seem to produce rather equivalent groups of problem youths regarding their prevalence rates of delinquency.

Table 1 indicates that the prevalence rates of all types of delinquency are quite similar for both cohorts. However, American youth seem to commit more acts of delinquency per person. Especially striking are the different frequencies in property offenses and the use of marihuana or hashish. Interestingly, the prevalence for group fights declines in both cohorts but the frequency for those Denver youths that are involved in such behavior increases over time.

The equivalence of both cohorts is quite striking because crime rates in the U.S. are considered so much higher compared to European countries (Shelley, 1985; Lynch, 1995). However, those comparisons are based primarily on index crime statistics. Self-report data show less impressive differences.[4] Our samples of problem youth differ only slightly. In both sites between 34 and 42 per cent are involved in some type of delinquency during any given year. Soft drug use contributes most to the total prevalence and frequency in Denver. In Bremen property offenses have a somewhat higher prevalence.

Table 1: Prevalence of Delinquency among Youths in the Bremen and Denver Cohorts in 1991 and 1994 and Frequency for Offenders

Delinquency	Prevalence (mean)				Frequency (mean)			
	Bremen		Denver		Bremen		Denver	
	1991	1994	1991	1994	1991	1994	1991	1994
Property Offenses	0.27	0.26	0.21	0.16	9.23	5.08	18.01	10.40
Serious Assault	0.16	0.08	0.11	0.10	6.25	2.65	7.61	8.78
Using Hashish, Marihuana	0.13	0.20	0.22	0.29	15.32	24.22	30.12	42.98
Group Fights	0.14	0.08	0.09	0.07	5.96	2.62	7.51	10.61
Total Delinquency	0.34	0.39	0.41	0.42	18.87	20.52	34.90	49.09

There is one final distinctive feature in the design of both studies. The Bremen cohort study has added an ethnographic, qualitative panel study. Sixty persons from the cohort have been interviewed with an unstructured, focused technique five times at interim dates, in addition to the standardized data collection of the cohort study. Such qualitative material is available for 18 persons who claim to be gang members at least for some time between 1989 and 1995. Thus we can use their accounts about their group membership to learn a bit more about the structures and dynamics of *Banden*.

GANG MEMBERSHIP

How many youth report gang membership in these two sites? Between 1988 and 1992, 14 percent of the Denver cohort claimed gang membership. In Bremen, the corresponding figure (1990–1994) is 13 percent. The measurement of this variable is quite similar in both sites. In Bremen the respondents have been asked the following set of questions:

44 Are you currently or have you in the years before been a member of a rather stable clique or group of buddies/friends? (yes/no)

a) in (1992)[5]

b) in (1991)

(if yes)

#45 Would it be right for any of these cliques to be called a gang ("Bande")? Did you call yourself that or have you been so called by others? (yes/no)

(if yes)

46 Which clique do you refer to?

(1992)

(1991)

47 (if yes) Did the gang have a name? ....

The question asked in the DYS questionnaire is simply:

Thinking about the school year between Christmas a year ago and the Christmas just past ...were you a member of a youth or street gang ? (no/yes)

Affirmative answers to this item are followed by items to insure that the group identified is a group that is engaged in delinquent behavior and has an identity such as a name, colors, etc.

Thus in both studies a name was considered a good feature indicating that the identified group may in fact be a gang or Bande. In Germany among the reported names for the *Bande* were the following: Radikale Onkelz Liga, Beat Boys, GH Power, Lawless Rebels, Skinheads, Bad Gang Blumenthal, Destroyers, Ghetto Kids, Tigers, Aumund Warriors, Nahkampftrinker (close-combat-drinker), Aysel, and Night Riders.

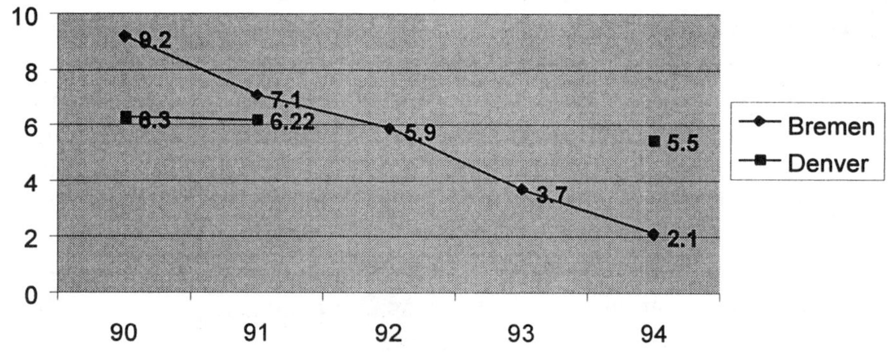

Figure 1. Proportion of Bande/Gang Members

Some comparative data may help to clarify differences and similarities of youth groups in Bremen and Denver. One indicator may be *duration* of gang membership. In Denver for the period 1989-1994, the mean duration of membership in gangs was 1.5 years; in Bremen it was 2.3 years. Surprisingly the American gangs seem to be more fluid or to have a higher turnover compared to *Banden* in Germany. Another hint may be gained from the *age grading* of gang-membership. As Figure 1 shows there are differences in the gang prevalence rate over time and between the two cohorts.

In Denver 6.3 percent of the cohort claim to be gang members in 1990 while the corresponding figure for Bremen kids is 9.2 percent. The proportion in Denver declines only slowly over the time to 5.5 in 1994 while the drop in the Bremen cohort is substantial (down to 2.1 percent).

One explanation for that difference may be that the entire Bremen cohort left school in 1989 while the Denver youths were only beginning to leave school in 1991 and school leaving continued in later years.

If gang membership is an appropriate behavior while youths are in school, it makes sense to expect that the proportion of gang members in the German cohort should drop after leaving school. This occurs when youths, as is predominantly the case for this German cohort, start to learn a trade in an apprenticeship. The drop would be even larger when they eventually enter the labor force.

Let us now turn to the question of whether gang members in Bremen contribute a similar amount to the total delinquency of their cohort, as do their American counterparts. In Figure 2 data for delinquency during the time span 1990-1994 (Bremen) and 1988-1992 (Denver) are presented.

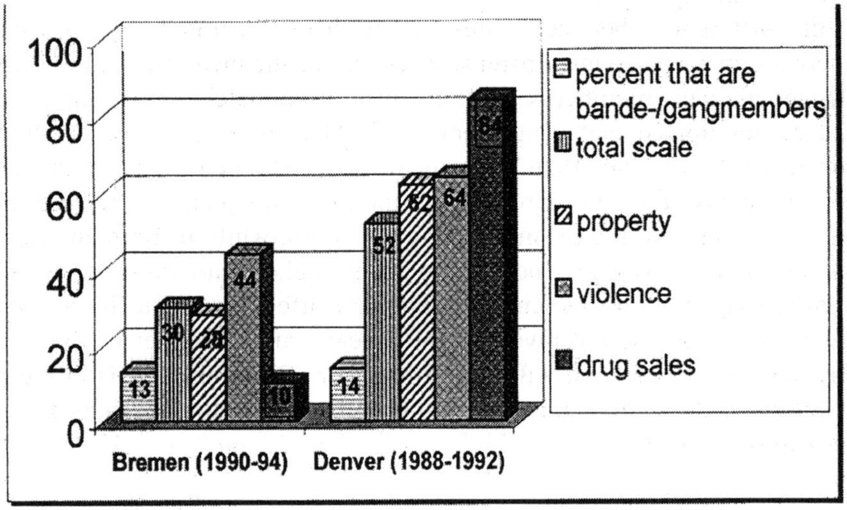

Figure 2. Proportion of Offenses Committed by Bande/Gang Members

In Bremen, 13 percent have been a member of a gang for at least a year in the '90-'94 period, and in Denver, 14 percent have been a gang member over the 1988-1992 period. As illustrated in Figure 2, gang members at both sites contribute an amount far beyond the level of the proportion in their cohort to the total delinquency, violence, and property offenses of the cohort. Two observations seem noteworthy, however. First, at both sites, gang members commit a substantial portion of violent offenses. Gang members account for almost half the violent offenses in Bremen and almost two-thirds of the violent offenses in Denver.

Second, for all types of offenses, the contribution made to delinquency by gang members is always substantially lower in Bremen than in Denver. Although gang members in Bremen account for a large proportion of delinquency, the difference in contribution to the total volume of delinquency between gang members and nongang youth is much smaller than in Denver. This is particularly evident for drug sales, where in Bremen, the contribution to drug sales offenses is actually smaller than the proportion of gang members in the cohort, while for Denver, and over 80 percent of all drug sales can be attributed to gang members.

This difference between sites is further illustrated by considering frequencies, or the individual offense rates. Since the mean frequency is higher in Denver and gang members contribute disproportionately to this higher rate, it would be anticipated that gang members in Denver would have substantially higher mean frequencies than gang members in Bremen. This is in fact the case. In Denver, for total delinquency, the mean for gang members is nearly ten times higher than the mean for nongang youth, while in Bremen, the mean for gang members is only about three times higher than for nongang youth. Similar findings hold for violence and property offenses. The influence of gang membership on delinquent involvement appears much stronger in Denver than in Bremen, and to call oneself a gang member (Bandenmitglied) in Germany may not imply the same magnitude of involvement in delinquency as it does for American street gangs.

IS THE "BANDE" EMBEDDED IN A WIDER NETWORK OF CLIQUES?

Let us leave the comparative analysis for a moment and describe more fully the available data for the Bremen cohort on youth groups. German youth tend to call their peer groups cliques. Clique membership varies from 56 percent of youth in 1990 to 48 percent in 1996. Clearly, many members, roughly half, of the cohort are at any given time members of a clique. This proportion is substantially higher than the proportion of the cohort that report being members of a *Bande*. There is only a small decline in clique membership over time, in comparison to the more striking decline in gang membership (from 9.2 to 1.9 over the 1990 to 1996 period). Also those cliques that call themselves (are or called) gangs seem to be joined more by teenagers than those in their twenties, while clique membership lasts far into adulthood.

It may also be asked whether gang membership is embedded in clique membership over the life course. That is, do some cliques become gangs and then later lose their gang identity? Or, are gangs truly a special kind of clique? To answer this question we look exclusively at those persons who report having been a gang member for at least one year during the time span 1989 through 1996. These individuals account for 66 episodes of gang membership over the years. For 26 episodes we have data for the periods before, during and after gang membership. For 27 episodes the data are left censored, so that only data for during and after gang membership are available. For six episodes the data are right censored, providing only before and during gang membership data. The uncensored episodes split into 10 having no clique membership before or after gang membership, three only before, six only after, and seven with both before and after clique membership. Of the left censored data, approximately one-half report clique membership after termination of gang membership, while the other half does not; and only a few of the right censored report prior membership in a clique. Apparently in some cases membership in gangs is preceded and or followed by membership in cliques, while in other cases this is not so. There is no definite pattern detectable. Quite clearly, in general, gangs are not simply on-going cliques that call themselves or are labeled "gangs" for some period of time. **Gangs are a unique kind of clique, with membership occurring most often during the teenage years.**

We further examined the delinquency rates of "delinquent non-gang cliques" in comparison to the delinquency of gang members. We distinguished members of cliques that had predominately delinquent friends, i.e., those who reported an above average number of delinquent friends and members of cliques with a lower than average number of delinquent friends. The delinquency of the members in these rather delinquent or in rather conforming cliques was compared to youth without commitment to cliques, on the one hand, and with gang members on the other. The delinquency rates of these four groups are given in Table 2.

Table 2: Mean Delinquency Scores in Relation to Membership in Cliques and Gangs (Bremen cohort study)[a]

Member of				
	No group	**A rather conforming clique**	**A rather delinquent clique**	**A gang**
1992	(n= 220)	(n=79)	(n=82)	(n=25)
Violence	.392	.063	.976	4.21
Property	1.593	.481	2.329	2.13
Drugs	.648	.063	1.280	1.75
All offenses[b]	3.844	1.139	7.415	15.48
1994	(n=171)	(n=113)	(n=82)	(n=8)
Violence	.309	.0531	.781	1.63
Property	1.442	.398	3.680	1.50
Drugs	1.515	.566	3.200	3.75
All offenses	4.514	1.309	10.888	9.75

a. Missing values for delinquency reduce the number in particular cells

b. The category "all offenses" consists of more than just the sum of the three indexes (drugs, violence and property); this score includes also traffic offenses and various other types of norm breaking (e.g., carrying concealed weapons, damaging property, etc.), excluding status offenses (which do not exist in Germany). It should also be stressed that this analysis of gang members' delinquency uses the whole dataset of the Bremen cohort, while the comparative Bremen-Denver dataset used in figures 1 and 2 refers only to types of delinquency that are identical or at least equivalent in both sites.

In both years gang members have by far the highest involvement in violent acts, although the small number of gang members in 1994 makes the gang estimates for that year somewhat unreliable. Gang members also report the highest (but not dramatically highest) involvement in drug offenses (which consist almost exclusively of drug use). Gang members have the highest total delinquency scores in 1992 (over twice that of any other group), but in 1994, members of delinquent cliques report more delinquency than do gang members. Property offenses are committed at the highest rate by members of delinquent cliques. Apparently, persons in cliques that identify themselves as or are called gangs are more involved in violence and may be more involved in drug use and in general delinquency than are other youth. However, heavy involvement in delinquency is not unique to gang members. Persons in delinquent (but not gang) cliques have the highest frequency of involvement in property offenses. Thus, there seems to be a blurred edge in the distinction between gangs and other delinquent cliques.

GROUP COHESION, BOUNDARIES, HIERARCHY, AND IDENTIFICATION: SOME DESCRIPTIVE DETAILS

Eighteen persons who claim to have been (or still are) gang members have been interviewed in an open form five times throughout the years 1989 to 1997. This ethnographic material provides some insights into the group structure of so-called *Banden*. A common feature of those youth groups is the expectation to support other group members if they get into trouble with outsiders.

In the hooligan scene (groups that meet for fighting during football games), it seems typical to join the group whenever one person wishes to participate in a fight against hooligans associated with another football club. Thus the delinquent activities happen occasionally and the members belonging to those scenes join the action or not, as they like. The same is true among graffiti-sprayers. They join occasionally for doing an act together and then split. Those are temporary cliques of individuals.

Gang members seem to spend much more time together. The more they have a history of fights against other groups, the more they tend to fear the situation of being on their own.

As Jim[6] recalls:

> You could no longer go places by yourself. You might have gotten into trouble. You needed to have one or two others with you. You were afraid that those guys would show up. They knew your face. They waited for you. Shit. You had to call somebody, telling him: Can you join me. I have to go downtown. Shit, forget it. (5th interview)

Group cohesion comes from a strong sense of supporting each other. Johann reports the rule:

> If my friend calls, I am deeply in trouble, here are 5 dudes who want to beat me up, then I jump into the car and drive to help him. I do not think a minute about possible consequences. I just do not want my friend to get hurt. It's a kind of codex. It's friendship. We know: I can call my friends anytime, two or four o'clock in the morning. They will come help me. (4th interview)

Boundaries have little to do with territoriality. They stem from ethnic backgrounds. Skins fight against Turkish groups. They recognize the 'enemy' from the outfit. Tom remembers:

> If two or three of us went to town, with baldheads, Springer-boots and bomber-coats and run into some Turks, that was it. We had to fight them. (5th interview)

Some gangs have developed some kind of hierarchy. Johann explains this in looking back to a *Bande* he intentionally left:

> The 'Rudel-Führer,' our high-rank leader, demanded that we do things which I did not want to do. All others obeyed but I did not. I just did not like that. Then they ignored me, isolated me. Eventually I said: ok, I can do without you, that's it. (5th interview)

The ability to leave a *Bande* depends on the importance of it for one's own identity. In many cases companionship within the clique makes the youths feel more powerful than they otherwise would be. Elmar, a longtime hooligan explains:

> I could say I am a 'Bremen City Boy.' That was my identity. You are somebody. Nobody gives you some shit. They are afraid of you... Usually when we met with other hools, we had planned to fight each other at a particular place. Even informed the police: Wait a minute, you must not go

> there. We want to be left alone... The thrill was being part of a group. When I go along the street by myself, the street is not mine. But if you once have been among a hundred, if you belong to them, then you believe you own the street even if you happen to be just by yourself. (5th interview)

Membership in those groups called *Bande* is demanding. One demand seems to be to participate in actions without any thought about how police or courts would judge the behavior. More important is that the group as a whole or its members look good; any necessary support is obligatory. Those cliques or groups are not organized to commit crimes or delinquency, but they tend to accept any norm breaking when it happens. Alternatively, one has to leave the clique. Would it be appropriate to call those youth groups "gangs" because they are referred to by their members as *Bande* but seem to have a rather limited cohesion, as the quotes above indicate? We are not sure of the answer to this question.

FINAL REMARKS

We began by asking whether there are "gangs" in Germany. Although we can not provide a definitive answer to this question, by comparing high-risk youths in Denver, Colorado, and Bremen, Germany, we detected some similarities regarding membership in youth groups. At both sites, over time, 13-14 percent of youth identify themselves as members of a "gang" or "Bande." Those youth who do identify themselves as a member of a "gang" or "Bande" contribute substantially and at a higher rate than other youth to the total delinquency of the cohort, especially violence. They do so, however, less in Bremen than in Denver. It was observed that Bremen youth who are members of a delinquent (but nongang) clique are also heavily involved in delinquent behavior, and commit even more property offenses than gang members, so that the distinction between gangs and delinquent cliques, at least in terms of their delinquent behavior, becomes blurred.

A particular difference between the US and Germany seems to be the relationship between gang membership and drug trafficking, at least during the period studied. In Bremen, very few members of *Banden* are involved in drug sales. In fact gang members contribute less to total drug sale delinquency than their proportion in the cohort, in striking contrast to other delinquent offenses.

In Denver, a high proportion of gang members are involved in drug sales and gang members account for the vast majority of drug sale delinquency. The different drug policy in Germany and the lesser relevance of opiates and cocaine in the German drug market may account for this difference. It raises the issue, however, of the relationship between American drug policy, the "War on Drugs," and the "American gang problem."

We close by noting that the use of cross-national research with empirical findings in examining issues such as the existence of gangs and raising the issue of the relationship of drug policies to gang behavior, as in this paper, suggests there may be value in such research. By developing and continuing such research efforts we may be able to understand better the meaning and significance of cross-national similarities and differences.

REFERENCES

Collins, R. (1979). The Credential Society, New York .

Junger-Tas, J., G.-J. Terlouw, M. Klein (eds.) (1994). Delinquent Behavior Among Young People in the Western World. Amsterdam: Kugler.

Klein, M. (1997). Gangs in the United States and Europe. European Journal of Criminal Policy and Research 4(2).

Lynch, J. (1995). Crime in international perspective. In J.Q.Wilson and J.Petersilia (eds.), Crime. San Francisco: ICS Press 1995, p.11-38.

Shelley, L. (1985). American crime: An international anomaly? Comparative Social Research, 8:81-95.

ENDNOTES

1 This research has been made possible by a grant from the German-American Academic Council in the TRANSCOOP program, with matching funds from the U.S. Office of Juvenile Justice and Delinquency Prevention (OJJDP). The two longitudinal studies providing the data for the comparative study are funded by Deutsche Forschungsgemeinschaft and OJJDP. The points of view expressed are those of the authors and do not necessarily represent the views or policies of the funding agencies. The authors are grateful for assistance and comments by Beate Ehret, Amanda Elliott, Eduard Matt, and Fred Othold.

2 For example, in § 244a Strafgesetzbuch (German Penal Code).

3 Lode Walgrave and others suggested this term during the Workshop in Schmitten.

4 See the comparative data provided by I. H. Marshall and V.J.Webb on the U.S. (p.339) and by P.Sutterer and T.Karger on Germany (p.177) in Junger-Tas, Terlouw and Klein, 1994.

5 Question asked at the second wave in 1993; later waves used corresponding years for reference.

6 Names have been modified to protect the identity of the interviewees.

Chapter 19

GROUPS OF VIOLENT YOUNG MALES IN GERMANY

Joachim Kersten
Hochschule für Polizei, Schwenningen, Germany

In Germany, the public debate on youth violence[1] has been focussing predominantly upon three items of crime and violence originating from groupings of young males:

Neighborhood cliques of German, multi-ethnic or in many cases migrant origin. Migrant origin means mostly children from Turkish (also Kurdish) families or from parts of former Yugoslavia, Algeria, and returned ex-patriate families of German background from Poland and regions of the former Soviet Union. Although parents and children do not speak German as a native tongue, expatriates have German passports.

Right-wing skinheads residing in parts of East and West Germany.

Hooligans in the context of soccer games.

In terms of quantity, neighborhood cliques by far outnumber all other types. They are the bread and butter stuff of youth crime be it property-related, vandalism, street robbery and extortion or crimes against the person. Skinheads are estimated at 8000 nation-wide with more than 2000 known by police as offenders, mostly of an assault-type of crime. The total number of Hooligans is estimated in roughly the same proportion, 8000 or more, and 2500 registered violent offenders.

In a nutshell, the following aims at two basic questions concerning characteristics of present groupings:

M.W. Klein et al (eds.), The Eurogang Paradox, 247–255.

1. Where can we locate street groupings ("cliques") and soccer hooligans (in another recently published English language article this author has described skinhead subcultures) in a typology of violent-prone groupings?
2. How can we differentiate between the style, the insignia and the focal concerns of neighborhood cliques and hooligans/*Nationalgesinnte* (right wing/nationalist/racist youth groupings)?

The most obvious common denominator for crime-prone present German groupings is their "action." Especially, when it comes to activities that cause harm to others or damage to public property this can be interpreted as an accomplishment of gender in the terms of Robert W. Connell (1987, 1995) and James Messerschmidt (1993). It is the behavior of nearly exclusively young males towards a situational claim of hegemonic masculinity, i.e.: displays of territorial protection, or the protection of "native" females, of German or ethnic pride and honor. This can be combined with displays of risk behavior, an aggressive "front," frequently involving assaults on "others": An additional emphasis is on things to do with driving and motor vehicles: reckless driving, speeding, stealing cars etc.

Bob Connell's chapter "Live fast and die young" in his paradigmatic (1995) work "Masculinities" provides an illustration for the meaning of "front" and "displays" of risk-seeking behavior for young underclass males. And across most of the Seven Seas we can observe striking similarities between what Connell describes for young Australians and what has been observed among underclass young males in both parts of Germany. Similarly, but without an explicit reference to gender theories, the French sociologist Pierre Bourdieu (1997) presents interview data from his study of underclass suburban life-worlds in Paris. With a migrant background and no educational or vocational skills, access to the labor market, to decent accommodation, and to a female partner is virtually out of sight. Displays of explicitly visible models of youthful masculinities, "real" men who deserve respect, and who protect the honor of their groupings, their ethnicity and, most important for feuds, "their" women, are also one of the main underlying themes of Luis Rodriguez' (1994) award-winning biography "Always Running." This story of a poor immigrant–his career of lost options, and bad habits gained in the barrios of Los Angeles–could also be told about other young males in segregated living quarters of *Aussiedler families (*expatriates from Poland and regions of what was the Soviet Union, particularly Kazachstan) or migrants from Turkey.

Bob Connell describes his Australian interview partners. Mighty Mal, strong like a lion, whose looks really earn him respect, can't read or write. Ed is a powerful fighter, and everybody is aware of that. However, everybody knows as well that against the police he doesn't stand a chance. Exactly the same could be said of urban young males in cliques of migrant background. They are called Macho-Turks because their displays of physical masculinity as male protectors and warriors are so clearly out of date and place. And they get them into frequent conflict with other cliques and the law.

Underclass young men, although representatives of the dominant sex, can take little advantage of the "dividend of patriarchy" as Connell, Messerschmidt, and Bourdieu point out in their case studies. They lack the resources to become marriageable or even a "family man": There is no regular income and there is very little when it comes to status. So they are left with their aggressive idea of "honor" and their displays of risk seeking, e.g. dangerous driving and other crime, staged in public with street corner and neighborhood audiences.

A down and out status is transformed into that of a rebellious hero, a man who earns respect and is feared because of his "front" and his "action." Such displays of risk-seeking, macho, underclass masculinities are "skilled, finely pitched productions mounted on a shoestring" writes Connell, but they lead their protagonists into a dead end road, with risk and confrontation as a **life-style**: Drug and alcohol abuse, car accidents, being perpetrators or victims of assaults; emotional and physical injuries and an extreme likelihood of criminalization are the outcomes of such compulsory life-styles of protest masculinity, a term originally coined by a pioneer of psychoanalysis, Alfred Adler (1927, 1928),[2] and filled with sociological meaning by Bob Connell. In such "front" realities of male-dominated youth violence, victims and offenders change roles quite frequently, and most of the disastrous violence remains, contrary to popular beliefs and reinforced media images within the very same community where such youths grow up to become bad boys. Becoming a good boy by being a bad boy was according to Talcott Parsons (1955) once the destiny of working class boys. With the demise of working class and working class culture, the factory no longer represents the real school of discipline for such youth. Paul Willis' (1981) research is somewhat outdated because the working class scenario that formed the culture of white working class males (a culture of beer, mate-ship, and football coupled with misogyny, homo- and xenophobia) has all but disappeared. Only Skinheads and Australians still believe in the working class mythology of the 19th and early 20th century. The current underclass and former working class youth are presently–at best–booked for tertiary sector jobs, feminized work that they deeply detest and find unmanly. This fuels their hate and their aggression. Their belief in violence as the most formidable means of protection, fighting, honor, is not completely outdated. It makes sense in their life-worlds as it does in Kosovo, Northern Ireland, and wherever Kurds congregate after the kidnapping of their leader "Apo" Öczalan.

SOCCER HOOLIGANS

In sociological and cultural terms Hooliganism is an entirely different, namely a socially and culturally "integrated" display of masculine rebellion. Formerly, soccer was a "life" event, a highlight of exactly that masculine white working class culture of the industrial urban regions of Britain and continental Europe that forms the link between protest masculinity, soccer, skinheads, hooliganism and main stream popular culture. Television has taken the "life" aspect out of soccer as much as it has had a deteriorating effect on other domains of "life" culture: music and theatre.

Hooliganism–as a subculture of non-marginal youths and young men–and soccer relate to each other in pretty much the same way as war and war crimes. Soccer is territorial. It is a display of "real" masculine virtues, risk-taking, and the physical use of the male body, equivalent to "real combat," and very similar to the culture of masculinity in underclass scenarios. Soccer as a prime time image of physical forms of combat masculinity serves a gender-specific purpose, aside from being a highly respected domain for making heaps of money for soccer clubs, corporations and media enterprise, and some successful business sportsmen. Soccer sells and promotes fossilized images of masculinity to largely young and old male audiences, and it is seen as playful, as a fair game, as sport.

Hooligans refuse to buy such fare, neither in the soccer stadium masses, nor–with peanuts and canned beer–as a passive consumer's delight in front of the television set. "Hools," as we call them, are not content with the abstract metaphor of territorial warfare. They take active part in the fight, in a form of a–so to speak–"living theatre." It is a living theatre with no director but it certainly has a script and an audience.

Also, there are rules for the confrontations amongst soccer hooligans. Lens, in Northern France, where German hooligans nearly killed a French police officer during the last World Championship, was an exception. If there were no rules for the regular warfare of the hooligans there would be hundreds, maybe more fatalities during each national or European soccer league season. But there are not. There are assaults, injuries, some quite serious, but they tend not to get reported. Hools are looking for other soccer mercenaries who are after exactly the same thing: to deal out blows and kicks without receiving too many oneself.

When hooligans go berserk, and that is what happened in the alley in Lens, France, they feel they are invincible. Lens was berserk hools against a single powerless representative of the most powerful enemy of hooliganism: the police. Soldiers that go berserk kill without fear and mercy. The American therapist Jonathan Shay has been working for many years with Vietnam veterans suffering from post-traumatic stress disorder (PTSD). In an exceptionally lateral approach Shay (1994) has drawn a parallel between the state of going berserk in the Greek Iliad, the territorial fight over Troy as described by Homer, and in the Vietnamese jungle. A mob of German hooligans, after having been chased by an overwhelming force of French police, turn into a small alley, while the main police body remained in the main street. In the alley German soccer hooligans went berserk against a helpless human being wearing a police uniform.

The state of exceptional mental and physical awareness made possible by stress hormones, adrenaline and endorphins, is exactly what hooligans are after when they travel to soccer games. This quest for the extraordinary, for manly fights, and for the masculinity of the mercenary found a very graphic description in Bill Buford's excellent book "Among the Thugs" (1991). The dangerous quest for the Holy Grail or the crusades also gave ample opportunity for going berserk in the name of one's Lord, the slaughtering business of noble men. Today's hooligans are middle class crusaders, in the name of no one but a silly ball game: All they desire is the same feeling of intensity of the moment that is behind the pains of marathon runners, mountain climbers or chess players. The home made narcotic is supported by situations where others are dehumanized and hurt, and also by the risk of getting hurt, in the extreme getting killed or caught. Hooligans are addicted to this state of high alertness and the feeling of invincibility like Siegfried after the bath in the dragon's blood. Like the average drug addict, they know that the state of euphoria bears high risks. It is mainly the perceived threat of being chased, harmed, hurt and injured, or arrested by police that feeds their flow. It is the flow of adrenaline. Fights are the ultimate, not the regular experience.

Hooligans look for an experience that PTSD Vietnam veterans desperately try to eliminate or at least get some control of in their lives and in the lives of their families and partners. While veteran patients (estimated at 30,000) cannot rid themselves of their experience, their living through loss, brutality and collective dehumanization, hooligans want a flavor of the fighting man's disaster, and they want it at a calculated risk. They use "legitimate" soccer warfare as a frame for micro-wars with other hooligans and police.

THE LINK TO RIGHT WING "ACTION," NAZI SUBCULTURES AND OTHER SOCIAL MOVEMENTS

Hooligans, Neonazis and right wing skinheads are not necessarily the same persons. But there are consistent links. In East Germany oppositional street youth groupings have emerged from a pool that has contained punk, skinhead and soccer hooligan elements, but not so much organized Neonazi youngsters. Hooliganism, as a subculture of soccer enthusiasm, was always on the very right wing of "working class" culture. And there, in its quality as a street culture, it has its overlaps with Neonazi skinheads and punks. Therefore hooliganism is compatible with right wing life styles but as such it is not a Nazi or racist subculture. The smallest common denominator of violence-prone groupings is not a political ideology but an underlying attitude of explicit intolerance and rigidity, typical for the right but also quite visible in other social movements (including some feminist activists and ecologists). The common feature of hooligans and loose right wing groupings, in contrast to neighborhood cliques and "gang" like phenomena is their "mob" quality, especially when they dehumanize and denigrate "others" in manhunts. Such mobs, whether hooligans chasing each other or skinheads/*Deutschnationale* chasing people of different color of skin or gays, only know how to attack. They exist only through movement, and they have no fixed hierarchies or sets of rules or orders. There is an element of being equals, mates, of egalitarianism in the mob culture. Our societies rarely provide space and opportunities for such aggressive forms of egalitarianism. The feeling of belonging comes from the mob's collective action.

The mob's members do not have to know each other to become a member. In cliques youths have to know each other but not in packs of hools. When it comes to violence, chasing, and dealing out blows, each hooligan scores for himself. He needs the mob because it creates opportunities for violence and a cover against being hurt oneself and getting caught too easily. Wolfgang Sofsky writes on the topic of mobs:

During the chase, cooperation of the mob's members is minimal. Division of labor is a spontaneous act. Hierarchies disappear when the mob is on the move. A mob can be ordered to move but it is not guided by orders but by people who set examples: They act and their action is visible to the others. Someone starts to lead and everyone follows and tries to be as fast as the person in front. The mob creates leaders, and they then lead the mob's way (Sofsky, 1996: 165).

Such mobs or packs of youths are not the material sought after by right wing parties. Such young men are not interested in power, in getting organized and being a party member. Sofsky comments: "mobs/packs lack a center of power. Their principle of formation is not organization but their status of being rivals. Hunting and chasing have a uniting effect but among the huntsmen competition is rife, greed for bounty, for head money, for the honor of being the best of the worst (1996:165)."

Rebellions of masculinity occur, as Tracy X. Karner (1998) has pointed out, because hitherto taken-for-granted access to dominance and privilege go forsaken for a larger part of the male population. The carriers of the rebellion are in the case of hooliganism not down and out underclass or ghetto kids, but middle class youths.

In debates on youth violence, the theoretical framework too frequently excludes the gender aspect of the groupings' style and action. Therefore the insignia and emblems of such male rebellions and their symbolism are not investigated with the necessary rigor. They are described as exotic but in reality they are obviously associated with pre-modernity or early industrialization. Such "museum images" of masculinity are important databases too often ignored, along with aspects of social and cultural background. Accordingly, the obvious differences in terms of gender, social class and cultural background as well as the similarities are not taken seriously.

The fire bomb mobs of right wing skinheads in Hoyerswerda, Rostock, and at the time of this writing the clique of right wing youths in Guben/Brandenburg at the Polish border who have chased a young asylum-seeker from Algeria to death, are a different brand. More often than not such youths and young men are not from an underclass background. In the Guben case they could not be taken into detention because of their "integrated" social background, and because the chase was not intentional manslaughter but negligently causing death.

Since German reunification such rebellions of masculinity carried out by street youths, skinheads and hooligans have been the focus of sociological concern. Germany has undergone an experience of cultural disorientation and extremely rapid social change, clearly recognizable from the outside. But the reality of cultural change, the consequence of which is always crime and a hitherto "unknown" quality of youth violence, is obscured to those who go through the experience. That makes the sale of apocalyptic visions declared as theory such a success. The rebellions described in this short and mostly exploratory chapter obviously relate to factors specific to the German situation (crisis of "national identity," influx of "foreigners"), and to factors that have to do with the crises of 19th and 29th century masculinities that cause similar rebellions of masculinity in other modern societies.

REFERENCES

Adler, A. (1928). Psychologie der macht. In F. Kohler (ed.), Gewalt und Gewaltlosigkeit. Zurich: Rotapfelverlag.

Adler, A. (1927). Understanding Human Nature (1992 translation: C. Brett). Oxford: Oneworld.

Bourdieu, P. (1997). Das Eland der Welt. Konstanz: Universitaetsverlag Konstanz.

Buford, B. (1991). Among the Thugs. London: Secker and Warburg.

Connell, R. (1995). Masculinities. Berkeley, CA: University of California Press.

Connell, R. (1987). Gender and Power. Cambridge, UK: Polity Press.

Karner, T.X. (1998). Engendering men: Oral histories of military masculinity. In L. Bowker (ed.), Masculinities and Violence. Thousand Oaks, CA: Sage Publications.

Messerschmidt, J. (1993). Masculinities and Crime: Critique and Reconceptualization of Theory. Lanham, MD: Rowman and Littlefield.

Parsons, T.et al. (1955). Family, Socialization and Interaction Process. Glencoe, IL: Free Press.

Rodriguez, L. (1994). Always Running: La Vida Loca. Gang Days in L.A. New York: Simon and Schuster.

Shay, J. (1994). Achilles in Vietnam: Combat Trauma and the Undoing of Character. New York: Atheneum.

Sofsky, W (1996). Traktat über die Gewalt. Frankfurt: Buechergilde Gutenberg.

Willis, P. (1981). How Working Class Kids Get Working Class Jobs. New York: Columbia University Press.

ENDNOTES

1 The public debate on youth violence tends to be a rather normative exercise, especially in youth sociology. At least since German reunification the most prominent theories of youth violence produce an apocalyptic vision on a routine basis.

2 Adler coined the term "protest masculinity" based on studies as an MD during WWI.

Chapter 20

CRIMINAL NETWORKS IN STOCKHOLM

Jerzy Sarnecki and Tove Pettersson
Department of Criminology, Stockholm University, Sweden

INTRODUCTION

This study employs a network analytical approach to examine co-offending. The aim is to test whether a network perspective can help with new approaches and a better insight into the character of juvenile crime in a metropolitan area.

The most fundamental difference between traditional social science and research employing a network perspective[1] is that network analysis stipulates the existence of observable relationships between the objects under study. Over the past few decades[2] social network analysis has become an increasingly common approach within the social sciences in general. It is still employed only rarely in criminological studies however, and this despite the fact that clear parallels exist between a network perspective and many aspects of criminological thought.

A few researchers, amongst others Reiss (1986,1988) and Tremblay (1993), have chosen to focus on the phenomenon of co-offending. They maintain that a proper understanding of co-offending would give us a fundamental insight into the etiology of crime, as well as a better understanding of the effectiveness of measures aimed at combating crime (Reiss, 1988:117).

It is well established that juvenile crime is to a large extent a group phenomenon. Membership in a delinquent group is often seen as a prerequisite for criminal behavior. This is especially true of learning and neutralization

M.W. Klein et al (eds.), The Eurogang Paradox, 257–272.

theories such as those presented by Sutherland, Akers and Matza (Sutherland, 1939; Sutherland, Cressey & Luckenbill, 1992; Akers, 1998; Matza, 1964).

At the same time, one might also claim that all those theories which associate crime with a working class, or perhaps a more generally lower class culture, or with different forms of subculture (e.g. Cohen, 1956; Miller, 1958; Cloward & Ohlin, 1960, Ferrell & Sanders, 1995) as well as the research tradition that has grown up around the American "gang" (e.g. Thrasher, 1927; Short & Strodtbeck, 1965; Klein, 1971, 1995), all stipulate the existence of a mechanism which both facilitates the spread of norms and values conducive to the commission of crime, and enables individuals to exert influence over one another.

The most widespread view of the effect on crime of friendships among young people however is that having criminally active friends is *one of several factors* that increase the likelihood that an individual will commit offenses. Even some proponents of the social bonding theory, which according to Hirschi's original (1969) statement does not regard relationships with antisocial friends as an important factor in the etiology of deviant behavior, have disagreed. They have claimed that, for example, given the existence of a strong relationship between the delinquency of a certain individual and that of his or her friends, certain aspects of learning theory ought to be incorporated into control theory to explain this (Krohn & Massey, 1980:536; Le Blanc & Caplan, 1993:287).

In summary, one might thus assert that as with any other social activity, delinquency could at least in part be explained with reference to the relationships an individual establishes with others. And it is just this quality that makes the network perspective so potentially useful in the analysis of crime.

The project carried out by Sarnecki in Borlänge[3] (1982, 1983, 1986, 1990) was the first criminological study where police suspects were examined, together with the offenses for which they were suspected, using the techniques of network analysis. Perhaps most importantly, the study showed that 47 percent of all the juveniles suspected of offenses in Borlänge during the six-year period covered could be linked to one another in a single large network. The members of this network, which included most of the town's highly delinquent youths, were responsible for the lion's share of all recorded offenses in Borlänge for which juveniles were suspected.

NETWORK ANALYSIS AND CRIMINOLOGY

Since the network perspective remains relatively unknown within criminology, we present some of the concepts basic to this field of enquiry and of the way these concepts have been applied within the confines of the current project.

The empirical material on which a network analysis is based consists of two elements: objects, commonly referred to as *actors* (such as people or organizations or other social groupings) and relations among these objects. A relation may consist of the transference of material resources, business transactions, joint participation in social activities, family ties, the spread of information, influence exerted to affect an attitude or anything similar. A *link* exists between two actors when they interact with one another on a specific relation (Wasserman & Faust, 1997).

For the purposes of the present study the actors (in most cases at least[4]) are individuals suspected of offenses by the police. The relation studied is co-offending, with links joining individuals suspected of having committed offenses together.

A *social network* comprises a limited number of actors and the relations among these actors (Wasserman & Faust, 1997:20). The boundaries of the networks in this study are primarily time-based. The longer the timeframe covered by a specific analysis, the larger the networks examined.

Simply because two individuals are part of the same network does not in itself imply that they have committed offenses together, however. They may well be connected indirectly via any number of intervening actors. *A network is thus made up of all those actors who, within a specified timeframe, are linked to one another either directly or indirectly, together with all the links connecting these actors.*

In those cases where actors are not members of a network, i.e., they have no known co-offenders, they will be referred to as *isolates*. It is important to note that an individual referred to as an isolate, in the context of an analysis covering a specific period, may well turn out to be linked into a network of co-offenders if the timeframe is extended. It is quite possible that the individual in question will have committed offenses with co-offenders in another of the study's six-month periods.

The study begins from the assumption that in most cases co-offending involves actors exerting influence over one another. At the same time, co-offending is seen as indicative of the existence of other kinds of relationship (which cannot be studied on the basis of police data) between the individuals in question.

The influence of actors on one another within a criminal network can be either *direct* if the individual has committed one or more joint offenses, or *indirect* if the actors are linked into the same network but with no known direct contacts between them. The intensity of this indirect influence decreases as the *distance* between two actors within a network (measured as the number of links separating them from one another) increases.

A further concept employed in the study is *network density* (also referred to as *link density*). A network is at its most dense when all the actors in the network are linked to all the others. The smaller the number of links present in relation to the maximum number possible[5] the lower the network density.

Some of the larger networks contain groups of actors with a considerably higher link density than the areas surrounding them. These relatively dense areas within larger networks will be referred to as *clusters*.

INTERPRETING THE RESULTS

The study covers all those individuals of age 20 or less who were suspected of one or more offenses in the city of Stockholm during the years 1991 through 1995, and who were registered as such by the police, and also their co-offenders.

It is important when working with police data to bear in mind that one examines only a fraction of the criminal activity that actually takes place. In terms of the present study this means that where the data show two individuals linked together in the joint commission of a single offense, it may well be the case that these individuals have also co-offended "invisibly" on several other occasions. Furthermore, the real networks of criminal relationships in Stockholm are significantly larger and more dense (they are made up of more actors and contain more links per actor) than those presented here.

Although individuals who are not linked in the data may in fact have co-offended, it seems reasonable to assume that the likelihood of two individuals having co-offended is higher if these individuals are indirectly connected (through membership in the same network) than if this is not the case. This is especially true for those individuals who lie relatively close to one another in a network.

In addition, when interpreting the results, we must bear in mind that the relationships between young co-offenders in reality involve a great deal more than simply the joint commission of criminal offenses. If we pay too much attention to the criminal ties linking delinquent youths, we miss a large segment of the social networks of which these individuals are a part [not least, to paraphrase Sutherland (1939), the contacts with models of conformist behavior]. At the same time, the results from Borlänge (Sarnecki, 1983) show that the most criminally active youths often commit offenses with their best friends and that the constitution of these individuals' circle of friends to a large extent coincides with their circle of co-offenders.

THE SUSPECTS (ACTORS) AND CRIMES (LINKS)

In total the study covers 22,091 individuals suspected in connection with 36,941 offense participations.[6] The number of actual offenses is considerably smaller since many were committed jointly by several individuals.[7] The principal population is made up of 19,617 individuals.[8] The youngest of these was five years old when he first became a suspect,[9] the eldest were twenty years old.[10] Girls/women constitute around 27 percent of the suspects although this proportion varies somewhat between different age groups.

The level of police registered re-offending varies greatly among the individuals in the study. The overwhelming majority (74 percent) is suspected of only one offense during the five-year period in question. The remaining 26 percent are suspected of between two and 44 offenses. On average the study population committed 1.63 offenses per individual over the course of the five years studied.[11]

Property crimes dominate among the classified offenses. Shoplifting is the most frequent offense category, accounting for almost a quarter of the offense participations included in the study. Participation in violent offenses is considerably less common than participation in crimes against property. Sex offenses constitute the most rarely seen offense category (0.3 percent), and drug offenses were also relatively uncommon (3.4 percent).

Of the individuals covered by the study, 8,825 (40 percent) had no known co-offenders. These individuals appear in the study as isolates. The remaining 13,266 actors did have known co-offenders and were thus linked to other individuals.

There is a correlation between the number of co-offenders to whom an individual is linked and the number of offenses for which the individual is suspected ($r = .24$). On average then, individuals with several links to other actors, are more delinquent than individuals with fewer links. This relationship does not hold for actors with more than 30 co-offenders however. These individuals have often committed relatively few offenses and the large number of co-offenders is the result of their having been arrested in connection with some kind of public order offense. There were a number of crimes of this kind registered during 1991 and 1992, and most of the actors who became suspects in connection with these did not find their way back into the police register during the remainder of the study period. When the 252 individuals (one percent of the study population) with 30 or more co-offenders are excluded, the correlation between the number of offenses and the number of co-offenders becomes much stronger ($r = .60$).

The linear relationship between the number of offenses and the number of co-offenders is described by the equation $y = 1.03 + 0.39x$, where y is the number of offenses and x the number of co-offenders. The number of offenses for which an individual is suspected thus increases with an average of .39 for every additional co-offender.

The Networks

Dividing the material into ten six-month periods creates 5,710 networks. In Appendix 1 there is an illustration of some of the networks. The individuals in the study are spread over these networks in the following way:

14 percent are linked into networks comprising six or more actors
20 percent are linked into networks comprising three to five actors
26 percent constitute the one-half of a pair of actors
40 percent appear as isolates

The Largest Network during the Period 1991-1995

As has been mentioned, the size of the networks expands as we extend the period examined. If we conduct a network analysis of all 22,000 or so individuals who appear in the study at some stage during the period 1991-1995, we find a large network comprising 4,390 individuals. This figure is just under 20 percent of the entire study population and represents 13,180 links (60 percent of all the links that appear in the material). The remainder of the population is divided into a large number of isolates, and other networks comprising up to 71 actors. The networks that are not linked into the single large network are thus strikingly small. They are also short-lived. None of them spans more than two of the ten six-month periods.

When we examine the network structure of the material as a whole, the large network assumes a central position. For this reason it will henceforth be referred to as the "central network." This central network would seem to be of considerable importance for the pattern of juvenile crime in Stockholm. It draws together a disproportionately large percentage of the most delinquent youths. For example, 95 percent of the 274 individuals suspected of ten or more offenses during the five year study period are to be found here, and the actors linked into this network are together suspected of 39 percent of all offense participations included in the study.

The central network contains 48 identifiable clusters with a significantly higher link density than the network as a whole. These clusters comprise just under half (46 percent) of all the actors in the network. Forty-seven of the clusters contain between four and 117 actors (with six and 857 links respectively). The remaining cluster is extremely large, comprising 1,459 actors and 6,928 links (seven percent of the individuals in the study but fully 27 percent of the links). Seventy-three percent of the 274 individuals suspected of participation in ten or more offenses are to be found in this cluster, which can be seen as the nucleus of the central network.

These results are very similar to those from the Borlänge study. In Borlänge we also found a large network which was of central importance for juvenile crime in the town, and into which a large proportion of the town's most delinquent youths were linked. In both the smaller town and the relatively large city there seems to be a central network which draws together a large proportion of the area's most delinquent juveniles and which accounts for a disproportionately high percentage of the offense participations in the area.

LONGEVITY OF CO-OFFENDER RELATIONSHIPS

The 22,091 actors in the study population are tied to one another with a total of 25,207 links. The vast majority of these links represent a single joint offense. Pairs or groups of actors suspected of co-offending together over a longer timeframe are extremely rare.

Table 1: Cumulative Frequencies of Pairs of Co-offenders over Six-month Periods

Number of Six-Month periods	Pairs of Co-offenders (cum. %)	N
6	0.00	2
5	0.00	8
4	0.00	18
3	0.37	94
2	2.53	658
1	100.00	25.207

Table 1 shows that around 2.5 percent of relationships between specific pairs of actors survive to outlive a single six-month period. Only two such relationships are sufficiently long-lived to appear in six of the ten six-month study periods. Information concerning the longevity of such relationships is limited as a result of the sampling procedure. This does not seem to have affected the results to any great extent, however. For those individuals who turned 20 in 1995, and who were thus unaffected by the age limitation, 3.5 percent of a total of 3,195 pairs of co-offenders appear in more than one of the six-month periods, while 0.7 percent appear in three or more of these periods.

Fourteen percent of the links between actors in the central network consist of offenses committed in more than one of the ten six-month periods. This percentage rises to 17 percent for those youths that turned 20 in 1995.

Longevity of network composition

Even if it is rare for a co-offending relationship to last longer than a single six-month period, it is possible that network composition might not change quite so rapidly (not every member of a network is directly linked to one another).

In order to examine changes in the composition of the various networks over time, a "macro-image" of the network data was produced. For the purposes of this analysis each network comprising six or more individuals from each of the ten six-month study periods was represented by a single symbol. Movements between the networks (i.e., when one or more actors present in a certain network during one of the six-month periods turn up linked into a different network during a later period) were represented as links. Networks comprising five individuals or less were excluded from the analysis.

The analysis comprises 327 networks tied to one another with 415 links. The results show that it is rare for offenders to move between networks. Only 16 percent of the total number of links covered by the study join three or more individuals who move between two networks. On average, each link represents 1.6 individuals.

Once again the results from Stockholm coincide with those from Borlänge inasmuch as longstanding networks are a rarity. Stability within groups of co-offenders seems however to be somewhat lower in Stockholm than it was in Borlänge. We find hardly any long-lived, densely linked networks that turn up in several different periods containing the same individuals. Quite the reverse, in fact: the criminally active youths in Stockholm seem constantly to be switching to different co-offenders.

There are however a few exceptions to this. There is a group of nine boys, aged 13 to 15, who were jointly suspected of theft and robbery both in the autumn of 1992 and in the spring of 1993. In autumn 1992, this group of boys was linked into a network comprising 34 individuals and in the following spring into another comprising 23 individuals. That is to say that of the 34 actors in the network from the autumn of 1992, nine turned up together in a network the following spring. A further eight of these 34 individuals were suspected of offenses in the spring of 1993, but in connection with different constellations of co-offenders and without being linked to one another. The co-offending of the group of nine boys seems to have ceased after the spring of 1993. However, two of them were suspected of a further joint offense (another robbery) in the spring of 1995.

In a few other cases, we find groups of between five and eight individuals suspected of co-offending in two separate periods, although these periods need not necessarily follow directly from one another. Such groups are always linked into larger networks in both periods however, and it is rare for two, or at most three, individuals to appear together in more than two periods.

DISCUSSION

The chief reason for studying co-offending among young people is that the joint commission of offenses is indicative of the contacts between the youths in question. Such contacts can facilitate both the exchange of information of various kinds and the exertion of influence over one another.

This is the first time juvenile crime in a metropolitan area has been described with the help of a network analysis. For this reason it is not possible to make generalizations on the basis of these results. The preliminary results from the Stockholm study nonetheless confirm many of the findings produced by the Borlänge study fifteen years ago.

As we have shown, the more criminally active youths occupy important positions in a central network. The distances between these individuals in the network are rarely very large which suggests the likelihood of a considerable exchange of information and influence among them. In Stockholm, as many as 73 percent of the study's most delinquent youths are linked into the nucleus of the central network, while this nucleus comprises barely seven percent of the study population.

What we do not find in Stockholm, on the other hand, are clearly defined, close-knit and long-lived groups of criminally active youths of a kind that were present in Borlänge.

It is not altogether clear to what extent the low proportion of lasting co-offender relationships is a result of the generally low clearance rates in Stockholm. We must of course assume that the actual number of offenses committed by the various pairs of co-offenders is higher than the number registered by the police. At the same time though, the results show the same youths re-offending with new co-offenders, which suggests that switching co-offenders is common and that the longevity of the relationships that comprise the networks is low. In all likelihood, long-lasting gangs of the kind found in North America do not exist in Stockholm.

Other findings from the project further support the contention that juvenile crime in Stockholm is not spread over a number of competing, close-knit gangs, as seems to be the case in the larger cities of North America for example. In an interview study carried out in 1995, representatives from the police and social services were asked if there were any juvenile gangs in the local area (Fondén & Sarnecki, 1996). The respondents identified a large number of groups of criminally active young people. Among these groups however, there were very few that the respondents felt were long-standing, and practically none of them used a gang name, gang symbols or a gang uniform. In none of these groups could the members be said to have developed the kind of "gang identity" which Klein (1995) suggests is perhaps the most important criterion when defining a group of young people as a gang. It was also uncommon for the respondents to have encountered persistent conflicts between different "gangs."

We find further confirmation of these conclusions in the findings of another study within the project. This study examined the ethnic backgrounds of those youths suspected of violent offenses during 1995 (Pettersson, 1998). The results show, once again in contrast to the situation found in North American cities, that criminally active youths in Stockholm rarely choose their co-offenders (or indeed their victims) on the basis of ethnic criteria. Most of the networks whose members have committed violent offenses display a mixed ethnic composition. Although the probability of individuals from a certain ethnic background choosing co-offenders or victims from their own ethnic group was somewhat greater than can be explained by chance, the majority of the links between co-offenders join individuals from different ethnic backgrounds.[12] In Stockholm, ethnic considerations do not appear to create the kind of barriers between different criminal networks that are often found in other countries (Klein,1995; Huff, 1991). One possible explanation for this may be that residential segregation of different ethnic groups is not as widespread in Stockholm as it is in many other places.

In other respects the picture we have produced of juvenile crime in Stockholm is rather more similar to that presented by American research on gangs. The criminal activities of the youths in Stockholm, for example, are also spread over a wide range of different offense categories ("cafeteria style" criminality; see Klein, 1995).

The police in Stockholm have also carried out a study of groups of criminally active youths. The police study made use of a questionnaire sent to the capital's local police districts, and the results, in contrast to those presented above, suggest the existence of a large number of juvenile gangs in Stockholm. Gang-related problems were reportedly particularly serious in certain suburban areas (Polismyndigheten ï Stockolms Län, 1998). Using the police study as a backdrop, Johnson (1999) carried out interviews with key figures from the police and social services in four of the areas portrayed as suffering the most serious gang-related problems. The interviewees felt that the police study seriously exaggerated the importance of gangs. The informants agreed that there were problems in the local community both with certain youth and with criminality, but they refuted claims that the youths had formed themselves into gangs.

Johnson (1999) also carried out in-depth interviews with a number of youths from one of the gangs mentioned in the police report. These youngsters live in an area portrayed as suffering from some of the worst gang trouble. The youths that were interviewed did not feel that there was a gang problem in their neighborhoods. Instead, they said that while they knew most of the young people in the area, they regarded them simply as friends and not as members in any kind of gang.

William-Olsson (1998) has also interviewed key informants and criminally active youths in one of the areas named in the police report as having serious "gang" problems. Her results are in many ways similar to those of Johnson. The people interviewed by William-Olsson accepted that there was a group of criminally active young people in the area. However, neither the informants nor the young people interviewed felt there was any form of close-knit gang involved, even if reports of the existence of such a gang had surfaced in the media on several occasions. As the boys themselves say, "The (...)[13] gang doesn't exist. We're just a group of friends who've known each other since we were small" (William-Olsson, 1998:19).

Conclusions regarding both similarities and dissimilarities between the situation in Stockholm and the situation elsewhere must nonetheless be seen as preliminary. Since the results concerning Stockholm and North America respectively have been produced with such different methodologies, their comparability must remain in some doubt. It would be interesting to apply the network methodology to the study of the structure of juvenile crime somewhere other than in Sweden.

In conclusion, this first attempt at studying the structure of juvenile crime in a metropolitan area by adapting a network methodology to a criminological perspective has not been without its problems. What the attempt has shown however, is that such an approach is sufficiently promising as to encourage continued efforts to refine and improve the application of the network methodology in the context of juvenile crime.

Appendix 1

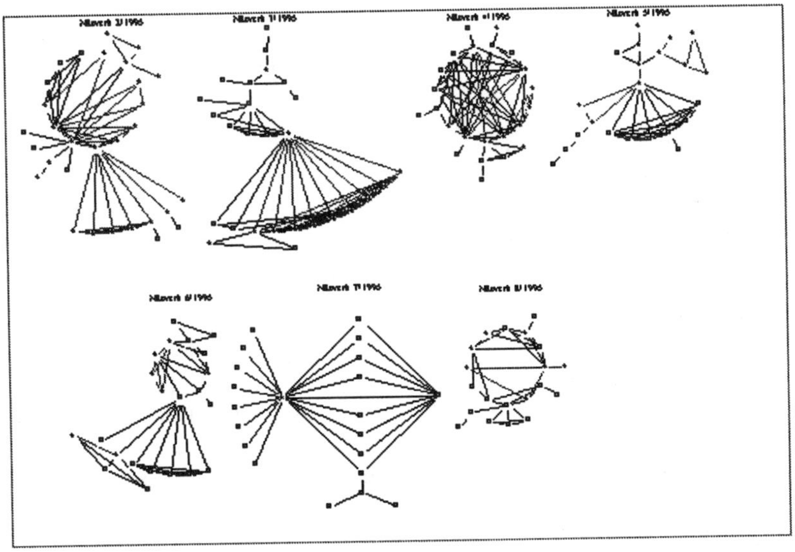

Figure1. Youths Suspected of Offenses in Stockholm in 1995 and Their Known Co-offenders (172 actors in total, 332 links)

REFERENCES

Akers, R. L. (1998). Social Learning and Social Structure. A General Theory of Crime and Deviance. Boston: Northeastern University Press.

Barnes, J. A. (1954). Class and committees in a Norwegian island parish, Human Relations 7:39-59.

Borell, K., and R. Johansson. (1994). Samhället som Nätverk. (Society as a Network). Lund: Studentlitteratur.

Cartwright, D. (1959). Studies in Social Power. Ann Arbor, MI: Institute for Social Research.

Cloward, R. A., and L.E. Ohlin (1960). Delinquency and Opportunity. Glencoe, Illinois: Free Press.

Cohen, A. K. (1956). Delinquent Boys: The Culture of the Gang. Glencoe, Illinois: Free Press.

Coleman, J. S., E. Katz, and H. Menzel (1957). The Diffusion of an innovation among physicians, Sociometry, XX, 253 -270.

Ferrell, J., and C.R. Sanders (1995). Cultural Criminology. Boston: Northeastern University Press.

Fondén, C., and J. Sarnecki (1996). Brottsliga ungdomsnätverk i Stockholm 1995. (Delinquent youth networks in Stockholm 1995). Stockholm: Samordningskansliet för brottsförebyggande åtgärder.

Hirschi, T. (1969). Causes of Delinquency. Berkeley: University of California Press.

Huff, R. C. (ed.) (1991). Gangs in America. Newbury Park: Sage Publications.

Johnson, M. (1999). En kvalitativ studie av Gäng I Stockholms Län (A qualitative study of gangs in the Stockholm area). Gäng I Stockholm (Gangs in Stockholm). Stockholm: Opublicerad stencil Kriminologiska institutionen vid Stockholms universitet.

Klein, M. (1971). Street Gangs and Street Workers. Englewood Cliffs, New Jersey: Prentice Hall.

Klein, M. (1995). The American Street Gang. Its Nature, Prevalence, and Control. New York: Oxford University Press.

Krohn, M. D., and J.L. Massey (1980). Social control and delinquent behavior: An examination of the elements of the social bond. The Sociological Quarterly 21 (Autumn): 529-543.

Le Blanc M., and A. Caplan (1993). Theoretical formalization, a necessity: The example of Hirschi's bonding theory. In F. Adler and W. Laufer, (eds.), New Directions in Criminological Theory. New Brunswick: Transaction Publishers.

Matza, D. (1964). Delinquency and Drift. New York: Wiley.

Miller, W. B. (1958). Lower class culture as a generating milieu of gang delinquency, Journal of Social Issues 14:5-19.

Moreno, J. L. (1934). Who shall survive? Foundations of Sociometry, Group Psychotherapy, and Sociodrama. Washington, D. C.: Nervous and Mental Disease Publishing Co.

Pettersson, T. (1998). Etnicitet och brottsliga nätverk bland ungdomar i Stockholm som misstänks för våldsbrott. (Ethnic Background and Criminal Networks among Youths Suspected of Violent Offenses in Stockholm) Barn - och ungdomsdelegationen. Stockholm: Regeringskansliet.

Polismyndigheten i Stockholms Län (1998). Rapport om kriminella gäng, rasism och främlingsfientlighet. (Report about criminal gangs, racism and xenophobia). Stockholm: Länskriminalpolisens Integrationsgrupp.

Reiss, A. J. Jr. (1986). Co-offending and criminal careers. In A. Blumstein, et al. (eds.), Criminal Careers and "Career Criminals," Vol.2. Washington D.C.: National Academy Press.

Reiss, A. J. Jr. (1988). Co-offending and criminal careers. In M. Tonry and N. Morris (eds.), Crime and Justice: An Annual Review of Research. Chicago: University of Chicago Press.

Sarnecki, J. (1982). Brottslighet och kamratrelationer. Studie av ungdomsbrottsligheten i en svensk kommun. (Criminality and Friendship Ties. A Study of Juvenile Crime in a Swedish Municipality). Stockholm. Brottsliga Brottsförebyggande rådet. Rapport 1982:5.

Sarnecki, J. (1983). Brottsliga Ungdomsgäng. (Delinquent Juvenile Gangs). Stockholm. Brottsförebyggande rådet. Rapport 1983:2.

Sarnecki, J. (1986). Delinquent Networks. Stockholm: The National Council for Crime Prevention. Sweden. Allmänna Förlaget.

Sarnecki, J. (1990). Delinquent networks in Sweden. Journal of Quantitative Criminology, Vol. 6, No 1.

Short, J. F. Jr., and F.L. Strodtbeck (1965). Group Process and Gang Delinquency. Chicago: The University of Chicago Press.

Sutherland, E. H. (1939). Principles of Criminology, 3rd. Ed. Philadelphia: Lippincott.

Sutherland, E. H., D. Cressey, and R. Luckenbill (1992). Principles of Criminology, 11th ed. Dix Hills, New York: Deneral Hall.

Thrasher, F. (1927). The Gang. Chicago: University of Chicago Press.

Tremblay, P. (1993). Searching for suitable co-offenders. In R.V. Clarkeand M. Felson (eds.), Routine Activity and Rational Choice. Advances in Criminological Theory, Vol. 5. New Brunswick: Transaction Publishers.

Wasserman, S., and J. Galaskiewicz (eds.) (1994). Advances in Social Network Analysis. Research in the Social and Behavioural Sciences. Thousand Oaks: Sage Publications.

Wasserman, S., and K. Faust (1997). Social Network Analysis: Methods and Applications. New York: Cambridge University Press.

William-Olsson, A. (1998). Ängengänget. En studie av ett brottsligt aktivt nätverk av unga män. (Ängengänget. A study of a criminal active network of young men.) Stockholm: C-uppsats I Kriminologi vid Stockholms universitet.

ENDNOTES

1 Barnes (1954) is widely held to be the first to have used the concept "social network." Theories and empirical studies in this field appear to have developed in parallel and to some degree independently of one another in several different areas within social science. The development of sociometric techniques in connection with social psychology was of major

Another early research initiative in the field was the study of how the prescription of new drugs was affected by relationships among the doctors doing the prescribing (Coleman, J.S., E. Katz, and H. Menzel, (1957).

2 For an overview of the more recent research in this area see Wasserman & Galaskiewicz (1994), Wasserman & Faust (1997) (and in Swedish, Borell & Johansson, 1994).

3 A Swedish town of 50,000 inhabitants.

4 In one of the analyses the actors are criminal networks and the relation studied is the movement of individuals between these networks over time.

5 The maximum possible number in a network can be calculated with the formula (n-1) n/2 where n is the number of actors in a network.

6 Official crime statistics in Sweden count offenses in more than one way. The offense participation count takes into consideration the number of co-offenders present at an incident. A single burglary committed by five co-offenders would be counted as five offense participations, for example.

7 Unfortunately it is not possible on the basis of the available data to count the precise number of offenses.

8 The principal population includes all those persons aged 20 or under suspected of offenses in the city of Stockholm between 1991 and 1995.

9 Individuals as young as this are extremely rare in the data. Children under 10 years of age comprise around 1 percent of those studied.

10 In practice, the principal population is defined on the basis of the year of birth. The eldest individuals included in the principal population for 1991 were born in 1971. Those included in 1992 were born 1972 or later, and so on.

11 It should be noted that because of the sampling procedure employed here, individuals of 21 years of age and over appear only to the extent that they commit offenses jointly with younger co-offenders. At the same time, any offenses committed outside the city of Stockholm do not appear in the data and given that the period covered by the data is fixed, the follow up period for any study of re-offending would vary from year to year. For these reasons the information outlined above is not suitable for the study of recidivism.

12 Of the links between co-offenders where the ethnicity of both the offenders is known, 65 percent involve individuals from different *countries* and 60 percent individuals are from different ethnic groups.

13 The gang's name, according to the media.

Chapter 21

GANG-LIKE GROUPS IN SLOVENIA

Bojan Dekleva
Department of Social Pedagogy, University of Ljubjana, Slovenia

INTRODUCTION–PREVIOUS RESEARCH

Writing about gangs and gang-like groups in Slovenia is difficult. The reason is that there has not been a lot of research done and there is not much empirical data available on gangs and other youth groups. The term "gang" and similar Slovenian expressions are not used very much in our media in describing youth deviance and crime. Both observations suggest that gangs are not (or have not been) something characteristic of the Slovenian scene.

Although there have been over 120 major research projects on crime carried out by our national Institute of Criminology since 1954 and approximately one third of them dealt with juvenile delinquency and youth deviance, there were only three of them dealing specifically with juvenile delinquent "groups" or "associations." The first one was carried out in 1966-1968 (Selih, 1968). Its author mainly analyzed data on "co-offenders and co-offending," that is juveniles who committed crimes in pairs or with more than one co-offender. The data were taken exclusively from the court and prosecutor's office records. Yet the focus of this research was not to explore the structures of these groups and their other psychosocial characteristics, but rather the processing of these offenders.

M.W. Klein et al (eds.), The Eurogang Paradox, 273–281.

The author of this article conducted the other two projects. In the first one (Dekleva, 1982) the data on "group offending" (defined as: at least three people together and related to the same group of offenses; at least two of them should be 14-18 year old juveniles) in the capital of Slovenia, Ljubljana, were analyzed. The researchers invited these delinquent group members (and their friends) to a suitable place, conducted semi-structured interviews with them and asked them to fill in some sociometric and other questionnaires. These data were compared to the official data taken from the police, public prosecutor's office and juvenile court records.

In the second phase of the project the researchers wanted to identify four (relatively structured groups of certain duration) of such officially known "delinquent groups" and to develop a kind of street group work approach to work with them. The declared aims of this work were to help to re-orient their group activities to a more socially acceptable direction, and/or to assist the process of the reconstruction of these groups to some other psycho-social structures which would be more supportive to their further personal development. The experiences demonstrated that such "open group work," close to their living environments (starting from the streets and squares of the new estates) is generally possible. However, the working structures (who should work with whom, how, when and for how long) are very unclear, as much as the outcomes of such work.

In the second research project (Dekleva, 1985), the researchers were looking for deviant or at-risk groups of youngsters in the streets, using non-formal ways (this time without the help and the involvement of the criminal justice system) of finding and contacting them. The researchers' idea was to make contacts with the street groups and with their local communities and to build–through street work and community work–some relational and institutional structures, which would make possible the additional community support for the non-deviant development and self-realization of these groups' members.

Coming back to the question of whether gangs have actually existed in Slovenia, I remember my traumas and frustrations in 1980 (when the second mentioned research was carried out). We were hardly able to find four groups which would at least somehow match our criteria (that there should be at least three youngsters who were perpetrating criminal acts for at least six months and who were likely to spend a good part of their leisure time together). After contacting and interviewing about 200 juveniles and after ten months of group work with the selected four groups, my conclusion was that there were actually no "real gangs" in Ljubljana. Being informed by Yablonsky's "near-group" concept, I concluded "that the structure of the majority of our delinquent sample could best be described as a structure of loosely inter-related network(s) of cliques, pairs, individuals and small groups, connected together with not much cohesion, of short existence, and typically found in newly built and relatively densely populated housing areas at the outskirts of the town." In these near-groups or networks, we were able to observe some of the elements of traditional American gangs, e.g., some territoriality, some inter-territorial conflicts and rivalry, hardly any differentiated age-grouping, but a low degree of criminal activity, and these structures seemed yet to be of short duration and not extremely important to their members.

After 1985 there have been no research projects on juvenile delinquency which would be specifically related to groups or gangs. My sources of information on gang-like phenomena have been from 1985 to 1997 only mass media, my children's and their friends' experiences (they were teenagers at the time), occasional discussions with one or two police officers and–not of the least importance–my students' experiences. Then in 1997 two of my students for their graduation theses analyzed official data on violent juvenile crime and on a relationship between the process of immigration and delinquency. In 1998 two other students did some field research on gangs and subcultures (in fact, deviant youth groups) in the framework of their degree theses. Lacking more serious and systematic research data I must rely a lot on my personal memories when describing the development of the gang-like youth structures in Slovenia.

During the late 1980's the issue of the youth groups came to the attention of the general public through mass media information on subcultural styles, subcultures and relations between them. I remember three incidents resulting in small local "wars" between different sub-groupings of youngsters, which belonged to different subculture (musical) styles in Ljubljana. All these "wars" took place in one dark square (or it may be better described as a small park on the inner side of a block of small houses) very close to the central meeting point of social night life in Ljubljana. In all cases there was a pair of groupings which were supposed to be there, to fight or to take revenge for previous (lost) fights. On one occasion they were rock punkers and pop music fans; on another occasion they were rock-punks and skinheads, and in still another case they were skinheads and ethnic minority group members. In all these cases the battles were anticipated and in a way "declared" in advance (which is true at least for the battles of revenge). Many of Ljubljana's teenagers (not only the explicitly subcultural or deviant ones, e.g. my children) knew about these battles and were looking forward to them. None of these groupings territorially belonged to that park, but it was of a highly strategic importance, as it was located in the middle of Ljubljana. These wars ended with some (or no) weapon use, some small injuries and some (or no) police interventions. As far as I know these battles were events of short duration and were not related to any structured grouping of youngsters which would stay together for a longer time and which would also be criminally active to an important degree. Some similar things have happened near some other parts of the town (concert halls, squads, subcultural centers), which were important for the (subcultural) musical (mostly heavy metal, hard core, punk) youth life.

After achieving the independence of Slovenia in 1991, the question of ethnic origin has become quite important. Acquiring of citizenship was conditioned by one's nationality, by the place of birth, by the time spent in Slovenia, by other citizenship, by having your own place of residence, by speaking the Slovenian language and similar things. Suddenly some part of the Slovenian population had a problem: either to acquire Slovenian citizenship, or to be doomed to be a "second class inhabitant," needing working and living visas for living and working in the same place as before. The developing economic competition and unemployment in the 1990s affected Slovenia's inhabitants, but non-citizens and citizens of non-Slovenian nationality were affected to a much larger degree. The situation was further complicated by the three waves of refugees coming from different ex-Yugoslav republics, mostly from Bosnia.

As regards the crime situation (and their mass media representation), there are three issues which have become important: organized crime (including arms trafficking), illegal drugs and drug trafficking, and bullying and peer (school and street) violence. The first and the last of the three issues are often supposed to be related to the non-Slovenian organized crime structures and to non-Slovenian youngsters.

THE RECENT SITUATION

About five years ago a new term appeared in wider use and began to be used mostly, but not exclusively, by young(er) people. This term chefoor can not be found in any dictionary and therefore has no formal meaning. I do not know its origin but I suppose that it is related to the term "chefoot," which used to be (and still is) a pejorative and offending term for Jews half a century ago.

The term chefoor is also mostly used in a pejorative manner. It has never been used–as far as I know–in any official document or in mass media, but children and youngsters are using it quite often, as a general offending word. Sometimes–if one says it to an actual chefoor–it denotes something very offensive, and sometimes–when saying it to one's friends–it just means: "come on, stop it, you are a fool."

In a small-scale pilot research (Lesar, 1998) consisting of surveys and interviews carried out with young people, it turned out that the term in its specific usage by young people denotes three meanings: 1. Somebody who is violent and quick to fight (has a macho behavior style), 2. Somebody of non-Slovenian origin (a synonym for this meaning is a pejorative term "a Bosnian," covering people of different nationalities, coming from the south of Slovenia, also "the southern ones"), 3. Having a specific style of clothes (shoes, trainers, jackets, also of very specific brand names) and a specific way of walking and bodily posture (of a street fighter). In summary, chefoors are "specifically dressed violent Bosnians."[1]

The emergence and much wider use of the pejorative term for young immigrants (they could be of the first or, more often, of the second generation) is in my understanding related to their worsened situation. Generally, it is related to the more insecure situation of a majority of Slovenian inhabitants, at least regarding their employment opportunities. Slovenians have become more aware of the presence of the "foreign" inhabitants and the places where they live. Although there are no typical slums or ghettos in Ljubljana, there are a few typical areas, which are supposed to be inhabited by a larger proportion of people of non-Slovenian origin.

At the outskirts of the town there is one local community (called Rakova Jelsa), where "only" non-Slovenians live in their individual houses. The houses have been built without any building license, sometimes also without the ownership of the "no man's" land (which actually belongs to the town). After many years of conflicts with municipal authorities the locations of the majority of these houses were legalized. For some decades this community has been known as one with the highest crime rates, regarding children, juveniles and adults. Three years ago the mass media published a series of reports on a group of youngsters from Rakova Jelsa, mainly on their acts of violence, street fights and some property crimes. After some time they became so famous that they agreed to be accompanied one night by a journalist and a photographer of one of the Slovenian weekly journals. The following week there were pictures of very explicit violence (which was said to be true, not just pretended for the photographer) published in the journal. These photos appeared along with statements from the gang members that they are the strongest, that they fear nobody and that the police prefer to stay away from them. The reactions of the public to these reports were furious and the criminal justice system made its moves. Today some core members of that gang, among them the most violent ones, are in prisons or juvenile residential institutions.

Besides Rakova Jelsa there are two other areas (housing projects Fuzine and BS3) of Ljubljana, which are famous for a lot of chefoors living there. The paths through or to these neighborhoods are supposed to be dangerous (but only for youngsters), and the public "knows" that there are a lot of drugs used by young people there.

This year, two of my students conducted their research projects on chefoors as a part of their degree theses. One of them (Lesar, 1998a) mainly analyzed the role of music in the socialization of members of different subcultures (including chefoors), while the other (Lesar, 1998b) explicitly studied chefoors' groupings and gangs and their self-concepts. He did it by using three kinds of techniques:

1. Using questionnaires and interviews, asking different groups of people (including children and youngsters in the above mentioned three typical town localities) "Who is a chefoor?"
2. Doing participant observation in a boarding home, where he works, observing frequent interactions, conflicts and fights between chefoor and other young people .
3. Doing fieldwork, partly participant observation, partly interviews with the group members, leaders and "key street experts," on who are chefoor groups, what are they like and what they do. In doing that, he used the snowball sampling technique and other kinds of street intelligence work.

He found out that being a chefoor is a very strong point of identification, and–what surprised us quite a lot–that "they" use the term chefoor among themselves quite a lot as a positive term, which gives them pride and a feeling of security. They said that people were afraid of chefoors, and if one goes to a disco, stating that he comes from Fuzine or BS3 or Rakova Jelsa, nobody would dare touch him or prevent him from coming in. After all, the security services at discotheques are very frequently composed of chefoors, too.

Samo Lesar (1998a) found many of the characteristics of traditional American gangs in two of three chefoor localities in Ljubljana.

- The BS3 group (or gang) has about 20 members, but in times of fights it grows to nearly 40 members.
- The Rakova Jelsa gang has three sub-groups according to their age: children 12-15 years old, youngsters 16-19 years old, and "grown-ups," over 20 years old, which seems to be close to the Mafia-like criminal structures.
- The importance of territoriality is not so big, probably because it seems that no other youth or subcultural groupings threaten them in their communities. At the same time, these areas are not strictly separated from other parts of the town; instead, they are relatively connected and integrated. All the same, it is important to know among chefoors, that those from Rakova Jelsa are "the strongest," but much more important is the fact that all of them are chefoors. Some of their statements (referring to the actual events or only mythical references) show that chefoors from other Slovenian towns are their allies and that they are ready to travel to other towns to give support in fights to other chefoor groupings.
- The specific ethnic composition of the gang does not seem to be strictly important or decisive. In these groupings one could find members of different ethnic groups of ex-Yugoslavs, and also some individual Slovenians, who accept the term chefoor, which means to them that they are tough and strong and fear nobody.
- Criminal activities of these gangs–besides the fact or the myth of violence–are not so clear. There is some dealing of drugs, some acts of breaking and entering, some auto thefts, some extortion on the streets. We do not have hard data on their criminal activities. But what is important for understanding their point of reference is the image that they talk about. This image is of a little bit older chefoor person (let us say 25 years old) whom one can "suddenly" see walk around with a lot of money, with an adult "gangster" dress and with good "connections." This image seems to be for some second-generation immigrants the most positive image they were able to find in their social surrounding (as relevant to them).
- Some of the chefoor groups (of younger boys) like to travel in the evenings to the center of the town to be around people, usually other youngsters.
- The use of media: they like to watch American movies on black gangs; they would like to be like them. They like Slovenian mass media reporting on them.

- The differentiation of "stupid" and "smart" chefoors, according to the "smart" ones, relates to the members of ethnic minorities, who–after achieving some social mobility (through good academic achievement)–do not need to identify with the chefoor stigma and are actually not chefoors any more. They have become either more ambivalent to the term chefoor or have outgrown it already. But one of the characteristics of the real chefoors (as explained by some of our field informants) is that they despise their parents as they have not achieved anything and they are nothing, doing only low-paid jobs "for Slovenians."

CONCLUSION

According to this study, it seems that we are witnessing in Ljubljana an early phase of the process of a development of the ethnic minority gangs.[2] On the one hand they seem to be similar to the compressed and on the other to the neotraditional gang type (Klein, 1996). It also seems that a development of these gangs is related to the worsening economic situation and changing political conditions in Slovenia and in the entire Balkan region. My personal concluding observation is that Slovenian (scientific and political) reflection of this development and the related social complexities lag behind the reality.

REFERENCES

Dekleva, B. (1982). Akcijsko raziskovanje mladoletniških prestopniskih zdruzb. (Action research of juvenile delinquent groupings). Research report. Institute of criminology, Ljubljana.
Dekleva, B. (1985). Preprecevanje odklonskosti mladine v krajevnih skupnostih. (Prevention of youth deviance in local communities). Research report. Institute of criminology, Ljubljana.
Klein, M. (1996). Gangs in the United States and Europe. European Journal on Criminal Policy and Research, 4(2): 63-80.
Lesar, Samo (1998a). Kdo je cefur? (Who is a Chefoor?). Degree thesis. Faculty of Education, Ljubljana.
Lesar, Simona (1998b). Pomen Glasbe v Socializaciji Mladine. (The Role of the Music in the Socialisation of Youth). Degree thesis. Faculty of Education, Ljubljana.
Selih, A. (1968). Nekateri Problemi Mladoletniskih Skupin. (Some Problems of Juvenile Gangs). Research report. Institute of Criminology, Ljubljana.

ENDNOTES

1 In doing small informal interviews on the meaning and the emergence of the term "chefoor," one of my colleagues, a professor at the Faculty of Education said, "I became aware of the term 'chefoor' at the same time, when I became aware that there are skinheads in Slovenia; in fact the son of my closest neighbor was one of the first skinheads I knew." My friend's 17-year-old daughter said one day last year: "Whoa, you wouldn't believe what happened to me this morning. A *chefoor* boy came to me in the street and begged me for some money." This is unusual in two ways: first, *chefoors* never beg, instead they **ask violently or threaten** you for money, and second, they never ask **women** for help, because they are supposed to protect them and to appear strong in front of them.

2 Situations in other parts of Slovenia are not well known to me.

Chapter 22

THE GROUP ASPECT OF YOUTH CRIME AND YOUTH GANGS IN BRUSSELS: WHAT WE DO KNOW AND ESPECIALLY WHAT WE DON'T KNOW

Conny Vercaigne
Leuven Catholic University, Leuven, Belgium

The objective of this paper is to provide a brief overview of the gang situation in Brussels. This task is not easy because knowledge on this subject is very limited and we have more questions than answers. For this reason we will put the subject of gangs in a larger context. First, we will situate Brussels in the Belgium context. Second, we will give general information on youth crime in Brussels. Third, we will focus on the group aspect of youth crime, and finally we will discuss the topic of gangs. Gangs are treated here as one particular form of youth group.

BRUSSELS

Brussels is the capital of Belgium and it's the biggest city. It is also the city that plays the most important international role in Belgium. According to 1991 data, Brussels has about 1,670,000 residents of which half a million (31 percent) are younger than 24 years. In addition, Brussels has the biggest number of "poverty zones."

The criteria used by Kesteloot (1992) to define a poverty zone are:

- the number of single-households is more than 40 percent

M.W. Klein et al (eds.), The Eurogang Paradox, 283–297.

- the number of laborers is more than 45 percent
- the number of houses with little comfort is more than 25 percent
- the number of Turkish and Moroccan people is more than 5 percent
- the average income per inhabitant is less than 250,000 Bfr. (approximately $6,500)
- the number of unemployed people is more than 15 percent
- the number of households with a telephone is less than 70 percent

Using these criteria, we find 9 percent of the Brussels households living in poverty zones, compared to only 0.4 percent of households in the rest of Flanders. In Brussels almost 40 percent of the households are located in neighborhoods in which at least four criteria are fulfilled; for the rest of Flanders this is only 4 percent.

Brussels is the city in Belgium with the most ethnic and cultural diversity; in Brussels there are more than 70 different nationalities, seven of which have more than 10,000 representatives. Brussels also has the largest number of foreign-born residents (30 percent, or almost 300,000 residents). The Walloon region has only 10.7 percent and the Flemish region 4.8 percent foreign-born residents. In Belgium, there are 15 towns with more than 25 percent foreign-born residents: 10 of those towns are situated in the Brussels area.[1]

Finally we see a concentration of crime. In Brussels over 120,000 crimes are registered every year, which is about 14 percent of the total crimes registered in the whole country.

YOUTH CRIME IN BRUSSELS IN GENERAL

Official data

An important source of information for official data on crime is the APSD (General Police Service). Unfortunately, the APSD only has information on the offense and not on the offender. As a consequence we can't separate the crimes committed by youngsters.

At the level of the public prosecutor the most recent information available is for 1993. In total 22,908 new youth records were opened (this is 6 percent of the total number of new records in Brussels); 14,627 records were still active, which sums to 37,435 youth records in 1993. Not all the cases are delinquency cases. Thirteen percent were cases of child endangerment, while an additional 30 percent involved charges against parents.

Information on the sex and age of the delinquent minors is reported in Table 1.

Table 1. Age and Gender of Delinquent Minors

Age	Male	Female	Total
<10	253 (2%)	55 (.4%)	308 (2.4%)
10-11	994 (7.7%)	162 (1.3%)	1,156 (8.9%)
12-13	3,413 (26.4%)	232 (1.8%)	3,645 (28.2%)
14-15	4,328 (32.4%)	421 (3.3%)	4,749 (36.7%)
16-17	2,882 (22.3%)	207 (1.6%)	3,089 (23.9%)
Total	11,870 (91.7%)	1,077 (8.3%)	12,947 (100%)

The information on the ethnic background of the minors is limited to Belgian nationality or non-Belgian nationality. Seventy-three percent of the minors have a non-Belgian nationality, a figure far higher than in many other localities.

Finally, 73 percent of the delinquency is against property (this category includes not only theft, but also vandalism, graffiti, etc.) and 10 percent are offenses against persons. The remaining 17 percent of delinquent offenses are not described in the report. Over a period of three years the number of crimes against property increased by 45 percent.

There is no information on the minor offender in the police data and information registered by the public prosecutor is very limited (no detailed information on nationality, on the type of crime, on the place of crime, etc.). We have therefore begun to register all records, at the level of the public prosecutor, on crimes committed by minors. In the long term, this should give us a general view of crimes committed by youngsters living in Brussels. Unfortunately this registration is not yet complete.

Survey data

In our research on Brussels we conducted a school survey with almost 5,000 youngsters. One part of the survey dealt with crime. The data gathered by this survey gives us more information on the so-called dark-number figure of crime; the results of our questionnaire reveal that most youngsters who committed certain crimes were not caught. Table 2 reports the prevalence of the types of offenses reported by survey youth and associated rates of detection.

Table 2. Admitted Crimes and Detection (percentages)

	Done last year		If done: been caught?			
Offense	Yes	No	Never	Sometimes	Mostly	Always
Using public transport without paying	46.0	54.0	77.0	19.5	2.0	1.5
Graffiti	13.3	86.7	87.9	9.1	1.1	1.9
Carrying a weapon	20.5	79.5	89.8	7.3	1.8	1.2
Using drugs	16.1	83.9	82.5	13.4	2.4	1.7
Vandalism	14.2	85.8	83.1	14.0	1.9	1.0
Shoplifting	33.5	66.5	78.7	17.9	1.2	2.2
Car theft	5.6	94.4	77.2	15.6	3.1	4.0
Stealing a handbag or a wallet	3.7	96.3	79.9	11.8	3.5	4.9
Troubling people on the street	13.0	87.0	77.2	14.8	3.4	4.6
Hitting somebody on the street	12.5	87.5	74.4	17.3	3.5	4.8
Selling drugs	5.1	94.9	86.0	8.2	1.9	3.9
Burglary	3.6	96.4	78.1	12.4	2.9	6.6

Table 3 reports offending data for males and females.

Table 3. Gender Differences (percentages)

Offense	Male	Female	Total
Using public transport without paying	47	44	46
Graffiti	17.6	9.1	13.3
Carrying a weapon	33.0	8.3	20.5
Using drugs	20.4	12.1	16.1
Vandalism	22.3	6.2	14.2
Shoplifting	40.1	27.1	33.5
Car theft	10.1	1.1	5.6
Stealing a handbag or a wallet	6.3	1.2	3.7
Troubling people on the street	17.6	8.5	13
Hitting somebody on the street	19.9	5.4	12.5
Selling drugs	8.0	2.2	5.1
Burglary	6.5	0.7	3.6

THE GROUP ASPECT OF YOUTH CRIME IN BRUSSELS

Official data

As already mentioned, there is no information on offenders in the police data. Information on the group aspect of youth crime is also missing, as it is in the public prosecutor's reports. As noted above, we therefore started to make our own registration of youth crime in Brussels. One of the characteristics registered is if the crime is committed alone or in a group. If several persons have committed the crime and information on the other offenders is available, we also register that information. In the long run, this registration should give us more information on the group aspect of registered youth crime (on the level of the public prosecutor). As already stated, these data are not yet available.

Survey data

In our survey we also asked if the youngsters committed their offenses mostly alone or mostly with others. The results are shown in Table 4, and are similar to reports of youth offending in many other western nations.

Table 4. Co-offending in Survey Reports

Offense	Done last year		Alone or with others?	
	Yes	No	Mostly alone	Mostly with others
Using public transport without paying	46.0	54.0	-	-
Graffiti	13.3	86.7	20.6	79.4
Carrying a weapon	20.5	79.5	-	-
Using drugs	16.1	83.9	8.8	91.2
Vandalism	14.2	85.8	16.0	84.0
Shoplifting	33.5	66.5	38.2	61.8
Car theft	5.6	94.4	24.5	75.5
Stealing a handbag or a wallet	3.7	96.3	35.9	64.1
Troubling people on the street	13.0	87.0	18.1	81.9
Hitting somebody on the street	12.5	87.5	46.7	53.3
Selling drugs	5.1	94.9	59.6	40.4
Burglary	3.6	96.4	20.6	79.4

- Means that the question was not asked for that offense

YOUTH GANGS IN BRUSSELS

Police data

Scholarly research on youth gangs or the group aspect of crime in Belgium doesn't exist. The only "hard" information on youth gangs in Brussels comes from the police Gang Unit (Cellule Bande Organisée). This unit was established in 1991 after several spontaneous riots in different neighborhoods of Brussels. Every year, all the police stations in Brussels (Brussels has 19 communities and every community has its police station) have to report on the gang situation in their community. For this report a gang is defined as "a group of minors whose behavior disturbs the public order and security." This definition is much broader than the legal definition of gangs which defines a gang as "every organization with the object of making an attempt on a person or property."[2] The gang unit determines whether gangs described by the police stations are also gangs or criminal organizations in the legal sense. The use of the broader definition by the police means that a lot of youngsters are registered and observed even when they don't commit crimes. This creates a risk of stigmatization and criminalization of certain youngsters who are just hanging around. Eventually this also can provoke violence or other delinquency.

In 1994 the gang unit worked out a typology of gangs. Four types of gangs, defined by unit, are as follows:

The gang with leader

The gang with leader consists mostly of youngsters from deprived neighborhoods, who find their role models on the street as they don't find them at home. If the first role model they find is a "destructive youngster," the chance is great that this youngster will be seen as a sort of leader. The youngsters in these gangs often have external features (e.g., shaved heads, marks on their arms) and their crimes are often violent. This violence is often used to get respect from the leader.

The spontaneous gang

Spontaneous gangs can be found at typical places for youngsters, like schools, sports clubs, and youth centers. In these gangs we find youngsters from all social backgrounds who are in a period in their lives when they reject the social order. The causes of this rejection can be the normal crisis in adolescence, bad influence of friends, etc. This rejection is translated into behavior like nuisance in the neighborhood, forbidden signs, throwing stones at the police, tags, etc. The unit claims that the visible presence of the police and enough organizations in the neighborhood often are sufficient to curb this phenomenon.

The ghetto gang

Ghetto gangs mostly occur in neighborhoods with high concentrations of immigrants. The youngsters are often confused as a consequence of the integration problems of their parents, the policy towards immigrants which is not always consistent, etc. As a consequence, these youngsters try to define their own territory where there is no rejection, where it is safe for them. These ghetto gangs become dangerous when the invisible boundaries of their territory are not respected.

The criminal organization

The criminal organization is the gang, as defined in the Belgian law. In this gang we find minors and adults. The ultimate goal of this type of gang is money. These gangs do not often use violence as it makes them too visible.

Table 5 (following page) shows the information of the gang unit for the judicial years registered.

Newspaper accounts

In addition to the information available from the gang unit, there are occasional articles on gangs in our newspapers. The first was published in *De Standaard* (February 7, 1996). On the front page we find the headline "*Brussels Youngsters in Splinter Gangs.*" The rest of the article on page 9 is entitled "*Youth Gangs in Brussels Get Increasingly Mobile and Violent.*" The catalyst for this article was the publication in the Belgian scientific magazine *Politeia* (Janssens & Janssen, 1996) of the article "Young and Quite Crazy." The author, a deputy attorney (member of the gang unit), stresses in his introduction that *"fortunately, the situation in Brussels cannot be compared with cities like Los Angeles, Sharpeville or Paris."* He continues with a description of the youth gang situation in Brussels and describes the special approach to this problem by the Brussels Attorney's Office. In the course of the article it becomes clear that youth gangs are not new in Brussels. Proof offered for that is the formation of the gang unit in 1991. The deputy attorney mentions also that there's an evolution in the youth gang phenomenon. "*We no longer see the organized gangs with a leader, lieutenants, working members and territories but we notice small groups of youngsters from different neighborhoods who quickly gather in view of particular activities (for example: car-jacking) and who disperse as quickly when the police appears.*" These smaller groups are called "splinter gangs."

Table 5. Gang Types Over Five Years

		Judicial year[a]					
		1991-1992	1993-1994	1994-1995	1995-1996	1996-1997	1997-1998
Number of new gangs		31	48	14	18	23	13
Typology of the gangs	Criminal organization	9[b]	14[c]	8	6	5	2
	Spontaneous gangs	-	6	2	3	1	2
	Gang with leader	-	2	2	1	5	-
	Ghetto gang	-	-	2	8	12	6
Composition of the gang	Only minors	-	3	1	4	3	1
	Only adults	-	9	6	7	4	3
	Mixed	-	36	7	7	16	9
Number of gang members	Minors	172	170	33	94	99	76
	Adults	-	423	105	191	109	62
Number of gangs using violence		-	14	8	13	18	11

a. For the judicial year year 1992-1993 we don't have the information.
b. In 1991-1992, the typology of gangs was not yet developed by the gang unit.
c. Only twenty-two gangs could be placed in the typology because twenty-six gangs showed characteristics of different types of gangs.

After reading such an article, one feels rather safe: the situation seems to be not that bad after all. The police are in control and handle the situation with a firm approach and, most important, American situations as in West Side Story are not yet in sight. Whoever wants to experience gang life without risks should–for the time being–go to the bookshop and read bestsellers such as *Gangs* by Bing (1992) and *Monster* by Shakur (1993).

On May the 4th 1996 another Belgian newspaper *De Morgen*, spends an entire page on "Splinters in the City" and the article does not address the remains of chopped down trees. The subject is once again splinter gangs. The article comments on the situation in three other Belgian cities: Ghent, Mechelen and Antwerp. It contains interviews of local residents, politicians, police commissioners and even a real gang member. As in the other article, the author states that: *"Belgium hasn't got any real gangs as we know them from the American movies, but small and casually created groups of neighbors and friends."* The police commissioner of Antwerp goes even further: *"For convenience's sake, we speak of gangs, but that is a heavy word... . As a matter of fact, neither Antwerp nor any other Flemish city has a youth gang worthy of that name. A real gang has a very strict and established hierarchy. We don't find that in these groups. When we apprehend the casual leaders, the group dissolves. Some boys disappear while others join a new group. Those things are not normal for a real gang. When a gang captain disappears, his two lieutenants take over, assisted by the sergeants."*

According to this article the situation in Ghent, Mechelen and Antwerp is not too bad after all. There are no "real" gangs and the police control the phenomenon by "*taking away the leader in order to dissolve the group.*" And above all, there is a very simple solution to this problem: "*Give those boys a job and a girl friend... their very own perspective for the future. It does not matter in which order! It just has to happen soon.*"

But alongside all this good news we should not forget the bad news. Cities like Ghent, Mechelen and Antwerp may not have a gang problem, but Brussels has. "*In Brussels, one does no longer talk about splinter groups. The capital counts about sixteen youth clans with an elaborated structure and hierarchy. Some of the members carry weapons and often communicate by means of GSM-phones. Under the supervision of some veterans, the younger members control their part of the city. They deal drugs, sell arms and, if necessary, they send out troops to settle something or to set up a punitive expedition"* (*De Morgen*, May 4th 1996). In other words, people who want to know the gang life better don't have to rely on Bing and Shakur any more. They can now experience it "live." What's more, we can now "hope" that this unique product "Gang Reality" will soon be available outside Brussels too. "*The real gangs can only be found in Brussels for the time being, but they are beginning to export their know-how to Flanders*" (*De Morgen*, May 4th 1996).

When we compare both newspaper articles, one thing becomes crystal clear: we may not be sure whether we have a gang problem or not, what it looks like and how big it is, but we do have a very elaborate vocabulary to talk about this problem. Those who want to take part in this explosive debate can take their pick from words like: "gang," "youth gang," "splinter gang" or "youth clan." However, the choice of words is not entirely free any more. Some participants in the debate have already claimed particular words. "*They are called youth gangs in popular speech, but are referred to as splinter groups in circles of social workers*" (*De Morgen*, May 4, 1996). The Attorney's Office uses no less than five terms: "delinquents," "gang," "gang with leader," "spontaneous gang," and "ghetto gang." The reader may find this a little amusing, but a scientist generally wants to be more than just amusing in his papers. After all, criminology is a rather serious business.

I would like to add to these recent newspaper reports some older ones. The first is from the *Gazet van Antwerpen* (September 28, 1994). The front page headlines were: *"Police fights youth gangs - Antwerp youngsters fight each other for a 'ter.'"* The article continues on page 9: "*The Same Old Story –Youth Gangs Have Always Existed.*" The reason for this article was an incident in which an 18 year-old boy, member of the Stella Maris gang, was stabbed. As a result, an Antwerp police officer was interviewed:

> They don't commit organized crimes yet. That's why I prefer to speak of groups, rather than of gangs. These groups also commit criminal offenses, but there is no question of purposiveness.... Youth gangs are a phenomenon in the United States but it doesn't fly over just like that. So we don't have to be afraid for the unbridled violence used by these American gangs in their struggle to control their part of the city. It doesn't seem to go that far in the city of Antwerp. ... Police officers investigating the formation of youth groups are unanimous: for the time being, there are groups that should be monitored closely. They commit crimes, but not purposefully.

Second, there were four articles on gangs in *De* Standaard as early as May 5, 1991. It is striking that they read almost exactly the same. *"Recent newspapers headlines give the impression that our big towns are terrorized by delinquent youth gangs. When we take a closer look, we can see that we are still far from the New York Bronx, where outlawed youngsters make the law. What we do have is a mass of deprived (immigrant) youth in marginal neighborhoods which are a constant and alarming hotbed for delinquency."*

The tone of these comments is very similar to the tone of the more recent newspaper articles. In fact, all the articles stress that Belgium does not know any real gangs and that even the word "gang" is too heavy for these groups. The logical question that pops up then is why the reporters repeatedly write about gangs just to tell us that they don't exist in Belgium. Isn't there a big risk that we are creating a gang problem? I admit, one swallow does not make a summer and some newspaper articles don't make a problem, but they do contribute to creating the problem. Whether we do or don't have gangs, youth clans, splinter groups etc., in Belgium or Brussels, the publication of another series of newspaper articles on this subject and one striking TV report might be enough to call up the gang specter which will persist in the mind of the public. From there, it's only a small step to "moral panic."[4] Groups of loitering youths will automatically be transformed into youth gangs while all crimes committed by a group of youngsters[5] are defined as gang delinquency or gang-related crime. This way, the "Problem" steadily builds up and the feeling of insecurity increases. The next step is the demand for interventions by the authorities. Ball & Curry (1995) point out that it is dangerous to frequently use definitions for gangs in which one of the criteria is that crimes are being committed. Working with such a definition excludes all possibly non-delinquent gangs and helps to establish the idea that youth groups always commit crimes. This image of youth gangs incites the citizens to demand a drastic approach to the Problem. "*The apparently irrational tendency to move from almost total denial when gangs first appear to overreaction when they can no longer be ignored, is to some extent a logical consequence of the fact that by this definition they are not gangs until lawbreaking has become their primary characteristic, by which time drastic measures seem necessary*" (Ball and Curry, 1995: 232).

The danger of this kind of image building in Belgium is quite real because, until now, the only available source of information on gang formation has been the gang unit. As explained above, the gang unit asks all police authorities in the Brussels district to draft a yearly report on the actual gang situation, using a much broader definition than the legal definition. On the basis of this definition the officials reported to the Attorney's Office the existence of 32 gangs in June 1991 (the year that the gang unit was established). Nine of those were eventually considered as "gangs in the legal sense of the word." This means as defined in article 322 of the penal code: "Every association of people with the objective of committing an assault on persons or properties is a crime or criminal offense which exists in the sole fact of establishing the gang." This definition clearly links the gang concept to criminal behavior in an organized manner. Since the objective of the Organized Gangs Unit is to dismantle youth gangs, they will focus on the gangs as defined in article 322. Moreover, the police will probably communicate to the Attorney only the information on gangs committing crimes and/or causing trouble.[6] The Attorney's Office will, in turn, gather information on the gangs reported by the police authorities. Gangs that avoid trouble and do not commit crimes keep out of sight until the day they might adopt criminal behavior and draw the attention of the police forces.

The aforementioned shows the probability that the image of gangs in Belgium may be grafted onto the concept of "criminal gang" or in judicial terms "delinquent gang." As noted above, the step towards a public demand for repression is then very small,[7] and contains the big risk that the "crime carousel" as described by Kutchinsky (1979) begins to turn: more repression which leads to more registered crime by so called youth gangs which in turn leads to a further demand for more repression... .

CONCLUSION

This paper on the group aspect of youth criminality in Belgium/Brussels makes clear that very little information on this subject is available. Until now no research has been done and the official criminal statistics are very limited. Information on youth delinquency in general is not available as police only gather information on the offenses and not on the offender. Information on the group aspect of youth delinquency is completely missing. On the specific subject of gangs, we have only the information from the gang unit. This information is interesting, but it is clear that it is limited by its source. Although the information on gangs is very limited, we see that from time to time newspaper articles are published on gangs. The striking thing in those articles is that they often stress that Belgium does not have any real gangs and that even the word "gang" is too heavy for these groups. The logical question that pops up then is why the reporters repeatedly write about gangs just to tell us that they don't exist in Belgium. Of course, the sound of "groups of delinquent youngsters" is less spectacular than of "gangs." Maybe some people cannot accept that America is still far ahead in that field–although our Belgian situation is not so bad after all! We have groups of delinquent youths (so much less than the real gangs) and by comparing them to the American situation we can still write about gangs, a terrific subject to write about, but a terrible thing to have. All in all, Belgium is such a nice country to live in!

REFERENCES

Ball, R. and D. Curry (1995). The logic of definition in criminology: Purposes and methods for defining "gangs." Criminology 33(2):225-245

Bing, L. (1992). Gangs–Jeugdbendes in Los Angeles. Amsterdam: Luitingh/Sijthof, p. 227.

Cohen, S. (1972). Folk Devils & Moral Panics–The Creation of the Mods and Rockers. Worcester: Billing & Sons.

Goode, E., and B-Y. Nachman (1994). Moral Panics–The Social Construction of Deviance. Blackwell: Oxford, UK & Cambridge USA.

Hendrix, P. (1981). Elementen van vertekening in de beschrijving over jeugdbendes. Een analyse van artikels uit 'Het Belang van Limburg' en de situatie in Limburg en Genk, Leuven, diss. lic. Criminologie.

Janssens, S. and C.Janssen (1996). Jong en goed gek - Jeugdbendes in Brussel, in Politeia, nr 1, p9-14.

Kesceloot, C. e.a. (1992) de sociaal-ruimtelijke structuur van het brussels hoofdstedelijk gewest. Leuven: Acte Geographica Lovansiensia.

Kutchinsky, B. (1979). Law, crime and legal attitudes: New advances in Scandinavian research on knowledge and opinion about law. In S. Mednick and S. Shoham (eds.), New Paths in Criminology, p191-235.

Shakur, S. (1993). Monster: Autobiografie van de Leider van de Crips-gang in Los Angeles. Amsterdam: Luitingh/Sijthof, 276p.

Schuyt, C.J.M. (1993). Jeugdcriminaliteit in groepsverband, in Delikt en Delinkwent, vol.23, afl.6, p499-510.

ENDNOTES

1 Given this concentration, one could have the impression that ghettos exist in Brussels, which is incorrect. We can only speak of ghettos when there are neighborhoods with almost exclusively one ethnic group. Brussels does not have those kinds of neighborhoods. People of Belgian origin are in the majority in almost all of Brussels. There are only a few neighborhoods in Brussels where a non-Belgian nationality makes up one third of the population.

2 This legal definition makes the existence of a gang itself illegal, even if no crimes are committed.

3 Hendrix examined one newspaper, Het Balng van Limbur, and gathered, in 30 months, 80 articles on gangs for her graduation paper.

4 Cohen's (1972) work "Folk Devils & Moral Panic" was the base of the moral panic concept. The concept has been further elaborated and refined by various authors since. The book 'Moral Panics–The Social Construction of Deviance' gives an excellent overview. See also Goode and Nachman, 1994.

5 One of the main characteristics of delinquency is that it is often committed in group. Literature on criminology states that 60 to 90 percent of all criminal activities are committed in group. For youth delinquency this percentage is even higher (Schuyt, 1993:499).

6 In the judicial year 1994-1995 the police reported 14 gangs to the Attorney's Office. Eight of those met the criteria of the legal definition of gangs. In comparison with 1991 the police reported fewer gangs, but a much larger part of them met the criteria of the legal definition. A hypothetical explanation of this fact is that the police are getting more selective in reporting gangs and that they report only those groups that they presume meet the criteria of the legal definition.

7 The establishment by the Attorney's Office of the special unit "Bandes Organisées" in 1990 is an example of the tougher (repressive) approach.

Chapter 23

A PROPOSAL FOR MULTI-SITE STUDY OF EUROPEAN GANGS AND YOUTH GROUPS

Cheryl L. Maxson
Social Science Research Institute, University of Southern California, Los Angeles, California

A primary goal of the Eurogang Workshop was to foster **systematic** research on gangs and youth groups in Europe. The question to be faced is what should the design of this research be? We hope that this effort would incorporate what we have learned from more than five decades of research in the U.S.– capitalizing on all our mistakes and reproducing none of them. Part I of this volume highlights some of the contributions of U.S. research; these topics were selected for their immediate utility to research in Europe. However, I want to highlight weaknesses rather than strengths of the U.S. research, to touch on the implications of those weaknesses, and to propose an alternative framework for gang research in Europe.

THE MAJOR MISTAKES

There is no shortage of critics of U.S. gang research. I have selected three problems that pertain most directly to the workshop's goals: 1) the "atomistic" nature of nearly all gang research in the U.S., 2) our failure to come to grips with the definition issue, and 3) the flirtation with theory. These weaknesses are often discussed within our research community; indeed these failings are quite obvious. They are problems that can be avoided, but not without considerable cooperation and flexibility among researchers.

M.W. Klein et al (eds.), The Eurogang Paradox, 299–307.

Atomism

The body of knowledge that we have slowly accumulated about street gangs in the U.S. is far too vulnerable in its idiosyncrasies. We fall back too easily on claims of gang diversity to account for conflicting findings when methodological diversity is an equally viable explanation. These differences of method, sample, and focus derive from our many separate disciplines, training, and interests, and reflect historical and political dynamics as well. While the nature of gangs surely differs over place and time, the nature of these differences is difficult to assess with our eclectic grab bag of methods and samples. The yield of our multiple methods is diminished by our failure to triangulate these methods in time and space, and most particularly, on the same groups.

There are examples of comparative work: investigators spanning multiple cities (e.g., Esbensen, Decker, J. Miller in this volume) and investigators in different cities who collaborate on some aspects of sampling design, instrumentation and data collection procedures, and analyses (e.g., Thornberry and Porter, Huizinga and Schumann in this volume). Still, the lack of true replications across time and place is a major limitation, and the generalizability of knowledge produced about particular gangs continues to plague our efforts to describe gang patterns.

The mass surveying efforts being conducted with law enforcement (see Curry, this volume) and Esbensen's school-based study lend themselves to replication far more easily than the ethnographic work which has contributed other forms of information about gangs. However, I think that ethnographic methods might be combined with broad survey efforts to capitalize upon the comparative opportunities that exist. *Rather than being selected for convenience, individual gang studies need to be situated in the context of both the overall gang-picture in the city and in comparison with other forms of youth groups.* This can be achieved by sampling gangs with reference to selected characteristics that are measured with common instrumentation.

That Ugly Definition Issue

About ten years ago, I participated in a two day meeting of law enforcement officials and gang researchers to attempt to develop a consensus on law enforcement approaches to defining street gangs and gang crime. The courageous Irving Spergel convened this meeting, and–surprising to no one–the group failed to agree (Spergel, 1988). The lack of consensus spans disciplinary identification although, given their more narrow concerns, law enforcement may do a better job of it than researchers. In some ways it is surprising that we researchers could produce as much as we have, given that we are rarely sure that we're talking about the same elephant, much less the same body part of the elephant.

Without delving into the varieties of definitions, it seems to be a critical first task for the European gang research effort to perform better than we did back in the Chicago meeting. There needs to be a common agreement on what to call "a gang" and a clearer definition of the borderlands. This is challenging because we don't yet fully know what gangs in Europe really look like, either in reference to the varieties we can describe in the U.S. or in comparison to the European groups described thus far. A different type of challenge arises from the tension between those who are concerned that raising the profile of the gang issue will generate "moral panic" and those who fear that denial of the gang issue will preclude early and effective intervention.

The message from Klein's description of our U.S. structures research (see Chapter 1) is that we would not want to limit this definition by territorial affiliation, sub-grouping, gender, age or ethnicity, although these are all characteristics that need to be assessed. Surely, we would want to include an orientation toward, or some level of commitment to, the group. Its members should know (subjectively) they are members, and they should be identifiable as such in their communities. The issue of criminal activity opens up a major area of definitional controversy among U.S. gang researchers. Yet it seems that a certain level of crime orientation in the group context may be a critical signpost in negotiating the territory on the borderlands between gangs and other law violating or "troublesome" youth groups which we assume to be ubiquitous throughout our respective countries. It may be that a group's orientation toward crime and the group processes that occur in the progression to violent confrontations is a distinguishing factor between street gangs and other delinquent groups.

Finally, we should be wary of a tactic that we often use to skirt elements of definitional ambiguity, that of identifying the types of groups that we are *not* talking about when we refer to "street gangs." In our own research, this often includes: motorcycle gangs, prison gangs, political terrorist groups, adult organized crime groups, and sometimes taggers (i.e., loosely formed groups whose sole activity is graffiti). While there may be denotable groups that the European research effort would choose to exclude, these may be important definers of the boundaries and such exclusions should be framed conceptually as well as empirically.

In summary, there are four primary elements that comprise a broad definition of gangs: 1) recognizable and denotable membership, 2) regular interaction patterns or association over a protracted period of time, 3) members' identification with the group, and 4) an orientation toward crime as a valued group activity. I recognize that each of these elements represents a continuum and that research observations may be required to find the "tipping point" wherein delinquent groups cross over to gangs.

A broad survey effort might describe the full range of law-violating groups (see for example, the range of youth group types in The Hague as described by Gruter and Versteegh, this volume). It is **critical** in a multi-city, multi-investigator study that there is agreement on the types of groups that fall within the primary field of study, and those that fall outside. Those groups that become the focus of intensive ethnographic approaches should fall well within the parameters of the four definitional elements described above.

Flirting with Theory

At best, U.S. gang researchers have danced on the fringes of theory testing; theory construction is pretty far beyond us. Of course, we pay homage to Thrasher and to Cloward and Ohlin, Cohen, W. Miller and Spergel. These works and others offer concepts which we sometimes attempt to test (see Short and Strodtbeck, 1965, for a systematic test of early gang theory), oft times with questionable operationalizations and rarely in systematically articulated frameworks. Much of the theoretical work in criminology in past decades attempted to explain gangs. More recently, gang researchers have drawn conceptual frameworks from broader delinquency or criminological theories (e.g., social learning, underclass, social control).

We need macro-level theories of gang emergence and proliferation; of group process and expansion; and individual theories on gang joining and desistance. This is perhaps the most critical of our failures. I would wish to offer our European counterparts a firm theoretical foundation on which a research design might be erected, but lacking that, I offer this plea instead: find the critical point in your data-gathering where you can step back as a group, integrate what you've learned, and direct your methods from a base of theoretically-derived principles.

IMPLICATIONS OF OUR MISTAKES

One arguable result of these limitations in gang research is that law enforcement has largely dominated U.S. gang policy and practice for the last decade or two. During the recent period of gang proliferation, our police, prosecutors, and corrections professionals became increasingly organized in their data systems, information-sharing networks and accessing of federal resources in support of their programs and needs. Certainly, they influenced the media far more effectively than researchers. We didn't present a strong countervailing case because we couldn't fall back on generalized descriptions or research that was relevant to their practice. Law enforcement first publicly identified the proliferation and they were the program entrepreneurs. And, even with all its limitations, for many questions, law enforcement has the only data with breadth (see Curry, this volume).

A second implication of the weakness in gang research is that prevention and social intervention programs have been largely unguided and under-conceptualized by empirical research and certainly by sound evaluation. At best we offer cautions based on a very few well-done program evaluations, and pull findings from other research with unknown applicability to the gang situations at hand.

So, my warning is clear: don't let this happen in Europe. Fight the compulsion to "do your own thing" and instead organize a systematic approach to gang research in multiple settings. Embrace common approaches to sampling, instrumentation and definitions. And above all, develop agreement on theoretical directions that will guide the collection of data on individual gangs.

THOUGHTS ON A MULTI-SITE DESIGN

The workshop's intention was to explore a coordinated process that can develop useful descriptions of European street gangs in such a manner that similarities and differences can reliably and validly be identified and not be undermined by methodological variations. We recognize that individual researchers have their unique interests and that any design should be flexible enough to incorporate these as well as place-specific variations. We hope that the initial effort will be undertaken with a consensus about common points of method and content.

I begin with the assumption that there is no readily available source for the information we seek, from law enforcement, service providers or the media. We must draw what is known from these sources, but a substantial effort must be directed to the streets, homes and hangouts of youth, using field observation techniques coupled with intensive interviews with community members and youth.

Accordingly, I propose a multi-stage research design that incorporates data gathering on three levels of increasing specificity. The first includes *city*-level characteristics that provide broad contextual information along which several city-sites might be arrayed. The second level focuses upon *neighborhoods* within these cities, selected for their relative concentrations of youth crime. The third level targets selected *youth groups* engaged in law violating activities, many of which should reflect the elements of the gang definition described above. These three stages require different data collection strategies and sources, and by design, different substantive foci. While I suggest specific directions below, these must surely be molded by the principal researchers being involved in the European research effort.

City Data

Information to be gathered at the city level should be readily accessible and generally comparable from one city to the next. Wherever possible, these should be drawn from systematically maintained databases, for example, World Health Organization, but may also be retrieved from local governmental sources. Potential city-level characteristics include:

- Demographic descriptions: city population size, ethnic and age distributions

- Socioeconomic indicators: employment and income data
- Public health indicators: drug abuse, teenage pregnancy, infant mortality
- Immigration patterns
- Crime data: age specific homicide and violence victimization rates, proportion of youth arrests.

Neighborhood Data

The intensive data gathering effort described in the next section is likely to be limited to a handful or even one youth group. To maximize the comparative utility of the individual group studies, it is critical that they be sampled from, or at least described within, the larger array of criminally active youth groups in a city. It is necessary to compile at least superficial descriptive information on a close to full enumeration of criminally active or "troublesome" youth groups in a city (see Gruter and Versteegh, this volume, as one example). Through conversations with law enforcement and other city officials, supplemented where possible by analysis of crime data, researchers might identify several neighborhoods that have the highest volume of youth crime. Within these half dozen or so neighborhoods, researchers can identify community informants (e.g., long term residents, youth service providers, school officials, clergy, and youth) from whom descriptions of active youth groups who represent a source of concern to the community may be obtained. Multiple informants for each neighborhood should be pursued.

The type of information that might be gathered for such groups includes:

- Rough estimate of size and longevity
- Gender and ethnic composition; indigenous or immigrant or mixed
- Age range
- Membership markers: name, costume, hand signs, colors, graffiti, tattoos etc.
- Territorial identification; residential patterns
- Subgroup or clique structures
- Nature of behaviors that present a threat or concern to the community, especially with regard to rivalries with other youth groups and to crime versatility or specialization.

This information can be used to create a single typology of groups from all included cities, which may be roughly comparable to what we developed from our U.S. research (Klein, 1996). Regardless of the form this Eurotypology may take, it provides a framework for sampling groups for the intensive work in the third stage. At the same time, the typology provides a broader city context–and multiple city contexts–within which the sampled groups might be described.

Gang or "Gang-Like" Group Data

The type and number of groups to be included in this stage of the study will depend upon several factors including the number of researchers in each city, access and cooperation of group members, resources, and the particular interests of the involved researchers. Selecting the same gang type for study in multiple cities would further the comparative goals of the project. In addition to the structure data captured in stage two, the other issues identified in the first workshop as important to the emergence of gangs in Europe should be explored. These are the spread of urban underclass, the diffusion of gang culture through the media and the role of marginalized, especially refugee and immigrant, populations.

The information to be gathered at this stage requires direct observation of group activities and use of group members as key informants. The Eurogang research consortium should provide substantive direction for this component, but topical areas might include:

- Origin: duration; entry or exit processes, recruitment patterns; attractions of the group
- Leadership or role structure; hierarchy or levels of membership
- Group interactional patterns, especially as they relate to commission of crime (e.g., role of crime in solidifying gang identity, instrumentality, intergroup rivalries); symbolic gang crime (e.g., graffiti, territorial challenges, intergang rivalries).
- Attention to media depictions of gangs; impact on group signs, symbols and rituals.

If we are successful, perhaps some American ethnographers might participate as well. The sad truth is that despite our many decades of research, this is information that is not gathered systematically in the cities and towns in the U.S.

In sum, the outcome over the next few years would be a set of systematically comparable street gang descriptions; a depiction of the broader youth groups context in which gangs exist; and a statement of the municipal settings that give rise to troublesome groups. In a word, we would begin to have **generalizable** knowledge.

REFERENCES

Klein, M.W. (1996). Gangs in the United States and Europe. European Journal on Criminal Policy and Research, 4:63-80.

Short, J.F., & F. Strodtbeck (1965). Group Process and Gang Delinquency. Chicago: University of Chicago Press.

Spergel, I.A. (1988). Report of the Law Enforcement Youth Gang Symposium. Chicago: University of Chicago, School of Social Service Administration.

Chapter 24

GANGS IN EUROPE: ASSESSMENTS AT THE MILLENNIUM

Elmar G.M. Weitekamp
Institute of Criminology, University of Tübingen, Tübingen, Germany

In reviewing the chapters on the European gang situation in Europe and looking at more information about the actual situation of street gangs, gang-like youth groups, and youth groups one finds some interesting developments. First, one cannot deny any longer that European cities have street gangs or gang-like youth groups. In accordance with the Maxson and Klein typology (Klein, 1995, 1996, and Chapter 1 of this volume), they are mainly specialty gangs and compressed gangs and not the older, traditional American gangs. These street gangs have to be differentiated from motorcycle gangs, prison gangs, hooligans, right-wing groups and neonazi gangs. Second, most Europeans seem to acknowledge the existence of youth groups, but do not consider them to be street gangs. This may merely be a matter of definition and takes attention away from the fact that we do indeed have street gangs in Europe. These groups appear to take over responsibilities and educational tasks the parents and families were for various reasons not able to provide any longer. Third, the European countries seem to be reducing official resources and programs for juveniles and adolescents. This will eventually lead and force youngsters to form and join gangs. Fourth, a society which shifts more and more to a "winner-loser culture" makes it very hard for young people today to get a good education or jobs, they are often excluded from fulltime, career oriented work, leading to this winner-loser culture (James 1995). Young immigrants in particular are the biggest losers since they are usually the least

M.W. Klein et al (eds.), The Eurogang Paradox, 309–322.

integrated and often live in poorer and neglected neighborhoods which can serve as breeding grounds for street gangs. Fifth, developments of crime and in particular violent crimes–which are mainly group offenses–point in the direction of an increasing street gang problem. For instance, in Germany to no one's surprise we find today in newspapers from small size to big cities reports about gangs and criminal behavior by gang-like groups.

By reviewing the gang situation in Europe as presented at the first Eurogang workshop in Schmitten we found that traditional gangs, as described in the American literature, can only be found in Russia since the mid-1960s. Characteristics of the traditional gangs are: they are large, territorial, are engaged in a wide variety of activities, have a history of self-regeneration, and have differentiated age or residence cliques. Salagaev reported that Kazan currently has 20 or more active gangs with 50 to 200 members, which are named, according to the territory of their activities. Economic stagnation leading to illegal economic structures can be seen as the reason gangs were formed in Kazan. The gangs have a wide economic network, corrupted connections, and special security groups. The gangs are hierarchically structured with strict norms and recruit their "fighters" from neighborhood youth. They are involved in a variety of crimes. Gang wars played a large role in the 1980s in Kazan, resulting in a substantial number of deaths. These wars stopped in 1992 when a law "not to divide the asphalt" was made and the gangs changed to start commercial activities. As a consequence every gang today has its separate brigades which are involved in specific enterprises. The gangs have a large pool of possible younger members, but only a small number become active gang members. The criminal gang activities include robberies, armed robberies, and the drug trade, but the main business is "solving problems" for businessmen inside their territory. According to estimates nine out of ten private businesses are under the control of organized crime and they pay between $50 to $200 per month to gangs for protection. A major object of gang activities, according to Salagaev, is involvement in banks where gangs get credit, which they never pay back. The Kazan gangs have branches in Moscow and St. Petersburg and some even go from city to city throughout Russia.

While the gang situation in Russia is clear and consists mostly of traditional, structured gangs, the picture changes a bit if we look at other European countries and cities. Mares indicates that for Great Britain only a few reports on gangs exist. This suggests that gangs are not considered to be a problem in Great Britain. This finding is supported by the fact that when we contacted the

Home Office in order to ask them to participate in the Eurogang workshop, they declared that they had no such problem and decided therefore not to participate. However, the descriptions of Mares about the Manchester area clearly give evidence of the existence of neo-traditional gangs. The Gooch and Doddington gangs are located in the most impoverished districts in the city and exist as social groups with about 90 members each, of whom around 40 are active gang members. The majority of the gang members are Afro-Caribbean and between 10 and 30 years of age. While some members deal drugs on an individual basis, this requires no formal leadership. The attainment of respect and power is very important. Original Gangsters (O.G.s) are the most respected members and having a reputation is an important feature of gang life. Designer clothes, sport cars, and having many women characterize role models within the area of the gangs and the stylistic features they wear are derived from popularized American gangs and Jamaican posses. However, besides reinforcing their "gangsta" style image through clothing style, music, and watching movies about gang life, the Gooch and Doddington gang members reject the idea that they are American-style street gangs. The gang members in Manchester are engaged in a lot of violence, often among members of the same gang.

Besides the neo-traditional Gooch and Doddington gangs in the Moss Side area, Mares reports the existence of compressed gangs in Salford and Wythenshaw. These gangs are mainly white, the members are between 14 and 18 years of age, and the life span of these gangs is limited usually to about five to ten years. Their criminal activities range from shoplifting and joyriding to extortion and robberies. The gangs are often located in impoverished metropolitan areas with very high unemployment, as well as low paying and insecure jobs. "Being hard" is the street gang attitude in Great Britain and economic changes led to the exclusion of a lot of youth who joined gangs in order to fulfill their need for cultural dignity.

Gruter and Versteegh and van Gemert report the existence of specialty gangs in the Netherlands, especially in The Hague and Rotterdam. Specialty gangs are fairly small, have a more functional role in a business sense, are territorial with regard to their victims' location rather than the members' residences, and commit only a few types of offenses. Gruter and Versteegh used the "T Model" in which the first step was to conduct a survey of community policemen in order to find out what kinds of groups exist in the community and how troublesome they are. They distinguished between youth groups engaged in troublesome behavior, non-serious crime, serious crime, and gang-related crime. Not surprisingly they were able to identify most youth groups as not gang-related crime groups. Only four such groups out of 98 were identified in 1995 and seven out of 127 in 1996.

By comparing the identified gangs with U.S. gangs Gruter and Versteegh found that the Dutch gang members imitate a lot of the typical behaviors like the outfit, gestures and language of the Crips. However, they engage in less armed-violence, have no territorial fights with other gangs, and they exhibit weak organizational ties. Van Gemert found a similar attraction of and romance with U.S. gangs for two gangs he studied in The Hague and one in Rotterdam. The Eight Tray Crips and Eastside Crips in the Hague are small gangs consisting of ten and seven members, respectively, noted in court files: they consist only of black males as members. They were on average a little over 15 years old, were born in Holland, and belong to the economically deprived group in the Dutch society. Neither group had a clear leader and the relationship among them was quite egalitarian. To become accepted as a gang member, one is tested by having a fight. In Rotterdam van Gemert described the Southside First Tray Crips, who were around 18 years old. The gang had eleven known members, all of whom were non-Caucasian, and the members used the sign language and the graffiti of the Crips. They wore tattoos and had some form of hierarchical order. In order to become a new member one had to commit a robbery. All three of these groups were engaged in specialized criminal activities. While the Eight Tray Crips primarily committed street robberies in small groups of two to four gang members, the Eastside Crips were mainly engaged in violent thefts in which the victims were often girls and acquaintances of the boys. The Rotterdam Southside First Tray Crips robbed shops in their neighborhoods, usually in pairs, and threatened to use weapons such as knives or firearms. A further common feature of all three groups was that they used violence, although they didn't need to use violence in order to carry out the offenses. The robberies were not very lucrative, but had the function of increasing the importance of the members in the gang. Van Gemert pointed out that culture could be a very important aspect when one looks at the gang situation in a particular city. In the Netherlands, which has a large Moroccan population, Moroccan youth groups from the Riff are often considered to be gangs. However, due to their traditional unwillingness to share and collaborate for common goals and the philosophy "everyone for himself," they are resistant to the formation of gangs.

Compressed gangs were identified by members of the Eurogang workshop in cities such as Copenhagen, Frankfurt, Manchester and Oslo. They are also of small or modest size, have little internal structure, can be territorial, and are versatile in their crime patterns. They exist usually for less than 10 years and are predominantly adolescent. Stevns reports the existence of about 15 to 20 street gangs in Copenhagen that have typically 5 to 20 members between the ages of 15 and 20 years; the majority belongs to an ethnic minority. They are poorly integrated in the Danish society and feel marginalized and discriminated against. They usually have poor education and have no or low paying jobs.

Quite similar gangs are reported to exist in Frankfurt by Tertilt and in Oslo by Lien. Tertilt reports that the Turkish Power Boys are characterized by brutality and street crimes and that the gang exclusively recruits sons of immigrant families and boldly proclaims to the world their ethnic identity. The use of violence can be seen as an attempt to free themselves from the low levels of self-esteem that has been forced upon them by German society. Lien also reports that immigrant youth in gangs are more violent than Norwegian ones and that the gang members are fearful of losing face and self-esteem. Ideals of masculinity based on physical strength are values that seem to rank high among immigrant gang members: the creation and spread of fear are the instruments they use to attain respect and recognition from their enemies and others. The parents of immigrant gang members usually occupy low-paid trades as unqualified workers and their children consider themselves as illegitimate children in society. The ethnically motivated violence as reported by Lien for Norway, Tertilt for Germany and Esterle-Hedibel for France can be summarized as an attempt to free themselves from the lowered self-esteem that afflicts immigrant youth in those countries. This is in accordance with Klein's (1995) claim that when gangs arise in a neighborhood it is because the environment has not been able to integrate and socialize parts of the youth population. Therefore the emergence of gangs is a side effect of a local community that does not work the way it should.

While we now assert the existence of gangs in European cities, the picture becomes more blurred when we look at the contributions of Huizinga and Schumann, Dekleva, and Vercaigne. They present mixed evidence for the existence of gangs in Bremen, Ljubljana, and Brussels. The authors hesitate to claim gangs in the American sense. Huizinga and Schumann, in comparing gang behavior in Denver and Bremen, expend quite some effort to explain why

Bremen and Germany have no gang problem while Denver and the U.S. have. Yet looking at the results of their comparison it seems evident that Bremen and therefore Germany has a gang problem even though the level of crime and violence is lower in Bremen than in Denver.

Dekleva for Ljubljana and Vercaigne for Brussels are also hesitant to use the term gang even though the findings they report indicate the likely existence of gangs in those cities. This hesitation reflects some of the discussion that took place in Schmitten during the first Eurogang meeting. The discussion about whether or not we have street gangs in Europe appears to be an artificial one, which has its roots in misunderstandings of the American society and related problems. While the U.S. stands for the best and worst on many scales, Europeans understand themselves as being more moderate and think the philosophy "from a dishwasher to a millionaire" may be applicable in America, but not in Europe. On the other hand the net of social security in Europe never can lead to the ugly realities of street people, ghettos, and poverty in the USA.

One can demonstrate these judgement differences by a simple example. When we show American visitors problem neighborhoods in Germany, which we consider to be very bad and almost unbearable for people to live in, we often hear our American friends making comments such as "nice working class neighborhood." In light of this, it is of no surprise that when Europeans are asked if we have street gangs, we answer quickly "no," since we have the images of American gang movies, slums, extreme poverty and highly violent youngsters with automatic weapons connected with the concept of gangs. That this picture of street gangs is wrong has been pointed out repeatedly by Klein.

It does not help the European onlooker in this context that the U.S. has the highest incarceration rate of the Western industrialized world, applies one of the most repressive criminal justice policies, still has the death penalty, executes record numbers, has almost more weapons in the streets than it has inhabitants, and fights "wars" against crimes and drugs. On the other hand the Europeans have no reason to have a holier than thou attitude towards the U.S. and deny the existence of gangs in the European context. The Europeans acknowledge the existence of youth groups or cultures which are indeed different from gangs and even agreed at the Eurogang Workshop on the terminology of gang-like youth groups since this seems to be less stigmatizing than gangs. This seems hypocritical: by denying the existence of gangs, as reported in Germany by Thiele and Taylor (1998, 162-65), we keep on dreaming about being the "better" societies compared to the U.S. Thus we ignore the signs of the time, which clearly point in the direction of gangs in Europe. Furthermore, we seem to do everything to create yet more gangs, and there exists the need to do something about these developments before it is too late.

Still, one should also not over dramatize the situation. We agree with Huizinga and Schumann that there exists, especially for Germany, no gang problem sufficient to cause abject fear among the public. This seems to be true for most of the European countries. We have found ample evidence, however, for the existence of gangs in Germany and assume that this is true for many other West European countries as well, since Germany shares many similar developments with them. The magazine *Der Spiegel* (no. 31, 1999) featured a major article on Europe-wide operating gangs of people from Kosovo and Albania who are extraordinarily violent and involved in a broad range of criminal activities. The *Schwaebisches Tagblatt* reported in July 1999 that a part of the city of Pforzheim is called "Little Moscow" because the percentage of Russian Aussiedler (immigrants with ancestors of German descent) has reached more than 70 percent. Drugs, drug dealing, and violence are rampant in this location and the youth formed the so-called Haidach-Gangs. The State Police Headquarters of Baden-Württemberg provided cases of gang activities for the year 1998 for the first time in numerous cities and sites of that state. The descriptions of the incidents clearly identify gang activity. We get similar reports from numerous other states and cities in Germany and throughout Europe, indicating that something on the gang front is happening.

A case in point is described by Huizinga and Schumann in one of the very few international comparative research projects on gangs. As pointed out earlier, they did find gang membership among the Bremen and Denver youth. However, the Bremen gangs seem low on territoriality, hierarchical leadership, and stability over substantial periods of time. The American youth commit more crimes per person and have a surprisingly higher turnover rate compared to the Bremen gangs. At both sites gang members contributed far more violent and property offenses compared to other members of their respective cohorts. Huizinga and Schumann found that the influence of gang membership was much stronger in Denver and that the commitment to a gang does not imply the same involvement in crime and delinquency for the Bremen gang members. A common feature of the gangs was the expectation to support other gang members, especially when they got in trouble with others, and to spend a lot of time together. The group cohesion comes from a strong sense of mutual support and common racial or ethnic backgrounds. The results clearly indicate that in both cities gangs exist with many common features, even though the Denver gang members were much more delinquent. More such research is needed in order to understand better the processes leading to gangs and their involvement in delinquency and crime.

Dekleva's description of the gang situation in Slovenia and especially the Chefoor gangs in Ljubljana suggests strongly that a gang situation is developing in Slovenia. Being a Chefoor means that one is violent and picks up fights quickly, is of non-Slovenian nationality, has a specific style of clothes, has a strong identification with the group, and has a specific way of walking and posturing. Belonging to the Chefoors leads to much pride and feelings of security for its members. In Ljubljana there are poor housing areas with a high number of immigrants, and according to Dekleva, his student Lesar found many characteristics of traditional American gangs in two of the three Chefoor localities in Ljubljana. These gangs have a size of 20 to 40 and the Rakova Jelsa gang has subgroups based on their age: 12 to 15 year olds; 16 to 19 year olds, and the grownups over 20 years old. Territoriality does not seem to play a major role and different ethnic backgrounds are no obstacle to joining the gang, even though the gangs are mainly Bosnians. The criminal activities include violent fights, drug dealing, extortion on the streets, as well as breaking and entering and car thefts. The Chefoor gang members imitate the U.S. gang behavior, watch American gang movies, and listen to "gangsta" music. Dekleva concludes that these developments with regard to gangs in Slovenia are related to the worsening economic and political conditions in Slovenia and the entire Balkan region.

Vercaigne, like Dekleva, is cautious in her description of the gang situation in Brussels and argues that she is not sure Brussels has a gang problem and, if so, how big it is. Contrary to that assessment she points out that the Belgians have a very elaborate vocabulary to talk about the gang problem. A further contradiction to her hesitancy with regard to naming gangs is the fact that the city of Brussels has a police gang unit that collects data on gang development in the 19 communities of Brussels. According to these records, Brussels contained 31 gangs in 1992, 48 gangs in 1994, and then declined afterwards to 14 and 18 in the years of 1995 and 1996. The last available records identified 22 gangs for 1997.

The police in Brussels distinguish four different forms of gangs. 1) The gang with a leader is typically a gang of youngsters from deprived neighborhoods that find their role models on the streets and often have common external features such as shaved heads or tattoos. 2) The spontaneous gangs are organized around schools, sport clubs and youth centers and reject the social order of society. The rejection leads to troublesome behavior and nuisance in their neighborhoods. 3) The ghetto gang can be found in deprived neighborhoods with a high concentration of immigrants. The ghetto gang members define their own territory in which they feel at home and which they defend violently when outsiders do not respect it. 4) The criminal organization consists of minors and adults whose main goal is to make money; violence is usually not used by these gangs since it enhances the chances of being detected. Vercaigne concludes that according to the police unit gangs do exist to a certain degree in Belgium, but that they are not "as bad" as their American counterparts.

In looking at the European situation, we have to conclude not only that gangs exist in Europe, but that the European countries are doing much to create more gangs and to develop a serious gang problem which might eventually look as bad as the American gang situation, a situation most people cannot even imagine for Europe. As we have seen above, all descriptions about European street gangs, despite some denial that they exist, share some common features. These are:

- gangs exist in deprived communities
- gangs often consist of minority or immigrant members of society either by race, nationality or ethnicity
- gangs are predominantly male
- gang members are almost always alienated, marginalized youth who are socially excluded from society and whose opportunities are blocked
- gang members are usually young and typically adolescents or young adults
- gang members are involved in all sorts of criminal activities with quite a range in the level of delinquent and criminal behavior
- gangs are stable over time and can exist for long periods of time

Pfeiffer's (1998) evaluation of juvenile crime and violence in Europe concludes that we have experienced a substantial increase in youth violence since the mid-1980s in the ten countries he reviewed. He sees the main cause for this in the shift of the European countries toward winner-loser cultures in which many disadvantaged youth appear to be the losers. Pfeiffer bases his argument on the findings of James (1995) who argues that at least three major elements are part of the creation of such winner-loser cultures:

> It is abundantly clear from many studies...that inequality in incomes combined with false promises of equality of opportunity, American-style of welfare support for the disadvantaged and poor job-quality are major causes of violence in developing and developed nations alike. From 1979 onwards in Britain, all three of these patterns were adopted as a deliberate government policy; the gap between rich and poor increased to pre-war levels, the amount and kind of state support for the disadvantaged was reduced dramatically; the quality of jobs available to young men decreased after union power to guarantee minimum wages and conditions of work was removed. These changes coincided with an unprecedented increase in violence against the persons since 1987 (James, 1995, 74).

Polk (1999) speaks in this context about youth abandonment. Young people, in his view, experience economic abandonment and these young people, who are the losers in the contemporary winner-loser culture, are caught in a dreadful developmental trap. Polk points out further that historically virtually all young people, at high, middle and low levels of the class structure, could look forward to a process of moving from childhood through schooling into adulthood with some combination of work and family roles. These prospects are not relevant anymore and the problem of abandonment is greater for those young people who leave school early and enter the labor force with little to offer in the way of qualifications, skills or experience.

In his work about the new urban poor, Wilson (1996) refers to a process in which work disappeared for this group of people. The lack of full-time work for this group leads to undesired consequences such as lack of money, delay of independence from parents, and problems in the establishment of sexual relationships, marriage and the establishment of a family. These individuals become stuck in a social and economic no-man's land, one where a central feature of their existence is that normal supports for identity as man or woman are not available. This is similar to Polk's developmental trap that forces young people to engage in complicated and innovative ways to struggle with their central identities as males or females. This development trap is even far worse for members of minority groups by race, nationality or ethnicity. Dubet and Lapeyronnie (1994) investigated the winner-loser hypothesis in France and found that a significant shift has occurred in social problems, including crime trends. They conclude that the social exclusion of marginal groups had become the key problem of the 1990s. They consider the criminal acts by the marginalized youngsters as an expression of their helplessness at being unable to live a normal life and their inability to gain access to society.

It is here that we can see the clear connection to violence and gangs. The situation of abandoned youngsters is such that issues of status and manhood are problematic and cry out for a solution. The lack of traditional pathways to define "who am I as a man" are, according to Polk (1999), especially applicable to gang formation, where one can compare one's status with that of others. The gang can change the rules of the game and can make the loser into a winner again.

There exist many signs in the European countries that we are on the way to create more winner-loser cultures that could serve as a fertile ground for the formation of gangs and the resort to violence as a way of contesting masculinity. Pfeiffer's (1998) research clearly indicates that Europe is experiencing a substantial increase in violence. In addition, Dünkel and Skepenat (1998) found for the State of Mecklenburg-Vorpommern, Germany, that group offending mainly causes the increase in violent crimes in that state. From group offending or offending within a group it seems not far from the formation of gangs, especially if any meaningful social policy and the opening of legitimate pathways for the youngsters to participate in society do not counter processes of youth abandonment.

I want to demonstrate this dangerous situation with the example of the German Aussiedler (immigrants with ancestors of German descent). These developments with the Aussiedler are fairly new ones, which started around the mid-1990s. I am convinced that any European country has similar problem groups, even though the Aussiedler exhibit some peculiarities. One of them is that the Aussiedler are immediately given a German passport and are considered to be Germans. According to Reich et al. (1999), since 1988 around two million came from the former Soviet Union to Germany, peaking with close to 400,000 coming alone in 1990. Germany used substantial aid packages in order to integrate the Aussiedler into German society. They received among other aid the so-called integration aid, which is a kind of unemployment payment. Up to 1993, this lasted for 312 days and German language courses were paid for 12 months.

However, new laws in 1993 reduced the amount of aid for the Aussiedler drastically. Integration aid is now only paid for 156 days and the language courses were also halved to six months. The so-called guarantee fund that amounted in 1991 to 450 million German marks, was reduced by 65 percent, and remains now at 180 million marks per year. This reduction in particular hurts young people, since this fund provided re-education, job training programs, and social integration support programs. In addition to these financial restrictions, the Aussiedler have to live at the beginning of their stay in Germany in so-called "temporary special housing arrangements." While they are supposed to leave these special housing units as fast as possible, they stay, for example in Tübingen according to Stoll (1999), on average two years in these units. These units are usually very cramped and the living arrangements are very poor and remind us of a ghetto-like situation where sometimes hundreds of people live. There exist no places for the young people, who are forced to hang out in the hallways or outside of the buildings. In general the people who live there have neither privacy nor common rooms which could be used for social activities.

The situation for the young Aussiedler is a particularly difficult one. While in Russia, they were considered to be a minority group because of their German descent and were labeled as German fascists. In Germany, even though they have a German passport, they are again a minority group and labeled Russians. In addition to their minority status they often have language problems and difficulties in schools. The school and/or job education they received in Russia is worth nothing in their new country of residence, thus blocking their legal opportunities and marginalizing them even more. It is no surprise that these young people form and join gangs in order to find a place where they belong and can identify themselves. Hanging out in groups was already very much part of their culture when they lived in the former Soviet Union, since it was often too dangerous there to go and hang out alone. In Germany they perceive the German culture and environment as too dangerous and these circumstances force them to hang out together and to form gangs.

Stoll (1999) reports the existence of gangs in the temporary special housing units of Tübingen and describes characteristics similar to the neo-traditional type of gang. The youngsters usually hang out in front of the housing unit and have a strong hierarchical order that is determined by age and experience in the country of the "enemy." For the Aussiedler these housing units are often the only possibility to find friends, especially in rural areas. When the families move away, the youngsters and young adults of these gangs often come back and are admired by those newly arrived or still living there because of the status symbols they were able to achieve. These status symbols are cars, clothes, and other forms, which indicate wealth. These older gang members then recruit younger ones from the newly arrived boys and use them for their illegal activities. The gang members are involved in a variety of criminal activities. A quick look in juvenile correctional facilities reveals that a disproportionately high number of Aussiedler youngsters are incarcerated. The group cohesion of the "Russian gangs" is particularly high, since in their country of origin they were already used to treating any outsiders and especially the State as the enemy and regulated conflicts among themselves. In addition, the Aussiedler youngsters exhibit a very strong machismo culture and attitudes in which a high level of violence is considered to be normal (Reich et al. 1999).

This brief description of the situation of the Aussiedler in Germany clearly shows that we are on our way in Germany to creating a serious and long lasting street gang problem. I assume that similar developments can be found throughout Europe, since all European countries have a serious minority problem, whose members live in general in poor housing arrangements, drop out of schools often because of language problems, have a poor education, are unskilled, hold often low paying jobs, are socially excluded and marginalized, and often look for an identity. The Aussiedler in Germany are in a way even privileged compared to other minority groups since the State provides them with integration privileges which are not available to other immigrants. If this group is forming gangs in order to cope with the circumstances of their new home country, the formation of gangs and gang activities seem to be an even more viable solution for other immigrant groups.

We in Europe have to open our eyes and tune our ears with regard to the existence of gangs and the emergence of a serious gang problem. We can no longer deny the existence of street gangs in European cities, even though they seem not to reflect the worst American gang scenario, which has been incorrectly implanted in the European minds by popular movies, books, music, and sensational press reports. Signs of emergent winner-loser cultures can be found in all European countries and their influence on the use of violence to gain one's aims cannot be denied either. I would like to conclude with a saying of Franz von Liszt who claimed at the end of the last century that "the best criminal policy is a good social policy," something that the European countries seem to have forgotten. This negligence can lead to serious problems: with regard to gangs we might be on a direct route to creating a very serious problem in Europe.

REFERENCES

Dubet, F., and D. Lapeyronnie (1994). Im Aus der Vorstaedte: der Zerfall der demokratischen Gesellschaft. Stuttgart: Klett-Cotta.

Dünkel, F., and M. Skepenat (1998). Jugendliche und heranwachsende als taeter un opfer von gewalt. In H-D. Schwind, E. Kube, and H-H. Kühne (eds.), Essays in Honour of Hans Joachim Schneider: Criminology on the Threshold of the 21st Century. Berlin: Walter de Gruyter.

James, O. (1995). Juvenile Violence in a Winner-Loser Culture. London: Free Association Books.

Klein, M.W. (1995). The American Street Gang: Its Nature, Prevalence, and Control. New York: Oxford University Press.

Klein, M.W. (1996). Gangs in the United States and Europe. European Journal on Criminal Policy and Research 4(2):63-80.

Pfeiffer, C (1998). Juvenile crime and violence in Europe." In M. Tonry (ed.), Crime and Justice: A Review of Research. Volume 23., pp. 255-328. Chicago: The University of Chicago Press.

Polk, K. (1999). Changing Patterns of Violence. Unpublished paper. Department of Criminology, University of Melbourne.

Reich, K, E. G.M. Weitekamp, and H-J. Kerner (1999). Jugendliche Aussiedler: Probleme und Chancen im Integrationsprozess. Forthcoming in Bewährungshilfe.

Stoll, F (1999). Von Russland nach Württemberg: Eine Studie zur Integration jugendlicher Spätaussiedler. Unpublished Master Thesis. Faculty of Social and Behavioral Sciences, University of Tübingen.

Thiele, G, and C.S. Taylor (1998). Jugendkulturen und Gangs. Berlin: Verlag für Wissenschaft und Bildung.

Wilson, W.J. (1996). When Work Disappears. The World of the New Urban Poor. New York: Vintage Books.

PART IV

Chapter 25

BRIDGING THE AMERICAN/EUROPEAN CONTEXTS: INTERVENTIONS, COMMUNITIES, YOUTH GROUPS, AND MORAL PANICS

The Editors

Part I of this volume presented an updated overview of gangs in the U.S. The most general purpose of these papers was to emphasize street gang realities and to dispel common myths and ambiguities about the American gang situation. Modern data, derived from both traditional and recently sharpened research methods, were presented to illustrate the paradox that beliefs about European gangs as different from those in America may be based in large part on false stereotypes of most American gangs. Any implications for European gang knowledge and practice must come from realistic images of the American situation.

Part II provided a series of recent depictions of street gangs, or gang-like groups, in various European settings. This constitutes the first compilation of such gang descriptions in the professional literature. As such, it stands by itself. In conjunction with the reports in Part I, it provides a much needed base for setting European street gangs in their own context, against the background of the far more numerous and established gangs of America. A comparative knowledge vacuum is thus considerably reduced.

Part III, by illustration and argument, sets yet another context, placing street gangs in possible contrast with other youth groups which are seen as troublesome but perhaps not deserving the stigma of "gang." This gang-vs.-group issue is seldom addressed in modern American literature, perhaps

M.W. Klein et al (eds.), The Eurogang Paradox, 325–338.

because street gangs have become defined in part by their antisocial or even violent behaviors and as such have become the province of law enforcement. In Europe, where the gang situation is emergent but sporadic, the distinctions become more important between gangs and informal youth groups, networks, youth movements, and other such categories. This is important for knowledge and certainly for the development of any gang-specific interventions.

Taken together, parts I through III raise the more practical, "So what?" questions. What are the implications for preventing or controlling European street gangs, and how might we best undertake research by European scholars about European gangs? This chapter discusses the policy and intervention issue as it emerged in the Workshop discussions.

The American experience with gang prevention and control has been highly varied over the past three-quarters of a century. As documented by presentations at the Workshop, it has been characterized by faith in its success, but only seldom by concerted attempts to document such success. Anecdotal evidence has been common, but testable evidence has been rare. What is known, unequivocally, is that attempts at prevention and control have failed to prevent the steady–and of late the dramatically increased–proliferation of American communities found with street gang problems.

Throughout the Eurogang Workshop, and especially during its final day, the participants struggled with and sought clarification of the issues related to the applicability of the American experience to the European experience. Inevitably, this also involved discussion of the broader American and European social contexts. Given the mixed picture of America's success with its street gangs, the discussion occasionally seemed surreal.

Nonetheless, the editors attempt in this final essay to summarize the issues briefly in order to move along the requirements for comparative gang research and its policy relevance. We offer as well some thoughts that may clarify the issues and set the stage for future discussion. We will elaborate on four principal issues; approaches to street gang intervention, community variations, gangs versus other youth groups, and moral panics versus denial.

APPROACHES TO INTERVENTION

The repertoire of approaches to ameliorating the gang problems in America is broad, and extends over time through seven decades of recorded attempts. Extensively reviewed elsewhere (Covey et al., 1992; Spergel, 1995; Klein, 1995; Howell, 1998) we list the broad categories only briefly.

Community mobilization Chicago-style

The Chicago Area Projects approached delinquency prevention, including gang activity, as an issue to be tackled by community residents themselves, with social agencies providing resources but not determining the actions to be taken. This "bottom-up" approach was unique in its emphasis on community definition of problems and community decision-making in allocation of resources. Still continuing in some areas after 50 years, the projects have not been assessed for effectiveness by independent, empirical research.

Community mobilization, generic

Here the attempt again is to empower communities to improve the street gang situation, but the decision-making is in the hands of community agencies. In some instances the lead is taken by law enforcement and takes on a control mentality. In others, the lead is taken by social service agencies, with an emphasis on finding alternative resources for gang members. These variations on community mobilization have become increasingly popular since the advent of the proliferation of gang-involved American cities in the 1980s, but they have not to date been subjected to independent, empirical assessment of their effectiveness.

Street worker programs

These programs were an outgrowth of the Chicago Area Projects, refined during the 1950s by the New York City Youth Board and independently evaluated during the 1950s and 1960s in Boston, Chicago, and Los Angeles. Street worker programs attached individual workers to troublesome gangs to transform them into less anti-social groups and to connect members to adult socialization roles and opportunities. The approach emphasizes the rapport between worker and youth, and initially accepts the gang structure as a given, to be worked with as a fulcrum for reform. All three major assessments revealed either no overall impact on gang structure and gang crime, or a counter-productive pattern of increased gang cohesiveness and increased criminal involvement.

Social service models

Approaches to ameliorating the gang problem through social services have been as varied as in any other field. Prominent among these have been individual and group counseling, remedial education, employment training and job finding, medical services, recreation, and religious outreach. Two points deserve special mention. First no concerted effort has been made to determine, empirically, which of these services is more or less helpful; normally, they are applied in concert rather than separately. Second, each service is particularly appropriate to only a portion of gang members. For example, some but not most have a drug abuse problem; some but not all come from dysfunctional families; some but not all are school failures; some but not all lack employment skills, and so on. The trick is to match service to need, not to apply one's favorite modality across the board.

In-school prevention

Most gang recruits can be found in the schools, so there is logic to attempting prevention in that setting. Two large-scale projects illustrate serious problems with the approach. In Los Angeles, a program attempted in about 30 middle schools has foundered due both to political problems (e.g., programs located in non-gang areas) and to conceptual problems such as failure to distinguish between the relatively small proportion of gang-prone youth and those at-risk of other problems. An independent evaluation has failed due to political intrusions.

Another program, modeled after D.A.R.E., the national drug education program, is located in schools across the country. It, too, fails to target the gang-prone youth specifically, and is–like D.A.R.E.–controlled and presented to the students by uniformed police officers. The curriculum has little direct relevance to gangs as a targeted group. An independent evaluation, initially hopeful, has recently suggested no effect on behavior.

Law enforcement suppression

Police crackdowns and task-force sweeps, heavy street surveillance, and special gang prosecution programs have been adopted throughout America. They are often bolstered by special anti-gang legislation and civil injunctions that increase the reach of the law beyond normal bounds, define gangs in a manner to increase their vulnerability to prosecution, and expand sentences upon conviction. Despite the massiveness of the effort, virtually no independent assessment of impact has been undertaken. Reliance on unsystematic, anecdotal evidence seems to have sufficed for law enforcement and politicians alike.

Two contrary examples have been described. In Reno, Nevada, the application of community policing specifically to a growing gang problem has shown promise. In Copenhagen, the use of police officers as mentors to gang members and their families contrasts dramatically with the narrowness of accepted suppression techniques. Other expansions of police interventions would seem to be worthy of exploration.

In sum, there has been a rather full panoply of gang programs in the U.S. While they have yielded some guidelines on what not to do–programs that build gang status and cohesiveness, or engage youth who are unlikely to join gangs in any case–they have yielded few if any models of successful intervention. One reason for this, of course, has been the failure to undertake serious, independent evaluations of program success. But other problems as well emerged from the Workshop discussions, several of them having to do with the lack of clarification of goals and targets of gang programming.

For example, it would be fruitful to distinguish between prevention, intervention, and suppression goals. Prevention programs are designed to reduce the entry of youth into gangs, or to limit the need for gang formation in the community. Practices associated with such goals, including procedures for identifying which youth are most gang-prone, will differ from intervention practices. These are designed to wean vulnerable members away from gangs or provide meaningful alternatives to gang participation. They include attempts to reduce gang cohesiveness generally in order to make the gang itself less attractive to members and recruits.

These prevention and intervention goals yield practices that are in turn different from those associated with gang suppression. Police and prosecutorial crackdowns are aimed generally at the most active and criminally involved gang members, and at members considered to be gang leaders. The purpose is "to take them off the streets" rather than to find life alternatives, to reform, or to rehabilitate. Conflicting goals yield conflicting practices but these are often ill-recognized in gang programs.

In a similar fashion, programs usually have failed to distinguish between youths' joining, persistence, and desistance from gang membership. Different practices are suggested by each. Further, distinguishing between individuals, as program targets, and gang structures, as targets, has been lazy. Short term targeting on specific members does little to reduce the factors related to the very existence of street gangs. Targeting gang structures provides a broad brush that fails to recognize the diversity of gang members' needs and characteristics.

Finally, a concern expressed by some of the American Workshop participants was the counter-productiveness of many well-meaning programs, due to the inadvertent strengthening of gang cohesiveness. It was stressed that most youth join gangs, not in order to commit crime, but in order to meet personal and social needs for identity, for status, for excitement, for a sense of belonging, and for a false sense of protection. Workshop participants pointed out that direct intervention and suppression programs may actually help fulfill these very needs. Cohesiveness is increased by providing sources of identity and status and excitement, and by reinforcing the sense that the gang is very special. Failure to assess this unforeseen outcome can doom an anti-gang program.

COMMUNITY VARIATIONS

While the American Workshop participants noted the programmatic difficulties just cited, their European counterparts raised issues of a different order, each based on different emphases in criminological endeavors in the U.S. and Europe. The few direct anti-gang programs mentioned in Europe, each a variation on American attempts, did not as yet find strong endorsement because it was unclear how well they fit the needs of an ill-defined European problem. Among these were a volunteer street worker program in Stockholm, a professional street work program for Turkish gangs in Berlin, the aforementioned police mentoring program in Copenhagen, a police gang intelligence operation in Frankfurt, and a prosecutorial and judicial suppression effort in Kazan.

The first of three principal concerns expressed was the nature of communities and social organizations in various European settings. One aspect of the American literature has been rather extensively covered, that of gang-community relationships. A useful summary is provided by Short (1996). A considerable variety of such relationships have been described. But American gang researchers have been far less careful to describe and contrast the communities that spawn their gangs. One gets the general impression–undoubtedly false–that any one-gang community is similar to most others.[1] One aspect may be particularly pertinent to the newer gang developments in Europe; in emergent gang cities, local community organization seems potentially to be a viable source of control, as opposed to traditional gang cities where more external input is required to guide and energize local social control.[2]

When the question of community organizations was raised among the European Workshop participants, such varied responses were received that the whole issue of a generic community conceptualization was called into question. The situation can be seen in the following capsule participant responses, each from a different scholar from a different home city:

- Most community action has had to do with developing opportunities for youth, and recently this has been "high-jacked" by specific problem–driven agendas such as the mobilization of victims as a political force.
- Informal social control is the norm, but to practice suppression has become prevalent, including the enactment of new laws that no one enforces.
- Ghettos are almost non-existent, so the American experience is less relevant. In many communities, local authority is strong but in migrant areas "community" is really a series of networks.
- Communities, many of them minority groups, are not reached by mainstream agencies, so that the legitimacy of agencies–especially the police–tends to be low.

- A system exists of a comprehensive community model. School, social and welfare agencies, and police collaborate in 80 percent of neighborhoods, set up local committees, meet regularly, and report to a citywide steering committee.
- For us, community-based prevention is a new idea, so we have many debates among ourselves about the meaning of "community." Current attempts take place only for deprived communities, thereby stereotyping them; one of them is even stigmatized by labeling it "Chicago."
- Community has different meanings in the northern and southern parts of the country. In the one, it can mean attempts to involve young people in local planning. In the other, it means street corner society. In both cases, the open presence of organized crime dictates much about the role of youth.
- In our country, there are no ghettoes but it is a growing concern to prevent the marginalization of certain communities. Crime prevention emphasizing local community resources is a development of only the last few years; ironically the communities having less, need to do more programming.
- With the decline of power among trade unions and other organizations, structural changes have been taking place such that local neighborhoods have become more of a focus. There are numerous examples now of multi-agency community-based programs. These work best when they include the migrant populations, but this is deterred by the non-citizen status of these groups.
- We need to have many community-based programs, but with recent political changes we've discarded a number of good things. Still, we continue to believe that communities should be responsible for their youths.
- The contrast can be great between informal social control levels from country to country. There is a story of a Dutchman on a train layover in Hamburg, Germany. He borrowed a railway luggage cart to walk to the famous Alster Lake while waiting for his connection and was repeatedly berated by angry citizens for his unauthorized removal of the cart. In the Netherlands, he could have pushed that cart from Amsterdam to Rotterdam and would never have heard a word from anyone.

Clearly, to the extent that these pictures reflect a true variety of community definitions and realities, gang research in Europe as well as gang intervention will benefit from cross-national comparisons only to the extent that clarifications of community contexts are realized. In a number of cities, such as Berlin, Brussels, Stuttgart, den Haag, and Stockholm, street gangs seem to come and go over time. These phases remind us that it is not merely the gangs that require our attention, but the gang-spawning communities as well.

STREET GANGS VERSUS OTHER YOUTH GROUPS

Several American gang scholars, most notably Fredric Thrasher (1927), James F. Short, Jr. (1996), and John Hagedorn (1988) have noted the evolution of street gangs from more "innocent" forms of youth gangs. This pattern of growth from playgroup to gang may help to explain the origin of some gangs, but how many is certainly not known. But since street gangs are not the most common form of troublesome youth groups (Miller, 1980) it is clear that most youth groups do not form gangs. American gang scholars have not devoted much attention to non-gang groups, perhaps to their own scholarly detriment.

In a number of European countries, there has been a tradition of research on various youth groups, with the result that Eurogang Workshop participants gave considerable discussion to what distinguishes most youth groups from street gangs. In the absence of a clear consensus on the definition of street gangs, two general positions were suggested, both with important policy implications.

The first of these is that street gangs exist at one end of a continuum of youth groups, the continuum being composed of level of disruptive or delinquent behavior. Gangs are "more serious" forms of group, and special attention must be applied to them because of their antisocial behavior. Thus most principles of youth group behavior and dynamics apply well to gangs, and group practices common to youth work generally will be applicable to street gangs.

The second position, emphasized in particular by some of the American participants, is that gangs are not simply more serious forms of acting out youth groups, but in becoming "gang like" they have become qualitatively different. Important to this position, although not shared by all the Americans, is that one of the defining characteristics of the street gang is its emphasis on orientation to criminal pursuits. As one of the Americans phrased it, there is a (vaguely defined) "tipping point" reached by a group of youth engaged in criminal acts where they recognize themselves as different from others due to their antisocial orientation. Different forms of group dynamics kick in at this point. An "oppositional culture" (Moore and Vigil, 1989) toward the non-gang world develops, and attempts to reform or control the group are reinterpreted by the members to reinforce gang bonds or cohesion. Under these circumstances, normal youth work practices become inapplicable or even counterproductive.

Two European participants reported variations on this latter position in describing briefly youth groups whose lower levels of delinquent behavior were noted and co-opted by adult criminals to "professionalize" the groups into more gang-like structures. Another European scholar, concerned with the arbitrariness of the "tipping point" approach as exemplified by these two reports, suggested a series of definitional criteria that might be applicable to the European situation. We present these here as the closest the Workshop participants came to a working understanding of how one might characterize street gangs in Europe.

1. Beyond-normal engagement in criminal (delinquent) activity
2. A level of social organization greater than the usual informal youth group
3. A degree of temporal stability
4. Indicia of group identity (name, rituals, clothes, signals, etc.)
5. Opportunities in space to come together with some regularity
6. Perceived blocks to social opportunities
7. A tradition as a group that can be passed on to new members. Connection with a specific territory may be common.

What became clear, as part of these discussions, was that European gang research must be located in the larger context of an understanding of other forms of youth groups. A congenial model for such research was suggested by the Dutch participants and demonstrated by the chapters in Part II by Gruter and Versteegh, and by van Gemert. It was referred to as the "T Model," wherein the first step is to undertake a census of the numbers and types of youth groups in a given jurisdiction. The second step, then, is to launch an intensive or in-depth study of the street gangs included in that broader census. Such a model, it was thought, might overcome some of the arbitrariness of gang definitions and help to avoid the problem of over-identifying gangs (also see Maxson's chapter in this volume). Variations on this approach, it was noted, had already been proposed in youth surveys and group censuses in three smaller Dutch cities and in Brussels.

MORAL PANIC VERSUS GANG DENIAL

No issue at the Eurogang Workshop raised as much controversy as this one: Might not the launching of coordinated gang research in Europe serve inadvertently to create or strengthen the existence of street gangs? Or, might there be more harm in soft-pedaling the gang issue, allowing it to fester without intervention and without explicit research attention? The first concern has to do with "moral panics," the second with denial of reality.

Stanley Cohen (1972) is generally acknowledged as first formulating the concept of moral panic as part of his study of the Mods and Rockers in England. He described it as a situation in which credible officials, for example police or the media, first called attention to a condition or a group of people. Thus defined by the officials as a threat to social order and values, stereotypes of the "offending" group are formed, and approaches to control are devised and applied. Implicit in the concept is the notion that the real threat is far less than portrayed.

Other writers have amplified the concept (see for example Goode and Ben-Yehuda, 1994), emphasizing the exaggeration of the danger, the disproportionate response given the low threat level actually posed, and the often temporary nature of the episode. Classic examples in the American gang literature have been provided, by Zatz (1987) in Phoenix, Arizona, and by Jackson and Rudman (1989) in California.

The concern was expressed by a number of the European participants in the Workshop, and echoed by at least one American, that undertaking explicit gang research in the European setting, where the youth group/relationship was unclear, could in some locations spark or accelerate a moral panic. The response from a number of the Americans and from Europeans already engaged in gang research was that the avoidance of the topic and relevant research would fail to inform public policy. The Americans cited numerous instances in the U.S. where gang denial by public officials served to delay gang prevention programs, perhaps until they could no longer be effective once the situation reached public consciousness.[3]

To some extent, these two positions were overlays on the distinction noted earlier, between gangs as extreme forms of youth groups versus gangs as qualitatively different. Those concerned with creating a moral panic tended to be those viewing gangs as the polar end of the group seriousness continuum. Those concerned with gangs as a qualitatively different phenomenon are those who tend to see gang denial as the greater danger. To the former, street gangs are a "social construction" of researchers, which could become a self-fulfilling prophecy. To the latter, avoidance was a lost opportunity for valuable research and for the advantages of data based policy formulation. Much of the issue is of course a function of the degree to which "real" street gangs are to be found in Europe and how serious a threat to themselves and others they represent. Both sides concurred on this at the very least: more study and more information is needed, and in the process, the Eurogang paradox must be resolved.

CONCLUSION

Four issues engaging Workshop participants have been highlighted: forms of intervention, the community context, the youth group context, and the danger of moral panics and gang denials. These Workshop discussions along with the chapters in parts I, II, and III have set a foundation for future work. Indeed, as this final essay is written and the volume prepared for publication, two follow-up workshops have already been organized, one in Oslo, Norway and one in Leuven, Belgium. The materials presented in this volume will be the starting position for those two meetings and their expanded set of European researchers. What must be faced in these meetings and in any subsequent activities they spawn is the direction that future research into gangs in Europe–or elsewhere for that matter–must take.

The current volume provides guidance in that it suggests the relevance of the American experience and also some of the cautions raised by differences between the American and European contexts. We suspect, as well, that European gang and youth group research will be more driven by policy considerations than has been the case in the U.S. The preparation and testing of various approaches to intervention is of value by itself, but it also promises a closer tie of researcher to gang member and gang community. The varieties of community contexts to be found in cities of many countries should serve to sharpen understanding of gang/community relationships, of ethnic differences in gang formation, and social responses to gang problems.

Setting gang research into the broader context of other youth group forms should serve to formulate better approaches to defining street gangs and understanding how they may differ from other groups. Research on gangs and on other groups cannot but benefit from the comparison. The disparity between the moral panic and denial concerns presents, we feel, a less well defined advantage. While we are sensitive to the moral panic concerns, the editors of this volume are strongly inclined to a more purist view of the research enterprise. We feel that research self-censored by fears of public or official reaction is likely to be tainted research, less valuable both to knowledge seeking and to policy setting.

Indeed, where interested gang researchers and scholars now exist, or where other researchers can be brought into the enterprise, we urge a concerted effort to assess current and likely developments. In particular, we urge comparative projects, across cities and across nations. We urge coordinated multi-method research, and in particular ethnographic or other forms that bring the researchers into direct contact with gang members and gang structures. Knowledge synthesis, for its own sake and for the sake of policy development, simply cannot evolve from one-location, one-method efforts. This is perhaps the most important if inadvertent lesson from seven decades of American street gang research.

REFERENCES

Cohen, S. (1972). Folk Devils and Moral Panics: The Creation of the Mods and Rockers. London: MacGibbon and Kee.

Covey, H.C., S. Menard, and R.J. Franzese (1982). Juvenile Gangs. Chicago: Charles C. Thomas.

Goode, E., and B-Y. Nachman (1978). Crime in Our Changing Society. New York: Holt, Rinehart, and Winston.

Hagedorn, J. (1988). People and Folks: Gangs, Crime, and the Underclass in a Rustbelt City. Chicago: Lakeview Press.

Howell, J.C. (1998). Youth Gang Programs and Strategies. Draft Report to the Office of Juvenile Justice and Delinquency Prevention. Washington, DC: U.S. Department of Justice, 1998.

Jackson, P., and C. Rudman (1993). Moral panic and the response to gangs in California. In S. Cummings and D.J. Monti (eds.), Gangs: The Origins and Impact of Contemporary Youth Gangs in the United States. Albany: State University of New York Press.

Klein, M.W (1995). The American Street Gang: Its Nature, Prevalence, and Control. New York: Oxford University Press.

Miller, W.B. (1980). Gangs, groups, and serious youth crime. In D. Shichor and D.H. Kelly (eds.), Critical Issues in Juvenile Delinquency. Lexington, MA: Lexington Books.

Moore, J.W., and J.D. Vigil (1989). Chicano gangs: Group norms and individual factors related to adult criminality. Aztlan 18.

Short, J.F., Jr. (1996). Gangs and Adolescent Violence. Boulder, Colorado: University of Colorado Center for the Study and Prevention of Violence.

Spergel, I.A. (1995). The Youth Gang Problem: A Community Approach. New York: Oxford University Press.

Thrasher, F.M. (1927). The Gang: A Study of 1,313 Gangs in Chicago. Chicago: University of Chicago Press.

Zatz, M. (1987). Chicano youth gangs and crime: The creation of a moral panic. Contemporary Crisis 11:129-158.

ENDNOTES

[1] In the American vernacular, "When you've seen one, you've seen them all."

[2] See the chapter by Thornberry and Porter in this volume for a brief description of emergent versus traditional gang cities.

[3] In one case cited by an American participant, his community argued that releasing his report on the evolution and nature of street gangs there would simply increase the racism already in full supply. His reply was that only by reporting the situation could steps be initiated to increase the resources and attention needed.

Contributors

David Curry
Dept. of Criminology & Criminal Justice
University of Missouri, St. Louis
8001 Natural Bridge Road
St. Louis MO 63121-4499
UNITED STATES

Finn-Aage Esbensen
Dept. of Criminal Justice
University of Nebraska at Omaha
1100 Niehardt Hall
Lincoln, NE 68588-0630
UNITED STATES

Scott Decker
Dept. of Criminology & Criminal Justice
University of Missouri, St. Louis
8001 Natural Bridge Road
St. Louis MO 63121-4499
UNITED STATES

Paul Gruter
Haaglanden Police Department
IKH
Analyse en Research
Postbus 264
2501 CG Den Haag
THE NETHERLANDS

Bojan Dekleva
Faculty of Education
Department of Social Pedagogy
University of Ljubljana
Kardeljeva pl. 16
1000 Ljubljana
SLOVENIA

John M. Hagedorn
Dept. of Criminal Justice
University of Ilinois-Chicago
Chicago, IL 60607-7410
UNITED STATES

Maryse Esterle-Hedibel
CESOIP
43 bd Vauban
78280 Guyancourt
FRANCE

Hans-Jürgen Kërner
Institute of Criminology
University of Tübingen
Corrensstrasse 34
72076 Tübingen
GERMANY

Joachim Kersten
Hochschule für Polizei
Sturmbühlstrasse 250
D78054 VS-Schwenningen
GERMANY

Malcolm W. Klein
Social Science Research Institute
University of Southern California
Los Angeles, CA 90089-0375
UNITED STATES

Cheryl L. Maxson
Social Science Research Institute
University of Southern California
Los Angeles, CA 90089-0375
UNITED STATES

Jody Miller
Dept. of Criminology & Criminal Justice
University of Missouri, St. Louis
8001 Natural Bridge Road
St. Louis, MO 63121-4499
UNITED STATES

Tove Pettersson
Department of Criminology
Stockholms Universitet
S-106 91 Stockholm
SWEDEN

Pamela Porter
Hindelang Criminal Justice Research Ctr
University at Albany
135 Western Avenue
Albany, New York 12222
UNITED STATES

Alexander Salagaev
K. Marx str. 68
Department of Public Administration
Kazan State Technological University
4420015 Kazan, Tatarstan
RUSSIA

Karl F. Schumann
Sonderforschungsbereich 186
Universitat Bremen
Wiener Strasse
Postfach 330440
D-28334 Bremen
GERMANY

Arne Stevns
Deputy Commissioner
Copenhagen Police
Politigården
1567 Kobenhavn V
DENMARK

Conny Vercaigne
Faculteit Rechtsgeleerdheid
Katholieke Universiteit Leuven
Hooverplein 10
B-3000
Leuven
BELGIUM

Terence Thornberry
School of Criminal Justice
University at Albany
135 Western Avenue
Albany, NY 12222
UNITED STATES

Elmar Weitekamp
Institute of Criminology
University of Tübingen
Correnssstrasse 34
72076 Tübingen
GERMANY

Frank van Gemert
Regioplan
Max Euweplein 36
1017 MB Amsterdam
THE NETHERLANDS

European Cities Reported tc